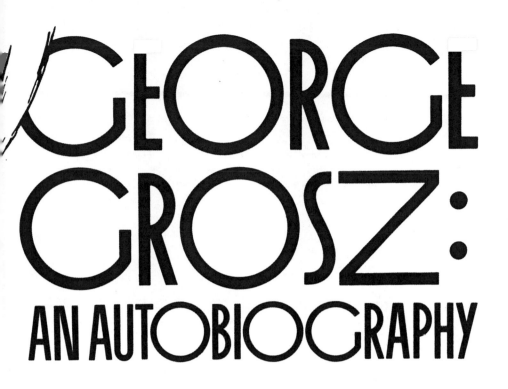

GEORGE GROSZ: AN AUTOBIOGRAPHY

Translated by
NORA HODGES

Foreword by
BARBARA McCLOSKEY

UNIVERSITY OF CALIFORNIA PRESS
Berkeley · Los Angeles · London

This book is a print-on-demand volume. It is manufactured using toner in place of ink. Type and images may be less sharp than the same material seen in traditionally printed University of California Press editions.

University of California Press
Berkeley, California
University of California Press, Ltd.
London, England
First Paperback Printing 1998

Ein kleines Ja und ein grosses Nein
Copyright © 1946, 1955 by the Estate of George Grosz
This translation copyright © 1983 by Imago Design Company, Inc.
Foreword copyright © 1997 by Barbara McCloskey

Library of Congress Cataloging-in-Publication Data

Grosz, George, 1893–1959.
    [Kleines Ja und ein grosses Nein. English]
    George Grosz : an autobiography / translated by Nora Hodges ;
foreword by Barbara McCloskey.
      p. cm.
    Originally published: New York : Macmillan, 1983.
    ISBN 0-520-21327-0 (pbk. : alk. paper)
    1. Grosz, George, 1893–1959.   2. Artists—Germany—Biography.
I. Title.
N6888.G742A2   1998
760'.092—dc21
[B]   97-37059
                                                    CIP

Printed in the United States of America

The paper used in this publication meets the minimum requirements of ANSI/NISO Z39.48 (R 1997)
(Permanence of paper)

CONTENTS

ACKNOWLEDGMENTS

We thank Peter and Lilian Grosz, Peter for his patience and kindness in making the archives of the estate of George Grosz available to us, and Lilian for her firsthand knowledge of the man and her editorial acumen, which were a truly enormous contribution.

Marion Wheeler's foresight brought this edition into being. Her energy and humor sustained us.

We are indebted to Larry Lorber and Stuart Penney for their generous and unstinting support, without which our work would not have been possible.

Special mention must be made of Uno Skolnick for his cheerful presence throughout.

All illustrations used are the property of the estate of George Grosz, with the exception of pp. 282-283, courtesy of the Fogg Art Museum, Harvard University, Cambridge, Massachusetts.

We much appreciate Lothar Fischer's kindness in allowing us to translate an extract from his monograph, *George Grosz*, Rowohlt Verlag, Reinbek bei Hamburg, 1976. It is a fitting epilogue to this book.

FOREWORD

Most of us know George Grosz as the brilliant satirist whose art and provocative career have become synonymous with the vibrant and troubled culture of Berlin's "Golden Twenties." His images of pompous officials, bestial militarists, bloated capitalists, and a simpering bourgeoisie occupy our popular imagination as incisive portraits of a fragile and tumultuous Germany during the years of Hitler's rise to power. Grosz's penchant for lacerating caricatures of church, military, and government leaders and his untiring attack on bourgeois hypocrisy landed him in court on three separate occasions in the 1920s. His frequent confrontations with the German authorities established his work as an outstanding and widely emulated example of politically committed art. By the late 1920s, the nationalist right regularly vilified Grosz as Germany's "Cultural Bolshevist #1." In 1933, he barely escaped Nazi persecution by emigrating to New York just days before Hitler was appointed Chancellor.

In this, his autobiography, Grosz spins out an account of his incendiary career as alive with visual interest and quirky detail as any of his by now famous caricatures. Autobiographies, however, can in some ways conceal more than they reveal. In reading Grosz's narrative, we inevitably remain beholden to what he cared for us to know about him. He warns us bluntly from the outset: "the reader should know that what I do not say, I do not want to say." Grosz says little, in fact, about his radicalization by the events of World War I, his role as one of the more outlandish Berlin Dada artists, and his place at the forefront of Dada's anti-art program in the early 1920s. He provides us with even less information concerning his international fame as the leading artist of the German Communist Party, which he joined shortly after its founding congress in December 1918. Who could guess from the autobiography's conspicuous silences that Grosz worked with Party initiatives throughout the 1920s? That he was involved in everything from signing petitions to illustrating the Party press, producing agitational placards, and chairing the Party's first formal organization of artists, the Red Group, founded in 1924?

But the way in which an author selects and retells life events is often more revealing than any unedited reportage could ever be. This is certainly the case with the Grosz we come to know, however obliquely, in the following pages. By delving into the circumstances under which Grosz composed his autobiography and setting the text into relief against the history of his life and art, we gain fuller insight into what continues to make Grosz one of the most important cultural figures of the 20th century. Alongside his vivid chronicle of the people, places, and events that shaped German history between the wars, Grosz gives us firsthand insight into the experience of exile and the profound forces that redefined U.S. culture during the World War II years.

This edition of Grosz's autobiography is a significantly altered version of the one that first appeared in 1946. In 1941, Grosz signed a contract with New York's Dial Press to cast his life story in words for a U.S. public increasingly caught up in the horror of events unfolding in Europe and anxious for insight into the culture that gave rise to the nightmare of Nazism. This explanatory imperative accounts in large measure for Grosz's obsession with defining for us his own Germanness, an obsession that haunts his autobiography's otherwise lively and humorous anecdotes with a deep and unrelieved pessimism. Grosz composed sections of the text in German, which were subsequently translated into English by his editor, throughout 1942 and 1943. The completed work was published in 1946 under the title *A Little Yes and a Big No: The Autobiography of George Grosz.*

A substantially revised German edition of the autobiography, which Nora Hodges presents here in her fine English translation, appeared in 1955. It contained a sensational new chapter concerning Grosz's trip to Soviet Russia in 1922, a chapter that originally appeared in 1953 as an article in the anti-Communist German-American journal, *Der Monat.* Its incorporation into the 1955 autobiography promised to illuminate what had remained obscured in the 1946 edition concerning Grosz's political involvement during the Weimar years.

The chapter tells of a commission Grosz received in 1922 from

Willi Münzenberg, head of a vast Communist-affiliated propaganda empire during the Weimar years. Grosz, along with the Danish writer, Martin Andersen-Nexö, toured for five months some of Soviet Russia's most famine-stricken areas in order to prepare an illustrated documentary on the plight of the Soviet state. Münzenberg hoped to publish the book in an effort to arouse Western support for food relief and technical assistance to the new struggling regime. It never materialized, however, and Grosz's only published record of what transpired during that time appears here in his devastating reminiscence.

Grosz rejects in his Russian account any glimmer of the revolutionary idealism that we might have expected from a young, radicalized artist. Gloom and suspicion, not optimism and hope, define his vision of the new Soviet regime, a regime populated not by courageous revolutionaries and empowered workers, but rather by colorless functionaries, petty bureaucrats, and faceless drones. Grosz recalls for us his encounters during his sojourn with an impressive list of revolutionary leaders, including Lenin, Trotsky, Sinoviev, Radek, Bucharin, and Lunacharsky. But in a few descriptive touches as deft as any stroke from his draftsman's pen, Grosz deflates one after another in a series of irreverent portraits distilled from his satiric repertoire of incidental and often pointedly incongruous details of clothing, gesture, and physiognomy. Published first in 1953, this chapter's wholly unsympathetic view of the new Soviet state tells us little in the end about Grosz in the 1920s. It tells us a great deal, however, about Grosz in the 1950s, his entanglement in the sensibility of the Cold War, and his eagerness to affirm publicly his by then long-standing repudiation of Communism.

Since the German publication of his autobiography, Grosz's account of his experiences in Russia has exercised profound influence over scholarly interpretations of his career. It has led some to speculate that his rejection of Communism and his desire to forsake politics altogether in his work dates from this consequential trip. Others have maintained that Grosz was never seriously political at any point in his career. His fierce artistic individualism, they insist, could never have allowed him to accommodate fully any prescribed political agenda.

If such a characterization sounds familiar it is because Grosz, too, insists on this understanding of his life and art throughout the pages of his autobiography. In more than one instance in the text, Grosz dismisses his political activities as nothing more than youthful naiveté and impressionability. With respect to his art, he may have once deluded himself, Grosz tells us, into believing that his political caricatures could serve the task of progress, but no more. He describes himself as an inveterate misanthrope whose deep contempt and skepticism could never have allowed him to dedicate his work to "the people" for long. With judgments such as these we are reminded once again of the time, place, and historical vantage point from which the autobiography was written. That vantage point is no longer at the center of a highly politicized 1920s Berlin art world, but rather at the cultural and political margins of U.S. exile in the 1940s and 1950s. Grosz's retrospective refashioning of his life and art intimates the precariousness of that life, a life in which he was torn between his German past and his attempts to adapt himself to the changed circumstances of his new American environment.

We first encounter Grosz in his autobiography on a bleak and mist-shrouded day as melancholy fog horns boom out over the Sound toward his home and studio on New York's Long Island. Grosz uses the hazy indistinctness and mournful quality of the setting as a metaphor for the murky and at times painful process of autobiographical remembrance on which he is about to embark. The eeriness of the scene also defines for Grosz the mystical and the irrational as intrinsic aspects of his German psyche, a psyche that he sets in stark contrast not only against the sobriety and pragmatism of his new American environment but also against the materialism and rationality he ascribes to the Communist doctrine he has long since, at the time of his writing, left behind.

As we know from his published statements and private letters of the time, Grosz had become increasingly skeptical by the late 1920s about Communism and Marxist theories of the historical inevitability of progress and human emancipation. Since Stalin's accession to power in the Soviet Union in 1924, Grosz's personal experience of Communism became a creatively stifling one as Party functionaries attempted more and more to dictate the form and content of his art. He also witnessed first hand the way in which the Communist Party's declared war on Germany's moderate Social Democrats effectively destroyed any hope for a united front against Hitler's rise to power in 1933.

For Grosz, Marxist notions of progress, reason, and materialism had become nothing more than a misplaced belief in "statistics," an outmoded faith in facts and figures that could in no way capture, let alone explain, the apparent irrationalism of current events.

What Marxist idea of history's ineluctable drive for freedom and workers' emancipation could possibly contend with Germany's present crisis? How could Marxist theory ever explain the seeming willingness of the German working class to enslave itself in ever greater numbers to the Nazis' martial pageantry and fatuous sloganeering? Grosz's disillusionment with Communism, coupled with his growing fear of the Nazi threat, prompted him to accept a timely offer in 1932 of a teaching contract at the Art Students' League in New York.

After his emigration to the U.S. in 1933, Grosz refused to allow his work to be used any longer for the Communist Party cause. For this he faced repeated condemnation. His Marxist friends, many of whom had fled to Prague, Paris, London, and other European havens in the wake of Hitler's accession to power, accused him of selling out to U.S capitalist culture. Members of New York's left-wing art world who had eagerly anticipated his arrival in 1933 also felt alienated by Grosz's new stand. To their dismay he claimed to see little distinction any more between Stalin and Hitler. In the midst of the Moscow show trials of 1936, Grosz committed his final judgment on the Communist Party to a series of drawings published in his last lithographic portfolio, *Interregnum*, that portrayed fascism and Communism as mirror images of one another. From that point forward, Grosz turned away from his past as a political caricaturist and began to work increasingly on traditional themes of landscapes, still lifes, and nudes in the high art medium of oil painting.

In letters to Bertolt Brecht, Wieland Herzfelde, and others during his first years in New York, Grosz made no secret of his desire to immerse himself in his new environment. He openly expressed to them his relief at finding a refreshing freedom in his new American home from the political fractiousness that had become so much a part of his daily life in Berlin. But his autobiography reveals another dimension of Grosz's response to the U.S., one that is decidedly less affirmative than the more positive image of America he promoted among his Marxist friends. Grosz's repeated references in the autobiography to his disdain for the masses serves not only to distance him for his readers from his Communist Party past. It also functions as a none-too-subtle attack on what he and other exiled artists and intellectuals perceived as the deplorable nature of U.S. mass culture.

As a Dada artist in the early 1920s, Grosz had emulated in his work the brash kitschiness of U.S. mass culture as part of Dada's

xii GEORGE GROSZ: AN AUTOBIOGRAPHY

explicit attack on the self-seriousness of German high culture. Now in the U.S., Grosz and other exiles, including Thomas Mann, Bertolt Brecht, and Ernst Toller who figure into his autobiography, came increasingly to envision themselves as bearers of a European high cultural tradition cast adrift in an unremarkable sea of consumerism, loud advertising, cartoons, Hollywood film, and popular music. Grosz describes for us his failed attempts to succeed in various mass culture venues, including popular journal illustration and Hollywood film. He attributes his failures once again to his Germanness, his ultimate inability to assimilate because of his "national heritage" of mysticism and irrationality, a sensibility fundamentally at odds, Grosz insists, with what he sees as the up-beat, no-nonsense pragmatism of U.S. mass culture.

Grosz's autobiography impresses upon us his overall sense of alienation in the United States and as such lends insight into the experience of exile during this tragic and historically pivotal period. He relies heavily on dream sequences and childhood experiences in unfolding for us his life story, a narrative strategy of psychological reflection that reinforces the general sense of interiority and isolation that we encounter in his reminiscences. For all his professed distrust of psychoanalysis and his lack of belief in its diagnostic possibility, Grosz's writing is nonetheless heavily imbued with its explanatory methods. A case in point is the reason Grosz gives us for his retreat from political caricature and turn in the late 1930s toward the high art themes of landscapes and nudes. He relates this dramatic change in no way to the larger context of radical leftism's decline in the mid-1930s and the New York art market's turn away from politically engaged art at that time. He explains this shift instead as an inevitable and inescapable return to his own origins, a reaching back to the sandy dunes and grasses of his small town, country-life childhood and a revisiting of his adolescent interest in trash literature and peep shows. In this he claims to have found his truer self from which the intervening years of artistic activism and political turmoil were nothing more than a long and circuitous detour.

Grosz's allegiance to traditional figurative art after 1936 placed him outside the latest avant-garde tendencies of the New York art world and the emergence of Abstract Expressionism on the eve of World War II. But Grosz's claims of isolation to the contrary, his autobiography demonstrates for us once again his unerring ability to place himself at the forefront of profound cultural change. In this sense he remains true to the avant-garde sensibility that made him such an influential interpreter of Germany's unfolding horror in the 1920s and 1930s. His interest in psychoanalytic thought betrays not only his reading of Freud during this period, but, more specifically, the impact of Surrealism on his autobiography's form and content. Since Salvador Dali's much-publicized arrival in New York in 1934, Surrealism's dream-like imagery and fascination with Freudian theories of the unconscious had eclipsed the overtly political art of Social Realism and marked the end of the Marxist left's heyday in the New York avant-garde.

The triumph of Freud over Marx and the retreat from politics to art which Grosz so movingly describes in terms of his own life trajectory thus mirrors a larger and consequential change in U.S. vanguard culture. It not only circumscribes a retreat in the 1930s from Marxist collectivism and dreams of a socialist future. It also charts the turn toward psychological interiority and emphasis on individualism that formed the ideological core of Abstract Expressionism and the political ascendancy of American liberalism during the World War II years.

Grosz and his wife, Eva, returned in 1959 to Berlin shortly before Grosz's 66th birthday. He died there a month after their arrival. As Berlin stands poised to become the capital of a united Germany once again, Grosz's descriptions of the raucous cultural life of Potsdamer Platz and Friedrichstrasse are nostalgic reminders of what an undivided Germany once was. His words remind us of how Berlin blossomed as one of Europe's leading cultural capitals before the horror of Nazism and the brinkmanship of the Cold War. They also remind us of the way in which his life, and the lives of all those touched by the tragic events of World War II, were irredeemably dislocated, torn asunder, and changed forever. With the disarming mixture of humor, insight, and skepticism that we know so well from his caricatures, Grosz takes us on a journey through these events. He brings alive the dreams and failures that have lost none of their potency for our contemporary culture as we continue to struggle with the legacy of the World War II years—years that Grosz so vividly captures for us in the following pages.

Barbara McCloskey
Pittsburgh
August, 1997

PREFACE

A foggy day, foggy and dense, as is sometimes our memory. From the hilltop where I now stand I behold the valley of my past as though looking out of my studio window on a wintry day. I see rolling masses of fog, milky, eerie forms, leafless skeletons of trees that look as though they had always been that way, as though they had never bloomed.

I am peaceful and have plenty of time. There is a warm glow from the electric heater. I love the hoarse, hollow boom of the fog horns coming over from Long Island Sound, excellent company for my wanderings into the mist of the world of past memories.

America is a pragmatic country that thrives on facts and figures, and that likes to have things recorded in sharp photographic focus. I am thankful that recollections cannot be photographed. It is not because many of my documents, letters, clippings and notes were destroyed by a bomb in the Berlin attic that my narrative is inexact. In all honesty, even if I had everything right here—my notes from World War I, letters, passports, family photos, love letters, all the things that attach themselves to a person during his active life like barnacles to a ship—even then I would not have come up to American expectations. I will not and cannot write an interview with myself.

This is an attempt at an autobiography, and the reader should know that what I do not say, I do not want to say. Yes, I love the twilight. And please don't mistake that for haziness or flabbiness, for even in twilight the eternal human form remains tangible and firm.

Much has been forgotten. But forgetting is not necessarily a sign of defective memory. The veil of the past is a kind veil that flatters the face of time. The contemporary pseudo-enlightened custom of ripping the veil to show all the ugliness, all the cracks and crevices, all the maladies that one can remember, should be relegated to the nineteenth century where it belongs. For me, mystery remains ever mysterious, and I cherish my inclination toward mysticism as a true part of my national heritage.

If I have become skeptical about progress, it is because of the experiences of my lifetime. Mine has been a time when the sweetest declarations of the brotherhood of man were voiced at the same time as the bloodiest wars in the history of our planet were being fought—solace and suicide in grand style.

The world of my ancestors was filled with spirits. Grasses, wind and earth were animated by invisible forces that had not yet been subjected to scientific classification. Those unknown natural powers were as terrifying as the atom bomb is to us today, even though we believe we understand its components.

My terrified ancestors sat in the branches of their trees, stones in hand, watching Brother Boniface as he went about felling their "holy oak." He cut down that holy tree with an axe that had been blessed by his holy God. Nothing happened. But fear has remained with us to this very day.

Maybe I too never became properly enlightened. Maybe I could have benefited from the rays of exact science and statistics. But I am what I am in this sixth decade of my life. Much of what I have seen and done, I saw and did as in a dream; so the dream sometimes seems more real to me than reality.

I am now trying to find myself through the bubbling mist of the valleys of the past. Much must remain veiled, because it was not meant to be clearly seen. Darkness will alternate with light, clarity with opacity, sweetness with bitterness.

Yes, I was a questioner, for curiosity is human. But in contrast to others who were satisfied with labels, facts and dates, I was not. Facts, to me, were something like corks that bounce up and down on the waves. For me, they were corks, and nothing but corks. Whereas I saw myself as a diver—until I found out that there is a limit to depth, too....

BEGINNINGS: POMERANIA

I only vaguely remember my father. He died when I was six. At that time we were living in Stolp, a small town in Pomerania. My father was steward and a working brother at the Freemasonic Lodge. The beautiful Lodge building was opposite the high school on a nice, quiet street leading to a large garden with tennis courts; in a second, less cultivated garden there was a mysterious, round pond full of tadpoles and frogs. Twilight tales ghosted that pond; it was said to be bottomless, a scary, endless hole overgrown with weeds and a paradise for mosquitoes. Only later, after it was filled in, did it become evident that it had been quite a modest little pond; and then all the hobgoblins and will-o'-the-wisps that our imagination had bestowed upon it disappeared.

Upstairs in my father's quarters, it was nice and cozy. I used to spend much time on the big rug by the warm, glowing stove, buried in sensational illustrations of the Russo-Japanese War or the German colonial troops fighting bravely in the African bush. Once a week the book club delivered the *Gartenlaube, Über Land und Meer, Fliegende* and *Meggendorfer Blätter,* and the *Deutsche Romanzeitung.* But nothing made me as happy as the *Leipziger Illustrierte,* which brought those wonderful drawings from the current theater of war—and there always was a war going on in far-away places.

Those pictures kindled my imagination. My father also sketched a bit on the large sheets of paper that covered the square table where cardplayers marked their scores at night. I remember sitting on his lap and watching the images take shape while he drew— little men, horses, soldiers—he had served in the Franco-Prussian War in the seventies, and had been at the Siege of Paris.

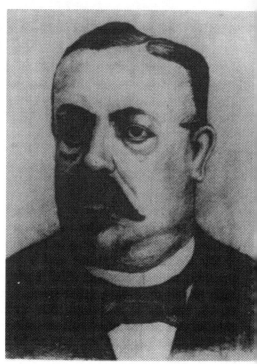

Young George Grosz and His Parents

My father had dark hair and blue eyes. He wore a mustache and a little tuft of hair on his chin that had been in vogue in the eighties and had not yet gone out of style. I liked being close to him and watching him manipulate the bottles and glasses. He was in charge of setting up the bar at the Lodge for the evening; I loved the bottles' different shapes and labels and the colorful pictures on the cigar boxes which I may occasionally have tried to copy.

A young noblewoman once came to paint on our garden porch. She only copied—it was a still life of peaches and plums—but I was enchanted. The way she rendered the melting, misty blue plums seemed to me the highest art, even if copied. I had no idea yet of becoming a painter, but how I would have loved to do something like that. I liked the idea of conjuring up something that looked like nature. This pleasure of straight, plain imitation has never left me. Sitting before a still life, time and again I see myself on that porch watching peaches and plums appear under the clever hands of that aristocratic young lady.

That was the first time I had seen real oil painting, with real tubes of paint. A great experience. I smell the spice of lavender and turpentine that hovered around her activity, every time I think of it. My greatest wish ever after was to own that sort of paint box and use it in the same way. The very tubes with their colored labels, the large one of white next to the small fat one of rose madder, the oval palette that I was once allowed to hold in my hand just like a real painter, the long brushes of hair and bristle, the knives and little bottles of resin: it was such a treat to look at all those things and see how they were used.

My father must have had a mischievous vein. Once on a moonless night he terrified my sister Martha and her friends by hanging a nightshirt on a rake and making it bob up and down. They squealed with fright, believing it to be one of those many ghosts that are said to inhabit Masonic Lodges. This building that the Masons used for their secret rites had a bad reputation anyhow. The neighborhood boys with whom I talked once in a while told me eerie things about the rooms upstairs: not of ghosts exactly, but there was supposedly a coffin there with the skeleton of the late Master of the Lodge. And somehow every Mason knew exactly when he was to die, not only the date, but even the hour....

That fed and directed my imagination. Except for a few social rooms, the upper floor was out of bounds, but I decided to explore that business about the coffin. So one day, when my father was going upstairs, I crept in stocking feet after him—only to be booted unceremoniously to the bottom steps of the first floor.

I used to enjoy spending time in the attic. In the middle of it was an opening under which a huge chandelier was suspended. You could look down into the large ballroom from there; the height made you a bit dizzy, and everything looked small, crooked, and funnily distorted: my God, what if the whole chandelier should fall down...! The charity parties were fun too, with all the pretty booths in the garden, the elegant ladies, and the fireworks late at night. The Lodge garden was great anyhow, modeled after the great parks of another century, harking back to an earlier great tradition. I loved the statues—cheap castings of Greek works—which peeked out of the foliage. We buried our canary there. I used to pick up paradise apples lying on the ground and collect them in a cigar box. Others were made into apple jelly. Sometimes when there were minor floods, my friend Seifert and I would build toy boats from bark and sail them around the harbors, islands and continents we constructed. I once built a real tent out of twigs, grass and moss, and would lie there for hours. The sun was shining, I was surrounded by greenish-golden twilight, and dreamed of adventures like those in my favorite books; I would, of course, be as infinitely good and noble as those heroes.

Today I sometimes yearn for that—how shall I say it—long-lost garden of my childhood. Life was without a care. Every summer we went to Stolpmünde, a Baltic beach an hour and three quarters away. My childhood was free of worries.

After my father's death, we moved to Berlin, where we lived on Wöhlerstrasse near Wedding, opposite a coal depot. I still have visions of those black crossed hammers, the coal trade's traditional sign, as an unhappy memento. Behind the fireproof wall was the typical city view of concrete and stone, and I longed for Stolp's woods, meadows, river and hay-scented summer days. My mother and aunt sewed blouses for a wholesale house, a job that was easy to get at the time: much work for low pay. Even though living was cheap and there was enough for our direst needs, now, there were always money worries.

Once in a while my big sister would come to see us and take me to a pastry shop or to Aschinger's. That popular pub near the Oranienburger Gate with its crystal and mirrored hot dog counter and the waitress in blue-and-white checks at the center seemed a fairy palace to me. Not far from us, on Chausseestrasse, were the barracks of the celebrated infantry regiment that would occasionally march by with drums beating and trumpets sounding. Because

I had known only hussars in Stolp, I enjoyed these different
uniforms. We lived in a really proletarian neighborhood, but of
course I wasn't aware of that at the time. The street teemed with
life and was full of children; the baker's bread smelled wonderful,
and a store with its window of trashy literature gave me lascivious
shivers. Actually I have never quite overcome the peculiar shudder
such lurid title pages give me.

I made friends with a bright neighbor who was my age and a
prolific reader and who took me to the public library. Franz Kügler,
that long-lost friend, was already talking about Haeckel and his
then popular *The Riddle of the Universe*. He was excited about
science and had a subscription to *Neue Universum*. I was greatly
stimulated by all that and it somehow improved me—that is, made
me full of good intentions—and filled me with awe for the inventiveness and ingenuity of man. Franz was also somewhat of a star-
gazer. There was something about him that attracted me and
pulled me out of narrowness and confinement. Our unconscious
dreams seemed closer to fulfillment when our thoughts, inspired
by popular articles and drawings, soared far away, high above the
coal depots, the teeming streets and crowded apartments of Berlin.

One day our luck changed. We moved back to Pomerania.
Bedded on our trunks, dozing through the night, we travelled back
to my beloved Stolp. Certain connections and recommendations
enabled my mother to become manager of the hussar regiment's
officers' club. The urgent, pressing cares concerning our daily
bread came to an end.

Looking back at my youth in Stolp, I can say that, in the main, it
was a happy time. I grew up in undisturbed freedom, as my mother

was busy all day with housekeeping chores, and was training new help besides. What a great time my friends and I had! We roamed the nearby woods and the banks of the river that flowed by our house. In those days there was still a huge meadow where people bleached their sheets. That was where we played cowboys and Indians. We shot each other with air rifles and homemade catapults. In one of the mighty, ancient willows we built a regular hunting box from where we terrorized the servant girls when they came to hang up the wash. Like real robber knights or Indians. The wet sheets, and particularly long underwear, gave us all the stimulus we needed. I still keenly remember the infamous battle against those underpants; it cost me my beloved gun, given to me by the club sergeant, Arndt.

We Indians and pirates were the terror of a small neighboring estate whose administrator with the peculiar name of Butterbrodt was our mortal enemy. We were often on the war path against him and his aides, and more than once planned a bloody death for him which included such niceties as hanging him head-first over an ant heap. So vivid was our imagination that we actually erected a stake for him. Every time Butterbrodt came along in his donkey cart he was the target for our verbal barrage delivered from behind the trees: Butterbread, freshly spread! He was very cruel to the donkey, an animal rarely used in Stolp, and as we were very fond of the beast, we felt we were exercising justice against its tormentor.

The Stolpe surfaces again before me, the little river that flowed past our house. In our youthful imagination it was the Hudson or the St. Lawrence, or even "Lake Glimmerglass." Sometimes timber was floated downstream to the small Baltic port, and we would ride along on it barefoot for miles. The logs then became

planks on one of the schooners of a Marryat buccaneer, and our catapult shots whizzed into the water. Occasionally we ourselves fell in. During one of those adventures I got under a slippery log and would certainly have drowned, had I not at the last minute noticed an opening above me. I had just learned to open my eyes underwater; that saved my life. I was plenty scared though, and on top of that got a sound thrashing when I arrived home all drenched and exhausted.

Woods, meadows and turbid nights on the moor come to mind again, puddles and small ponds. We would go out with specimen boxes and glass jars to catch all sorts of salamanders and lizards for our private zoos. Flowers and plants were carefully pressed and cataloged—only to rot later in the attic? No, not quite.

Our mentor for all this was our popular science teacher Herr Marquardt, who made us laugh. With him we used to wander through the countryside, his old-fashioned cape floating like a banner over our forays into the world of frogs, insects, bugs and butterflies. Schooled in the tradition of Humboldt, he aimed indefatigably to imbue his pupils with that great spirit of humanism.

I remember brooks bordered by willows where we caught river lampreys. At home they were pickled in vinegar and olive oil; they tasted wonderfully sour, and had no bones. It took patience to catch alburns, those hand-sized fish in the Stolpe. You had to sit for ages with your rod and worms before they would bite; but when pan fried, they tasted better than any of the big ones bought in the market.

And those marvelous, hot, innocent summer days when we were allowed to go and help with the haymaking, and then sank dead tired into those gingham feather beds to sleep dreamlessly till the rooster crowed at five in the morning. The bushes were laden with gooseberries and red currants, which we would pick lying on our backs and roll into our mouths until our tummies swelled up like

balloons. Utopia! You had to go past the saw mill to get there; the fresh boards smelled pleasantly resinous, and the saw buzzed like a big bumble bee on those cloudless July holidays.

We would cut rushes, strap them into two bundles to use as life preservers, and teach ourselves to swim, jumping in and out of the Stolpe like frogs. No need for instructors or bathing trunks. Every Saturday night we were scrubbed with soap in a tin tub brought into the big room next to the kitchen, with water heated on the stove. My cousin and I bathed together to save water and fuel and that usually ended in a small flood—to the distress of my aunt, who intervened with a snapping wet rag—and tears and water mingled on the floor.

It is good to grow up in a small town, half in the country. Nature is everywhere close at hand. Fields and meadows started right behind the houses and it seemed as though the wind blew fresh and strong straight from the sea. Just right for a growing boy. Concrete, asphalt and stone had not yet insulated you from the earth beneath. My love for grasses, for the constant motion of the wind-swept dunes, and even my concentration upon seemingly small things may stem from these childhood impressions. But even then, the mighty city of mechanical toys and machines began to appear on the horizon like a mythical, adventure-laden piece of reality.

My cousin wanted to be a commercial artist (he had an exquisite talent for drawing and painting and became quite well known in Berlin later on). He was apprenticed to a decorator, where he started to work his way up from the rank of house painter. Through him I met his boss, Herr Grot, who lived next door. He had studied in Munich at the well-known school of Wilhelm von Debschitz and with his big, black beret and blond Vandyke beard, he behaved like a real artist; he even owned an original drawing by Albert Weisgerber, whom he greatly admired and frequently mentioned. (Weisgerber was then drawing caricatures for the Munich magazine *Jugend* in a distinctive, sparse black-and-white style. He was later known as one of the few great new talents; his painting leaned toward the younger French, especially Cézanne. Unfortunately, he was killed in the early weeks of World War I.)

This interior decorator-painter Grot saw a sort of picture story I had done. I had painted a scientist who had an adventure with a whale. He had been swallowed, and after all sorts of comic happenings—or so they seemed to me—he came out at the back end. I admit that it was rather secondhand, but not copied; I had never heard of the Swiss, Töpffer. I did know Wilhelm Busch, loved him dearly, and had therefore made up verses that were properly rhymed, neatly written into my school notebook and colored with crayon.

As it happened, Herr Grot found me sufficiently talented to participate in the Sunday morning drawing course that my father had also mentioned. My artistic appreciation was of course not very well developed. My hunger for images, nourished as it was merely by those family magazines, meant that my artistic appreciation was not well developed at all; it was usually sensational impact rather than artistic value that attracted me. Now this was different, and new. Grot's little collection consisted mainly of art pages from *Jugend* and such. His folders astonished me: it was all completely new. Grot was also the first person to direct me to God's natural world, for which I remain eternally grateful. He often went out himself on free days and did landscapes, mostly in tempera.

I must add that this decorator still maintained a tiny bit of a great tradition. It was still customary to paint the hallways of the better houses with flowers or landscapes with swimming swans. A tiny piece of the tradition of Tiepolo remained. And, honest artisan that he was, Grot preferred to obtain his models for decoration straight from nature rather than the customary pattern book. That was good, of course, and he was a man one could learn from. In Grot's own description, he was a "linear stylist."

This term is meant to explain *Jugendstil*, art nouveau, best described as a mixture of water lily stalks and Japan. All lines swing, bend, curve and recurve, deviate and rejoin in half-rounds until the ornament is completed. A veritable spaghetti-orgy of lines. Marbling was used to produce a spiral motif caused by putting oil on water. Kolo Moser in Vienna was the originator of this "style." But I knew neither that, nor a lot of other things, when I was taking Grot's drawing course.

Based on the famous modern Munich teachers, Debschitz and Kunowski, Grot had figured out a system that, to me at least, seemed utterly distorted and complicated. Using the head of a live model, usually an old man, one was supposed to discover "form." Discovering the form meant to circle around the paper with not too soft a pencil, round and round like a bicyclist gone crazy, until eventually out of all the circles and ovals there emerged a sort of expression of nature. That maneuver was supposed to be the "search" for form. The actual purpose—possibly a long-forgotten baroque tradition by Bellangé, some misunderstood system of engraving or whatever—was never clarified. I had naturally thought one should begin with one single line if possible, but there this peculiarly circuitous route was chosen; I accepted it all in silent devotion and without contradiction, raced my pencil round in circles like a madman, and was happy when Mr. Grot praised me.

Besides myself, there were only five others in the course: an artistically inclined officer (in civilian clothes, of course), a forest ranger, a youngish lady and an elderly one, and my cousin. Outside of the class, I went my own way and looked for my own models. One of my favorites, for example, was the famous and infamous Eduard Grützner, whose art book I had received for Christmas. I never got tired of gazing at his pictures of monks and of drinking scenes. At night, with snowflakes falling soothingly outside and the regimental band playing a cakewalk to cheer the officers upstairs, I would often sit in the small front room and copy a Grützner picture with a hard, well-sharpened pencil by the light of the oil lamp. I would sit and sit, hearing nothing, until the stupid lamp started to flicker before going out. All the way into my dreams I still had my hard pencil and was drawing feasting monks, lulled by Abe Holzmann's then popular cakewalk, "Smoky Smokes."

Then again I would design daring, free compositions, for I also loved the historical painters, and the books were always full of mighty, armored military pictures. My free compositions were small, but maybe...maybe some day I too would paint with giant brushes and buckets full of paint onto huge sheets of canvas? Thoughts like that made me dedicated, mellow and satisfied. Damnation, to be that sort of a painter, that was really something. I would be overcome by the happiness of creating, in a completely youthful and innocent way. Possibly at the same time my friend, Heini Blume, was dreaming of an expedition up the Nile, surrounded by crocodiles and Muslims—a brave Livingstone....

Mostly I drew pictures of knights with romantic castles and drawbridges high in the background. I drew horses and soldiers in antiquated uniforms by their camp fires; also romantic itinerant journeymen taking leave of the mill down in the valley by the forest's edge. The soldier-scenes stemmed mostly from upstairs in the officers' casino where there were hundreds of water colors, large and small, of men in uniform or simply paintings of uniforms themselves. There were oils there too, immortalizing the military feats of the Blücher Hussars; I remembered a cavalry attack by C. Röchling for a long time. During the Russo-Japanese War, of course, I drew battles with lots of rows of little soldiers, as well as the Port Arthur naval battle with its beautiful spray from crashing shellfire.

An indelible impression was made on me by the horror shows at country fairs. They always had a stall with two galleries and peep holes through which you could look at pictures, cleverly lighted by lamps from the right and left. Sometimes real objects, strategically placed, would lend the picture greater reality, so that it seemed as though you were actually stepping into it. The illusion of perspec-

tive was always enormously alive. In those pre-cinema days such panoramas satisfied the everpresent need for art and reality. Here people who liked drama and action—and that means just about everybody—really got their money's worth. I well remember to this day those horror paintings, primitive despite all their clever lighting. Even with the raw style and artistic flaws, the pictures were unusually effective in an impressively lively, simple and yet suggestive way. I still consider this type of art as a kind of atrocity reportage and something that is absolutely right, in fact in its way ideal. It seems to me that it continued an old, healthy tradition of visual education for the broader mass of people, a visual education that did, however, include some art. In these days of fragmented vision—as, for instance, in film—this visual experience no longer has the meaning it once had and probably never will have again. Now that art people and snobbish collectors are looking for new things, they occasionally discover some of these nearly extinct paintings. They are starting to be measured with the exacting criteria of fine art, but these were pictures for plain folk who wanted nothing more from art than pleasing representations.

The pictures were rough and sturdy, and undoubtedly painted without any artistic ambition. But this very absence of sophistication possibly lent them something basically human, the same sort of touching quality sometimes found in the work of talented amateurs. That at least is the way I feel today, at a time when three or four interpreters and art historians are needed for every painter. Those old pictures are simply lacking in any theory, or need for anemic exaltation. On the contrary, bright red blood was an important ingredient of their subject matter. Our modern educators and pedagogues would not pay much attention to this. One must not forget, however, that in those days the laws governing public decency were strict, and anything openly bloodthirsty was prohibited. In Europe, for instance, prizefighting was not permitted on humanitarian grounds and could only take place in private, almost secret, clubs.

Everything that we experience today as so repulsively commonplace began first during World War I and continued thereafter. The vulgarity of public life that we now accept was then still tempered by a mild aristocratic regime. Some of the old humanism established by the great poets and thinkers was still alive; the time of concentration camps, of mass executions, of race and class hatreds had not yet come. But I somehow had premonitions. I felt in those pictures some of the horror and the destructive spirit of the elements, and the little human flea in the midst of the great design. The proletarian element, the brutality of eternal direct action, yes, that was something one could really wallow in.

It was 1910, and one was not yet blunted and cynical. If one or two unemployed men died of wood alcohol or a rotten herring in a shelter, the whole German press got excited; that's how sensitive they were. The rare attempted assassinations of Russian potentates were enormous events. It "could not happen here." So the effect on my childish mind was all the greater when I saw that in pictures.

Pictures have an inexplicable magic. The imitation of life was then taken for life itself, as is now often true of the cinema. You identify with the heroes, imagine taking active part in the story, and practically become one of the little people yourself. What I am recounting in such detail may possibly have had an influence upon my later life and maturity; who can tell? Many people have forgotten these things, so why did they happen to affect me so strongly? Was I chosen to endure horrors? Was a superior force predicting, even though simplistically, the atrocities, the blood and the murder that was to come? At the time it wasn't clear. I merely enjoyed it all, as many boys today enjoy American comics. We were simply delighted with everything: with the wide world, with pirates, especially with wars against wicked, treacherous natives, preferably shooting poisoned arrows. In other words, it was not the world of factories and offices, or any sedentary, money-making activity that inspired us. It was simply a beautiful daydream. Some people, particularly artists, hold on to that all their lives.

How many people live within us? One upstairs, one in the middle, and one in the basement? Maybe an extra one somewhere tied up in a locked closet? I distrust psychology and psychiatry. They explain and explain, they try to get to the bottom of the secrets of the human heart and the human motivation. I maintain, however, that you may be able to hint at the demon in man, but not dissect it. Of course we have learned things, we have even perfected science to some degree in the course of thousands of years, but then we pay for it on the other side. We have certainly acquired spectacular pieces of knowledge, advancing to artificial hearts and television. But that is all. The demon remains: pain, death, love, hatred. Every generation has to live it all over again. What does my experience mean to any other flea of a human being?

Getting back to those horror-show pictures: some damned exciting scenes come to mind. For instance a fire in the Paris métro. Orange flames, mixed with smoke, ooze out of a narrow tunnel, a passage of death. Dozens of tiny, singed human fleas crowd in mortal terror toward the exit, while a mashed heap, trampled by the fleeing crowd, lies like burned matches around the platform.

In order to give a better view, all these panoramas were composed with an expansive horizon. Overwhelmed, the people appeared as tiny insects, which of course they really are.

Surely I must have been influenced, even though not consciously. Something was stimulated in me here that surfaced again later, when I first saw futurist painting. It is the sense for depicting contemporary life and the realities of the world. It seems significant that one of my first oils had an actual murder as its subject. To this day I toy with the idea of painting in the manner of those panoramas. Does that mean that I am still the little boy who wants to wish back his childhood?

Every time I saw another bloodcurdling picture in one of the itinerant show booths, a vague and eerie feeling came over me of the unknown horror and crime of a veiled and unexplored world. I was enraptured, but perplexed. Behind all those peculiarly painted assassinations, incendiaries, manhunts, executions, catastrophes, shootings of rebels, sinkings of ships and collisions of trains, I suspected the romance of an untracked world of great dangers and bloody adventure. Still the melody and drama that I so loved was not yet without fear. That world, it seemed to me, could not be experienced in our small Pomeranian town: a little, gifted boy knew nothing yet of the wise Chinese whose travels are confined to his room.

In those days I would read a heap of blood curdling novels of a type that has been long extinct. They were called backstairs books because peddlers sold them as serials to the housemaids behind the kitchen stairs. You had to sign a receipt obliging you to take all of the hundred installments. They cost ten pennies each and had an exciting picture on the cover, equal to the panoramas I have described. This was folk literature, primitive heroic stories which had been modernized. So-called educated people of course did not read such stuff. Many educators and reformers stormed against this kind of literature, claiming that it ruined intelligence, taste and character. (This just might be true of high literature too; the trouble may well have started with the printed word. As I have stated, I am not a reformer.)

I read a lot of these books. I got them mostly from an obscure little library owned by a crotchety old woman. There was a sort of stationery store in front where she sold pens, pencils, blotters, school supplies, paper goods and all sorts of notebooks. The back room was stuffed full of cheap books and packages of those old penny-dreadfuls tied together with twine. Klara Menning sat there, with spectacles and cane, reigning like a witch out of Grimm's fairy tales. She attracted children, and many a boy fell under her spell. It was a fabulous store; at street level, it looked like an untidy attic, all in a mess and full of dust. The antique gas lamp that was always lighted purred like a cat and kept the place in a Rembrandtesque semi-darkness that made it even cozier, and encouraged us in a little harmless snitching. A puppet hung in the doorway, and a white cardboard skeleton next to a hunchbacked pantaloon. Grotesque masks lay above in tattered boxes, a false beard next to slates and erasers, and wrapped slate pencils in a glass. It was a wonderful, fantastic junk heap. Christmas decorations from many years before were still in the window. Then, as was to be expected, there was a huge blue-black cat who was present everywhere; it was said that he could walk upside down across the ceiling like a fly. There were also silver threads for Christmas trees—or were they ancient spider webs? Finally, of course, there were those backstairs novels that the servant girls apparently resold here for a few pennies, full of grease spots, as signs of their former readers.

"Hatred and Love, or Two Women Under One Roof"; "Robber-baron Zimmermann, Friend of the Poor, Terror of the Tyrants"; "Sleeping Beauty, or the Pursuit Round the Globe"; "Buried Alive for Twenty-Five Years, or Dagger, Cross and Love"; "The Poachers, or The Robber's Bride in the Bavarian Forest." Beautiful titles. I read all the volumes I could buy, and we culture-hungry boys lent them to one another. There was a good deal of similarity in the action, but that minor flaw did not matter. The more fierce and unlikely the action, the more elated I was about the daring adventures and robberies that were almost as fantastic as fairy tales. Marvelous how robber captain Zimmermann managed to hang on to the platform of the prison tower with one hand while holding his rescued beloved with the other, as the river Elbe raged below. His pursuers departed above—after unknowingly treading on his clutching hand.

There was a serial called "Wenzel Kummer, the Terror of the Bohemian Forest, or the Secrets of the Casemates of the Fortress Brno" that I wanted to acquire for my library. The peddler knew

me and settled for payment by installments; but I only got as far as volume thirty-five, and then I ran out of money. Crying silently, I had to return those thirty-five volumes. That was my first encounter with the principles of modern economics.

These books really turned my friend Erwin's head. Setting himself up as a gang leader and brandishing an ancient pocket pistol, he threatened a harmless old woman on her way to market at a quiet street corner. Scared, she gave him her wallet, then went to the police. Erwin had already spent fifty pennies on chocolate cake with whipped cream when he was arrested. He was thrown out of high school, branded a youthful offender, despised by everybody, and the only job he could eventually get was as a salesman in the local department store. Erwin had won almost all my library from me in a card game, so this was the retribution for his luck in gambling.

At that time a whole new series of thrilling adventure stories came from America. Little stationery stores had them hanging on string straight across their shop windows. Each issue was self-contained and cost twenty pennies, but considering the larger size and the colored cover—new and very attractive—you gladly paid the higher price. The first series was about the brave explorer and Indian-killer, Buffalo Bill. Then came the superhumanly clever detective, Nick Carter, who defied and defeated every danger. His heroic deeds in the underworld inspired me to make some dramatic drawings. My cousin Martin had to serve as a model on Sundays dressed in one of those difficult modern suits. My school chum Hodapp even wrote a play in which Nick Carter and the infamous crime king Carruthers had a very dangerous adventure with a private electric chair. For these scenes I also did some vivid drawings inspired by those covers.

The literary quality of these publications was the same as that of the old penny-dreadfuls: the good old Dumas school. Compared to the movies, which now often satisfy the ever-present need for backstairs literature, the level was about grade-B Hollywood adventure.

It was always the goriest stories that attracted us, the real bluebeard ones. Again and again it was the locked room or the forbidden key. We devoured these spicy stories at the same speed as we ate the coconut flakes that ruined my teeth. Unfortunately, the uncouth reality of Pomerania gave the world quite a different look than the pretty colored covers of those tales. Many of these lovely stories occurred in America, in romantic prewar America. I do not know whether this early reading was responsible for the passion that I still have for America to this day. We all were inspired to dream of foreign lands—and America was considered quite All Right.

We would often bicycle to the railway gate of our little station and wait for the Paris-Petersburg Express to pass through once a week. It was always a sensation. While the train stopped for a few minutes, those elegant foreigners would get out to stretch their legs; they might buy a newspaper or frankfurters, drink a glass of beer or brandy standing up, and disappear again. Then the huge locomotive would start up, and sometimes one could glimpse the face of an extraordinarily beautiful woman behind a half-opened window; an actress, maybe, or even one of those dancers whom we knew only from the spectacular, colored postcards then in vogue…*Dining Car, Compagnie Internationale des Wagons-Lits* —slowly the shiny golden letters would float by, glistening pleasantly as the train speeded up. Then maybe a flash of waiter-white moving nimbly in the dining car, or the chef with his funny high white hat waving to us. Our youthful longing for the wide world would follow the yellow-brown cars as they disappeared.

One day in August huge billboards were put up in the busiest parts of town; shortly thereafter they were covered with colorful posters. Whoever did not know yet from the newspapers or by word of mouth could now find out that the world's greatest circus, Barnum & Bailey, was about to arrive. That white Pullman car with its golden decorations and foreign letters pulling into the side track of our little station seemed like a visit from fairyland. I spent all day roaming the circus site. Everywhere there were exciting new things to see. Rumor had it that there would be simultaneous shows in three rings. Construction went ahead with extraordinary speed and precision, apparently according to a plan of cooperation that I could not understand; everyone knew his place and part exactly.

The town itself seemed more lively than usual. Lots of country folk and farmers had come in to look. They ogled the exotic circus characters that would appear here and there around town. I marveled at an open carriage full of odd people with their heads covered. I recognized from the posters that the shapeless one of enormous girth must be the fattest man in the world. Beside him sat a person whose face was covered with a black cloth; judging by his mass of wild hair, that could only be Lionel, the hairy lion man. The tiny gentleman on the jump seat whose head was also concealed, but who wore a gorgeous uniform with much gold, must surely be the famous General Tom Thumb.

That freak display made a sharp impression on me. What boy would not have been enchanted by circus life? I would have given anything to roam the world with the rope dancers and jugglers, and to live in such a lavishly gilded white coach. (Not as myself, of course, but as a famous acrobat or trapeze artist.)

And then there were those gorgeous, heavy-hipped, tightly corseted female artists, in contrast to the concealing fashions of the day. This was your chance to focus your opera glasses upon their full fleshy beauty. Those heavy thighs in silk tights played a great role in my fantasies.

How mysterious, how beautiful the world beyond our confines must be—the world we glimpsed through these artists! A few days after their departure the entire magic was gone, and the little town seemed to me like a plundered Christmas tree, more desolate, more empty than ever before.

PEEKING INTO THE THIRTEENTH ROOM

I t had been a hot September day. After I had finished my homework, I went to see a friend of mine who lived nearby. I wanted
to borrow the book about pirates that he had got for his birthday
and that I had been looking forward to for a long time. It had
become dark, and the gas lamps in the street where he lived with
his parents threw only sparse light on the houses, set back behind
little gardens. My friend's house stood even further back, where
the street ended and truck gardens began. It was one of those old-
fashioned, one-storied Pomeranian houses; the living quarters
were not exactly at ground level, but the windows were at the
height of my shoulders, the roof ascended from there to a point,
and there was a sort of garret at the top.

I went through the garden, closing the big, wooden gate behind
me. I wanted to go in through the back door that my friend and I
always used. That entrance was next to a sort of tree nursery, back
of which were only long vegetable beds and the outlines of the
greenhouses in the truck garden. It was almost pitch dark that
evening, and nobody was around. I noticed some light in two
windows, hardly visible, because it came through small heart-
shaped holes in the solid wood shutters. It was not unusual to close
those shutters from the outside because of the strong wind that
often came in from the Baltic; the shutters offered good protection
from wind and weather.

I thought my friend would be at home. I waited a moment and
was just about to shout hello and knock to announce my presence
before entering the house, when it occurred to me to take a look
and see whether there was actually anybody in the room. Kids
seem to get ideas like that. I also thought I could surprise him more
that way. So I decided to let out the Indian war whoop that we had

both read about in one of our bloodcurdling Western pulps. In my mind, the house had already become a cabin in a clearing near the prairie.

It so happened that a large wooden box had been left in front of one of the windows. I sneaked up very stealthily, imagining my friend bent over a French composition or our hated math homework. I held my breath and carefully stepped on to the box. There was a slight creak. I waited, then put my eyes to the opening in the wood shutter. There were curtains inside the window, but of course they were divided in the middle; besides, it was easy to see through the curtains' open weave. A large oil lamp threw a cozy, yellow light onto the red plush cover on the table and into the room beyond. Suddenly I noticed that this was not my friend's room at all. Of course—it was the one next door. The darkness had confused me. This must be his parents' room, their bedroom, for the lamp showed part of the beds across from me to the left.

I was suddenly seized by an extraordinary excitement. I had the feeling of treading forbidden paths. The Westerns went into oblivion. A sensual feeling invaded me. I felt weak—but it was pleasant, somehow—when I suddenly noticed that there was a woman in the room....I immediately recognized my friend's aunt who had come from the big city to help in his father's business. A wild lusting curiosity grabbed me with devilish claws. All my good intentions were gone. I must have been about fourteen—still half young boy, but on the verge of breaking out from the chrysalis of childhood into adolescence. My friends came to mind. I remembered conversations, ambiguous remarks they had made....

A woman in that room! Something pulled me in. I felt as though I were being pricked by tiny red-hot needles. Driven by a passion that I did not yet understand, I stood rooted and observed the woman.

She now moved nearer the lamplight. I watched her take a middle-sized mirror that probably belonged over the washbasin and prop it against a shelf. Then she took off the lamp shade so as to get more light. I noticed an alcohol burner on the table, the sort that women used to heat their curling irons. There were some combs and a hairbrush next to it, and a few hairpins. Some bottles were there too, probably hair lotion and cologne or perfume, and a tube of skin cream. A coffee cup stood on a newspaper—next to it, a little box of carved wood lined in blue, with sewing things: needles, some of them threaded, in a pin cushion. Spools of silk thread, a metal thimble, a few loose, white, whalebone stays and some pink elastic completed this still life.

Without really being able to make it out, I suspected that a shiny black dress lay on the bed. At the wall in back was the washstand with its basin on top, flanked by a pitcher and a pot of hot water—I noticed the rising steam. Right! the mirror *had* been removed. I noticed the hook over the washstand, and the lighter color of the wallpaper where it had been hanging. Beneath it was a colorfully embroidered cloth, reading "Awaken Happily Every Morning," on which the capital letters were decorated with ornaments and flowers. The scalloped edges of this white cloth were embroidered with red silk. Next to the mahogany washstand was a wooden towel rack with towels, and next to that, a conical sponge holder of white celluloid with a little red bow on top. A washcloth was spread on the edge of the marble top of the washstand, presumably to dry. Below, in the shadow, was a big porcelain pail for dirty water, with a lid and a rattan handle hooked on two porcelain knobs. Next to the pail I saw a chamber pot, also porcelain, decorated with ornamental flowers. It made me think of a big, green cabbage.

I really don't know why this is all so vivid in my memory. Was it because of my inherent powers of observation, or was it because my excited imagination related it all to the woman in the room? I see it as vividly today as I did that memorable evening. I forgot God and the world. Passionately my eyes absorbed that room and everything in it.

I was overcome by an extraordinary, eerie feeling of pleasure. My friend's aunt walked back and forth, entered the circle of lamplight, pulled up a chair, sat down, brought the mirror closer, and started to busy herself with her face. She squeezed a blackhead, took a cloth and wiped it, leaned back, yawned suddenly and stretched her arms. Then she leaned forward again, fiddled with her ear lobe, and turned her head slightly toward me while taking off her earrings and putting them on the table. She picked up a hairpin and scratched her head with it. On impulse, she stood up again and disappeared to one side toward a chest of drawers half out of the light. I heard the creak of a drawer being opened, whereupon she came back to the table with a piece of white underwear, ladies' drawers...! She pulled over the box and poked around, looking for something. She found it, a roll of blue silk ribbon which she threaded through small holes in the embroidery and tied into bows. She picked up her coffee cup, took a sip, and went back to her work. Finished, she threw the drawers onto the bed where the black dress was, stood up, moved the chair sideways out of the light and—I had a hot flush—started fiddling with her blouse. Blouses, in those days, had high necks and were fastened in the back with hooks and eyes. My God, I thought, my God, and went weak, for I had never yet seen an undressed woman except in pictures, and that was mere paper....

Things were quite different in those days. Women wore skirts that went all the way down to the floor and sometimes even dragged after them. They were tightly laced in the middle; wasp waists were still in style. Everything was covered. Bare skin was never shown. A well brought up lady was not even allowed to cross her legs; she might possibly show her boots, but never where her leg began. That was the way it was in the strict, respectable bourgeois families. Those very prohibitions may have caused the indescribable fascination of catching a glimpse of what was so strictly concealed: bare skin.

I do not know. It seems inconceivable today that nudity would so obsess the imagination of our awakening adolescence. Oddly enough, while I was standing by that shutter with burning cheeks, my thoughts went to Hilda Giese and Alice Zöller, little school-mates our own age whom we very innocently admired, and some-how I had to compare them to the woman in the room. No, they were quite undeveloped teenagers in gym blouses; they did not have the figure-eight shape of grown women; except for their braids and skirts, they were rather similar to us boys. Nothing exciting about them. Just childish fun. I also remembered fat Willi, the pinball boy, who had been my rather dirty-minded mentor for human affairs, and my friend Gützkow, who once gave me a fantastically obscene description of a naked woman whom he had observed through field glasses on the dunes of Stolpmünde.

In the meantime, the woman had opened her blouse, and I gazed with delight into a heart-shaped cleavage. Her large, full breasts were pressed upward by the fashionable corset of the period. They lay like two ripe peaches in a basket, and the basket was decorated with lace, in the manner of a fashionable fruit shop, because fashion decreed that a chemise be worn under the corset. Now she took off her skirt. It fell like a shell out of the reach of the lamp into the circle of shade on the carpet. A shimmering petticoat followed. It, too, sank onto the floor. They are like skins, I thought, entranced by the sight of such bursting open.

My friend's aunt must have been about thirty-eight at that time. She was a so-called stately woman, the type then preferred by men. There was at first a little gossip when my friend's father

brought her into his house: she came from the big city and was better and more fashionably dressed; that alone was enough to raise suspicion in our small Pomeranian town. Nothing specific was known; supposedly she had had a love affair or something, but that was only gossip, for nothing really was known. And her behavior was always flawless, even toward us boys.

She was statuesque, of middle height, dark hair, not really black, but dark. She wore it in braids around her head....I stood there, transfixed. Everything around me dissolved. My eyes were in that room. She now stood in the light, half undressed. Those white batiste drawers with the blue silk ribbon were long, all the way down to her knees. Though generously cut, they fit tightly over her strong thighs. They were tied round her waist with a band. I saw her robust calves in black stockings narrowing down to high button shoes that seemed inordinately small.

I had never seen anything like this, had only daydreamed of it. She leaned over, picked up the skirts from the floor, her full womanly hips emphasized for a moment, tightly encased in white batiste, and casually tossed them onto a chair.

Around me not a sound—had anybody come at this moment, I would have been caught, so absorbed was I in fascinated observation. She went to the washstand and returned. Now she reached back and unfastened something, raised her legs and stepped out of the drawers. Her chemise, a bit crumpled, rustled down like a cascade. It was fairly long. She picked up the drawers and put them by the skirts on the chair. Now she was standing in her chemise, corset, and bodice. She took off the bodice, revealing the tightly laced corset that pushed up rolls of flesh, visible even under the voluminous chemise. Now she laid her arms over her breast and started to unhook the taped white stays of her corset; that took a good deal of effort, I could almost hear her breathing. The top of the corset broke open, releasing her large breasts, allowing them to gush slightly downward, still framed by the lacy triangular decolleté of the beribboned top of her chemise.

The corset was placed with her other garments. She was now in her chemise. She hesitated a little, raised her hand to her head as though to smooth her hair, passed it down over her chemise: unconscious movements, probably. Then she sat on the edge of the bed, pushing the black dress aside, put her hand up to her head again to pull out a large hairpin.

Leaning over and crossing her legs, she used it to unbutton her shoes. I could now look into her decolleté and see her full breasts hanging like ripe fruit. She had taken off her boots and rolled down her stockings. Only then did I notice that she had been wearing garters. Her movements shifted the chemise a bit, revealing the rosy flesh of her heavy thighs, where the garters had left marks. The light fell fully onto her, there at the edge of the bed. She stopped for a moment, yawned again, passed her hands again over her chemise, and sat up. With delight I noticed her breasts standing high under the white batiste, like little mountains. Suddenly she stood up, touched her armpits and, working with both hands, wriggled out of her chemise.

Breathlessly I watched this soft, voluptuous, fully developed female body slowly emerging from the white shell. The very furniture in the room seemed to participate in this spectacle. Did the chair not stretch its back to see better? Did the lamp not seem to flicker? In breathless excitement I absorbed it all. I was troubled, but enchanted. So this is what a woman looks like! These two halves!

She turned away and displayed a gorgeous back. Delightedly I contemplated the rosy, wide globes of her bottom with its funny little dimples. I noticed the rolls of fat that voluptuous women often have, and with happy surprise I discovered something dark, like a large furry heart, below her lightly rounded belly.

She moved around quite naturally, for how could she know that anyone, let alone I, was watching her? She stretched, rubbed her body and thighs, went to the mirror, raised her arms and started to let down her hair. She had the same dark hair in her armpits. Like small oases were these tufts of hair, in a large, smooth landscape of fleshy dunes, as though one could retire here thirsty, to rest after wandering through the hot, large and small dunes. She took hairpins out of her hair, keeping some in her mouth, laying others on the table. She also put a sort of toupee there that women used to wear to make their coiffure look rounder and higher. Her hair now snaked down and covered half her back. She looked for a large hairpin that had fallen down, leaning over and turning her back toward me. She did not immediately find it, and again I saw that dark, heart-shaped something push forward between her thighs....

I felt feverish. I was shaking with excitement, couldn't tear myself away. It was enchantment. How was it possible for this respectable bourgeois lady to suddenly produce such a totally different impression? Was this metamorphosis? I hardly recognized my friend's aunt, the way she moved around in her birthday suit.

"After Durer" [ca. 1

Something had peeled off with her clothes. This was the fruit itself, the pure female gender complete with all its attributes. It was full of curves, rosy white, brownish shades of flesh, blue veins shining through white skin. I suddenly thought of a horse I had seen, a whitish-yellow, fallow mare. Wasn't her rump just like that? This was my first experience with a naked woman, and it affected me to the marrow. It was immense. I felt the man awakening within me. How I would have loved to be in there with her, senseless, crazy, to caress her and kiss her—all those curves, those folds, the fur of the dark heart with the split in the middle. My knees went weak. I could not tear myself away.

Suddenly I heard a noise and voices. This time, the sound reached my consciousness; I was dazed and shaking, but remembered to be quiet when stepping off my box. Somewhat paralyzed, I got caught on a nail, fell down, and made a noise. I broke into a cold sweat (from fear? or from the excitement of my adventure?) and got up as fast as I could. Ran as fast as I could to the garden gate and out. I made it. Thank goodness the road was not paved, so the soft earth dampened the sound of my steps. I got home exhausted, bewildered and stricken. The image of this naked, Rubensesque woman has stayed with me and to this day, I have never overcome that first impression.

And I have really never wanted to get over it. That picture remained hanging in the gallery of my mind for a long time. That is, it is still there; later, I was able to bring it to life. And every so often, when I am painting, I look up and see that woman in the lamplit room. It is as though an unknown force was showing me an emblem, something eternal. For as long as we exist, we shall have the symbol of the female nude: woman as the eternal source and continuation of our race.

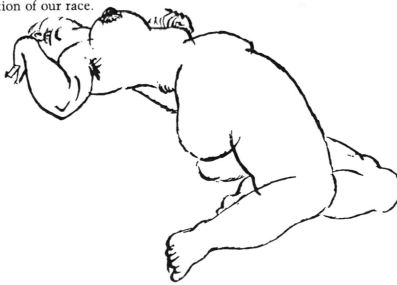

I KNOW WHAT I WANT

One day I became acquainted with the book dealer Schönboom, the idealistic owner of Stolp's largest book and art-supply store. I often stood before his store windows, enviously contemplating the beautiful painting paraphernalia which I so loved, the cases, the canvas stretched on frames, ready for use. A whole painter's studio was there, as yet unused; and how I would have loved to buy some of it! But on my meager allowance, those lovely things were out of reach.

Once when I was buying some paint there and exchanging a book in the lending library, I got to talk to the owner. Thereafter, I was allowed to spend all the time I wanted in the store's art department to look at all the reproductions. A small step forward to my unknown future.

I copied an illustration from the *Gartenlaube* that interested me greatly, a picture by Professor Werner Simmler entitled *Surprised*. Two poachers with blackened faces were caught in the act by the gamekeeper. They were just about to gut an unlawfully shot deer. One of them, terrifying to behold, was raising his rifle; the question now was—and this was the moment of suspense chosen for the picture—who would shoot first...I adored that picture. I copied it lovingly, putting all the ability I had into my work. I was very pleased with the result. When it was finished, my benefactor Schönboom put it neatly framed in his store window, making me and my friends very proud indeed. But imagine my joy when my work was sold a short while later to the owner of an estate, and Herr Schönboom handed me 4 marks 85 for it! It was a wonderful feeling to be paid for something that had been such a pleasure to do.

The book dealer continued to be my patron. He had a country

house not far from town with a lovely, well-tended garden where I was occasionally permitted to visit him. We would wander up and down between knowledgeably planned flower beds. Bending toward a rose, he would engage me in very serious pedagogical talks. One day in a hidden corner of the garden, he suddenly stopped in front of me, looked straight into my eyes in a kind yet strict way, and said emphatically: "I believe you are wandering down a bad path."

I got very red in the face, mumbled something incoherent, and left a little later, deeply worried. Truly, I would immediately begin a new life; the very same day I destroyed my little picture collection of beautiful, half-dressed women that I had assembled from the erotic crime magazine *Reporter*. Though I had never heard of the playwright Wedekind, I did the same thing his character Moritz Stiefel did: full of good resolutions, I drowned the shredded pictures in our newly installed water closet. I felt I was a sinner. I subjected myself to such searching judgment that the eating of meat seemed to be the source of evil (influenced by a gruesome propaganda leaflet I had just read). My mother could not understand why a juicy roast of beef suddenly left me completely unmoved.

Schönboom was the genuine old-style German book dealer, always somewhat didactic, and ever conscious of his cultural mission as an emissary of the book trade. He spoke with understanding and scholarly kindness, emphasized by the slightly raised index finger of a German high-school teacher, an erstwhile type he actually resembled. His gold-rimmed spectacles, reddish beard, humanist ideals of education and memories of travel in Greece are still with me. Father of a family, he had two precocious and unusually impertinent children, and a wife who looked artistic from afar and wore sensible clothes; he believed in a semi-meatless diet and sponsored a youth-temperance league.

I went on drawing and copying all sorts of things. A series of water color postcards done in the manner of the celebrated flower painter Katarina Klein was promptly sold and reordered. My bent toward humor, let alone satire, had not yet appeared, though there were occasional indications of that later gift. So enchanted was I with Wilhelm Busch, whom I had just discovered, that I spent the better part of a night copying his whole nymph story—until the pen literally dropped from my hand.

From bound volumes of the *Fliegende Blätter* from Schönboom's lending library I copied mostly Adolf Hengeler's work. With great

patience I tried to grasp every single line of the woodcut or reproduction and copy it exactly. I used special caligraphy pens to copy
the poetry which it illustrated. I also liked the pen drawings of old
Wilhelm von Diez very much. In a copy of *Daheim* I found an
article about him and a number of reproductions of his drawings of
the Thirty Years' War; after that, my "free" compositions showed
a lot of freebooters and Swedish soldiers. Then came sepia
drawings; with a pointed paintbrush and some sepia paint, I tried
to achieve the sort of effect that I had seen in drawings by Schwind
or Ludwig Richter.

Inspired by Eduard Grützner's studies of interiors, I tried to
render cellar motifs with barrels and wine bottles; not having any
monks to copy, I would add an old volume or goblet instead. I
would draw whatever came before my pencil, anything and everything around the house: yard, kitchen, cellar—baskets, a pair of
shoes, a ladder leaning on a fruit tree, our dog Witboi in his basket,
and an entire rear view of the officers' casino. I would take my bike
to find farm cottages and landscapes to draw. I would just draw and
draw, happily, heedless of questions or problems; if I emulated
Grützner one day, I might follow one of the historic battle painters
the next. Reading about the famous Adolph von Menzel, I resolved
to follow his example and keep on drawing, wherever, whenever,
while standing, lying, sitting, sleeping. Menzel's motto to the
effect that pure, hard, constant work was more important than
talent greatly impressed me.

Gradually and ever so gently, the later Grosz began to appear,
already showing a little bit of his cloven hoof. I tended more
toward dream than sarcasm, but was sufficiently objective an
observer to recognize the laws of might and right that were to
become the leading principles in my concepts of life and society. I
am not implying that I had a mature knowledge of life and human
nature at the age of 14 or 15—not at all. What I mean about the
laws of might and right was that I recognized a certain degree of
brutality among boys; if attacked, you parried as well as you could.
Likes and dislikes were settled by fists. Simply that.

Da Abt erschrak, sein Lieblings-
wein
Zur Stärkung nach der Mette
Sein Mittelchen zum „Schlafe
ein"
Des Abends vor dem Bette!
Doch dacht' er, Rahst kommt
mit der Zeit
Und füllte die Panne heiter
Und tat dem Ritter brav
Bescheid —
Herr Leupold, der trank wei-
ter
Und trank so ungewaltig fast
Wie das-Thor bei den Riesen,
Dann aber sank er zu seliger

An experience comes to mind that happened when I was a little boy in Berlin. I was a daydreamer at the time, had just come from Stolp to the city, and was in a new school. I was very much alone. I felt far away from Stolp. As I stood in the school yard during recess, it was all so strange, and Berlin so new. I had not had time yet to make any friends, so I stood there, half dreaming. I was just about to take a bite of my unwrapped sandwich when I was hit hard in the back by a boy running past, and fell full length on the dirty ground with my face in my sandwich...I was as if paralyzed. Annihilated. Though I saw the boy running away, I was incapable of following him or risking a fight. I really don't know why; it must have been more than just an ordinary blow in the back. I remember being frozen inside with hatred and fury, but somehow had to swallow it without protest. Odd. Later on I learned my lesson, and much later even became one of those who knocked other sandwich-eating, daydreaming boys down. But I certainly have not forgotten that experience to this day. Even now I am often subject to the immense malice, loneliness and forlornness that I felt in that schoolyard.

Again and again I have encountered that type of person, in almost all walks of life; it seems as though that experience had been the discovery of a deeper law of brutality, coupled with an ever-present malicious joy in others' misfortune.

Oh, when I think back to my growing years, how unclear it all is! Who guided you? Who and where was the puppeteer who made the puppet hop and dance like all the other puppets? We did go to church. It was our duty to attend church to prepare for confirmation, a very important religious event, particularly for a Protestant. Protestant ceremonies have nothing like the mystic pomp and magic attraction of Catholic rites. All told, it was an almost animalistic, amorphous kind of life. We were much like insects, it seems to me now, looking back at it. There must have been a bit of the reformer in me too, alongside the artistic dreamer. I hardly know where that came from. There had been a clergyman in the family, his old portrait in his black coat with a white collar hanging in the parlor, but nobody, not even my mother, knew much about him. He was known to be from my father's side, but that was about all we knew, as the portrait got more and more faded.

I mean by "reformer" an inclination to participate, a precarious inclination of knowing things better than others and, as a typical reformer, I often did know better. I succumbed to all sorts of ideas of reform that were very much in the air at that time. Those were the days when Victorian prudishness was beginning to be punctured by enlightening ideas. It was the time of Ibsen, the time when the middle-class world started listening to reformers, the time that let in fresh air. I embraced all those theories, and those of the Danish teacher, I. P. Müller, who advocated a cold water rubdown by an open window every morning, and who was opposed to corsets and high collars. Women were still wearing long skirts then, and if one actually had her hair cut, she would have been considered a crazy innovator.

My tenacity, patience and industry certainly came from my mother's side. My grandfather had been a basketmaker in Finsterwalde; from him came my ability to persevere, and concentrate when necessary, my manual dexterity and my sense of ornament— to weave the components of a picture together like a basket. Maybe my pictures outwardly seem like baskets; that there is, naturally, something inside those baskets is something else again. I believe drawing may have originated in man's inborn sense of braiding and weaving....

My enjoyment of life and lots of good food and drink is also inherited; that is simply a German trait. As to drinking, I remember an uncle, a basketweaver, who was reported always to have had one mighty bottle of schnaps standing next to his basket, even early in the morning. He got to be quite old though, and when I saw him at the age of 74 at his wife's funeral, he was a fine old man, not at all shaky or peculiar. Supposedly he had almost given up drinking at the age of 65, but remained a heavy smoker.

In Stolp I went to the high school. The boys in my class were mostly country boys, sons of landowners, government officials and ambitious middle class families. Their sons were to go "up" in the world, so they needed a high-school diploma which, in turn, entitled them to one year of training and officer rank during compulsory military service. Without it meant serving two or three years as an enlisted man, which was not all that tempting.

In those mild, quiet prewar days, nobody in our high school had heard about modern principles or methods of education. Student government, for instance, was inconceivable and probably actually impossible. We were brought up by cane, a cane painted with the national colors, black, white, and red. Our teachers were all Protestant and reserve officers, and their aim was to achieve as military an education as possible. They would admonish us by saying, "Surely you want to be a good soldier some day—so shape up!" That usually worked.

We took the old Prussian, spartan ideal for granted. With manly fortitude, we pulled the seats of our pants tight to receive the five or six blows from that cane. The cane would sometimes be named after the last one thrashed. It was bad, but flattering at the same time, when the order came: "Krause, get Grosz from the desk!" The cane was kept next to the chalk and eraser in the teacher's desk, and a special cane warden was designated each week—an honor comparable to that of the provost in the ancient Prussian regiments who saw to it that the willow rods were good and flexible for running the gauntlet.

It may be that this was the only way to deal with thick-skinned Pomeranian youngsters. Nearly every teacher used corporal punishment, and each had his own special method. One named Knapp had devised a particularly degrading punishment. To start with, his looks were quite unpleasant. He had a terrifying type of face, often seen on North German security guards or jailers. The frightening aspect of his cold, somber features was heightened by

his preference for rough wool suits that covered him like animal skin, stressing his ferocity. Sitting at his desk, he would make the delinquent student stand at attention before him, hands pressed to thighs, face straight forward. After staring disapprovingly at the boy for a while, he would twist his heavy signet ring into his palm, pause again for some time, then suddenly deliver a hard blow on the delinquent's face, shouting, with great scorn, "You ox!" The insignia of the ring left a painful imprint; and while those who always have to laugh at everything did laugh, you slunk back to your chair in shame.

Such were the approved principles of education. There were only a few exceptions among our teachers, and they were unable to get our respect. Instead of being popular, they were considered weak and were teased and tortured. Some of them, when annoyed beyond endurance, would throw their huge bunches of keys at us and chase us round the school benches, shouting hysterically and swearing at us: "Criminals...You'll end on the gallows...Get a revolver for the beast...!" It was a bitter battle, with victims on both sides. At times I had that half-tragic, half-comic feeling that we stood up better than our teachers. Both sides had become callous and since this was the way it was, nobody could do anything about it. The only way to deal with those bespectacled tyrants was with cunning, trickery and bright ideas.

A collective subterranean will was constantly vigilant and steadily intent to undermine the holy authority of the cane. Minor ruses were acted out with great theatrical skill. With groveling innocence you would offer your services to fetch science materials, or pretend helpless agony for bathroom permission—only to disappear like a flash round the corner, and devour a piece of still-warm apple cake from the nearby bakery. Such fairly harmless infringements of our rigid school discipline were as dangerous as real adventures: anybody caught outside during school hours got a merciless hiding or, even worse, would have to stay after school, thereby spoiling a free, beautiful June afternoon.

Many of my teachers were odd characters, funny drill-sergeant types with barrel-shaped bellies, amazingly limp trousers, impossibly badly fitting collars and peculiar pince-nez. They looked exactly like their caricatures in prewar *Simplicissimus*. How much inadequacy and failure they must have represented! No wonder those of us who went to school in those days still have recurrent nightmares. Our teachers were dictators, and we pupils had to keep our traps shut. (We obviously intended to act the same way when we grew up.) Remembering my school days, I can think of much amusing mischief, but I can never get rid of a certain sour, moldy smell.

One day, the inevitable happened. I was "discharged," as they say in the army. Simply thrown out. Herr Pingkwardt, an assistant teacher, boxed my ears, and in fury I struck back, thereby increasing the "bad" group's admiration for me. My mother humbled herself and went to implore Director Mörner for forgiveness, but he remained hard. His reply to her plea for another chance was: "Your son is corrupting the whole class; elements like that must be removed without consideration. Changing the faculty decision is out of the question, Mrs. Grosz; you can always try some other school. Good day."

Despite my audacity, I did not feel at all good. I hid in the laundry room like a sick animal, wept about the worry that my expulsion had inflicted on my mother, and brooded gloomily about the insecurity of my future. Getting enrolled in a school in another town would cost money, plus the additional expense of living away from home. Everything was ruined. A piece of my dream had disappeared in collision with the real rules and the powers of this world. So stupid. But that was it.

◆

Black clouds hung heavily over a future which was as unclear and formless as an impressionist picture. I preferred my daydreams to the serious pursuit of heavy thought. Oh, it will work somehow, somebody whispered inside me. I did not know then and I don't know to this day whether that "somebody" was strong or weak. It was countered by my Protestant vein: Work, be good, prove yourself, show what you can do—that was the other "somebody." Whether it was the heritage of the tippling innkeeper or my hardworking mother who supported the family—no matter, I saw myself as a good lithographer and would manage my two years as an infantry private....

As soon as my first tears had dried I returned from my self-imposed exile in the laundry room, bicycled round town as though nothing had happened, and started gently talking about my dearest wish of becoming a painter. My mother did not like the idea at all. Being a practical woman, she would rather have had me finish school in a nearby town and go on to a career as a government official, the post office, for instance. She was quite right, of course. That type of job has security and a pension, whereas an artist has no sort of security whatever, let alone a pension. That is the way the world order has settled it, and no committees on progress can change it. Nevertheless, a civil service career did not appeal to me at all: secretly, I was already standing on a high ladder before an enormous canvas and painting a huge historic picture. People with that kind of bug in their heads do not have the making of civil servants.

It was extraordinary how firmly those ideas were settled in my head, considering the lovely, free, school-less time I was having; I certainly did not want to give up this great chance of doing whatever I wanted all day long. And the fact that my friends were still subjected to the severe Stolp school discipline made me enjoy this respite all the more....

One of my best friends was Heini Blume. We were both addicted to penny-dreadfuls and both dreamed of the dangerous adventures we would have when we grew up. Heini planned to go to Hamburg, enlist as a cabin boy, and jump ship in Brazil. His passion for Brazil came mostly from his stamp collection; Brazilian stamps had beautiful, romantic pictures. Another attraction in our friendship was that Heini's father had an inn that provided stabling for horses, an important service in small country towns. All the small farmers of the neighborhood would come here on Saturday evenings after market, unharness their horses in the backyard, and meet in the front room. Many of them brought bread, bacon, sausage, and cake tied in colored handkerchiefs, and bought beer and schnaps from Heini's aunt, who tended bar in a green blouse. Schnaps was usually consumed straight from the bottle that was passed from mouth to mouth. Behind the counter were larger bottles, beautifully curved, with indentations for fingers to grasp; those later went out of use and became collectors' items as flower vases for interior decorators. The schnaps glasses were very solid, as were the coffee cups, designed for customers who were none too gentle; rightly, by the way, as thin glass or delicate china would have splintered in the gnarled hands of these farmers, masons and fishermen. The solid crockery on the counter and the tables made a beautiful still life, almost like an old Dutch painting; it was in harmony with the whitewashed walls, decorated with beer posters with folksy slogans. The men drank heavily, and some brawlers used the glasses that fitted their hands so well to fortify their blows. I will never forget Heini's father—a tall, strong, bearded man—dashing out of the front room, reaching under the counter, quick as a flash, for an arm-long rubber tube and swinging it indiscriminately at the brawlers. A pool of blood mixed with liquor on the sand-strewn floor was the result.

An emaciated old man was always sitting next to the counter, rawboned and sunburnt, in ragged brickmason's clothes. When

Heini was there and his aunt happened to have left, he would shyly pluck at Heini's sleeve and beg him for a drink. Heini would then get one of the big bottles, fill a decanter to the top—and in a flash, his eyes devoutly closed, the man would pour the spirits down his throat. Heini would also give him a handful of so-called Russian cigarettes with filters, out of a box that was always on the table. Both the booze and cigarettes were the cheapest available, but that made little difference to a person seeking numbness and oblivion.

This lonely, permanent guest became a good friend of Heini's and mine. It turned out that he had participated as a volunteer of the colonial force in the Herero campaign in German Southwest Africa, caught malaria, been wounded, and returned to his home town of Stolp at the end of his military adventure. Now he was done for. His war stories, medals and souvenirs may have got him some attention at first, but after a little while that stopped, and people merely laughed at him. "Look, there's that African again, telling his endless stories about how thirsty he had been in the colonial force..." He got to be boring, and hardly anybody would stand him to a beer or a drink.

Work?—No, that was no longer possible, he told us as we three were lying in the sun on the roof of the bath house by the Stolpe. "How can I work, plagued by that permanent thirst? You see, they all get that in the colonial forces, they all do, that confounded thirst...It drives you crazy, you see, Heini, the sun and the dust and more sun, and at night your marrow freezes in your bones, and that damned Witboi had either emptied or mucked up the water holes...thirst, boys—boys, thirst, you can't understand yet what that means...A guy in our squadron went completely nuts—he pissed in his hat and drank it...Yes, that's the way it was—Georg, give me that bottle and the matches—now I'll tell you what we used to do with the Herero women...."

He used to tell us the most wonderful stories and adventures. But every story took place in the tropical sun and the hot African bush and always ended with a terrible drought. "You see," he would say, "out there I got dried out like a prune. You get to be like a sponge out there. And in here (he pointed to himself) you feel as though something were on fire. Yeah. So that's why I have to keep on quenching it, keep on quenching it," he said as he reached for his cherished bottle that Heini secretly had managed to fill for him again before we went swimming. He was no longer able to work, but he was able to throw smoked cigarette filters, still moist with saliva, so skillfully at the whitewashed ceiling that they hung there like stalactites. Not a paying skill, however. One day he was

taken away and put in some institution. He had been seized by
tropical frenzy and went berserk with a bottle of booze. We, Heini
and I, were very sad to lose such a good companion and his
fabulous stories.

Not until a long time later did I understand what sort of person
he really was, that relic of a victorious campaign. For most people
he was a sad leftover, one who went astray, who could not find his
way back and therefore went to ruin in drink and misery; for Heini
and me, however, he was a romantic hero who had passed the test
of great perils, just the way (or nearly) they do in books. We never
saw him as he appeared to others. For us he was like a used, torn,
much read book, full of exciting stories, and that was quite appropriate. Actually he was a predecessor of those who got to be known
after World War I as "the lost generation."

Another friend of mine was the son of a prosperous butcher, Ite
Denzer. I can still see his father: a big man with one blind eye
standing behind his chopping block, the triangular top of his long
butcher's apron worn over his chest like monastic garb, a cleaver
in his hand to split a cutlet—like a symbolic figure. Doré could
have drawn him. He was a butcher and looked like one, not like a
doctor or a musician, and his hand was made to wield a cleaver, a

mallet and the various butcher knives, not the bow of a violin. A solid, strong, slightly brutal hand, that hand of Ite's father—but actually that was not what I was going to talk about.

Chemistry was the profession that Ite and his brother wanted to pursue. They spent much time in their room doing experiments, and there was always something smoking or sizzling. But it was not only pure science that they were practicing. They were also fabricating liquor from some sort of liquor essence. A man by the name of Reichel was advertising his wonderfully simple invention. By sending in a few marks, you could get (by return mail) a package of powders and pills, with instructions on how to brew any liquor in the world by the mere addition of a little alcohol. No previous knowledge was needed, no big apparatus, no filters or any such thing. All the liquors of the world. Enclosed were about twenty sorts to try out: starting with simple rye schnaps, then Podbipita (a Polish cavalry drink), on to a potion that cured cold feet and intestinal obstructions, to the king of all liqueurs, Benedictine or Chartreuse (yellow or green packet). Ite brewed like an old monk, and one Sunday morning after church he asked me to come over and watch his chemical experiments. Instead, he served me his newly brewed liqueurs. We were about 14 or 15 years old at the time, and I remember that we got really drunk. I staggered home, feeling very jolly at first, then got terribly sick and swore that never, ever again I would touch anything that had to do with liquor or alcohol...A promise that I naturally could not quite keep, as I was to meet many another Ite Denzer after church—symbolically, I mean.

Then there was Paul Friedrich's father, a cabinet maker. I have kept one of his sayings: "Don't spare the glue, my boy, don't spare the glue." We liked to hang around the wood turner's workshop and the wood sculpture studio. Zucker was the sculptor, Hoffmann the turner. Filthy language flowed from their mouths, but that did not bother us. All we wanted was their skill—and literally in a minute Hoffmann would make the greatest tomahawk out of a waste piece of leftover wood. Zucker, blaspheming and cursing away, would carve us excellent daggers that we then decorated with tacks from the upholstery shop. So we got the best weapons, swords, hatchets and daggers that there were, quite apart from the fun of climbing around all those staked wooden planks.

My supposed satiric talent appeared now and then. I tried it out once on a harmless barber, a sort of Henri Rousseau, passionately addicted to oil painting. In the midst of all the barber shop paraphernalia—brushes, combs, hairpins, soaps, toothpastes, perfumes and all the sweet splendor of a barber's display—stood his newest oil painting. In gilded frames you saw hunting scenes, animal studies, deer in the snow, a little too-raspberry colored sunset over a heath and a sail boat in a storm on waves of seltzer-bottle green. On market days, art-loving farmers would stand before the shop window full of admiration; after Master Hingst had skillfully soaped and shaved them, some of them would buy a picture. Looking back, there is a lot to be said for Hingst's shop; it was reminiscent of the days when a painter was also an innkeeper, a doctor, a barber, a mayor—or vice versa. As you entered his shop to have a haircut, you would often find Hingst painting. His enormous, curved palette and his artfully done hair in which a comb was often stuck made him look like that obsolete type of artisan whom you still might see in Paris. It was an interesting experience to have your hair cut while smelling a mixture of turpentine and linseed oil on one hand and shampoo and hair tonic on the other.

This engaging character was a thorn in the side of decorator Grot, my painting instructor. His studies in Munich had taught him what "true" art was and he therefore considered himself Stolp's artistic conscience. To him, this painting Figaro was a cultural disgrace, his pictures were dangerous trash, and he was ruining the taste of the people of Pomerania. Herr Grot liked to spread his ideas among his friends by issuing an occasional pamphlet, *Stolper Bilderbogen*, in which he satirized particularly ridiculous local events with his own line drawings and verse. Master Hingst's trashy pictures were a perfect topic for Grot's ridicule. In my desire for artistic education, I listened to everything he said, and believed his carefully chosen words.

I decided that I personally had to do something to combat the corrupting influence of the barber's painting, so I devised a biting satire for Grot's pamphlet. I made a line drawing of Master Hingst beating brownish foam in an oversized chamber pot, ready to lather a customer with his "art." This was supposed to be satirically symbolic, and I thought my idea was very original and biting. I made up a witty text for it too, borrowing from zoology. Unfortunately the whole thing was never printed; due to the lack of satirical appreciation in Stolp, and resulting financial difficulties, the *Stolper Bilderbogen* had to be discontinued until further notice.

Somebody told me that a lot of money could be made by doing caricatures. That misinformation led to my producing a lot of silly line drawings. The ideas were not my own, and I got lost in the

search for style. I was looking for simplicity and humor and tried to find my own style by studying old and new comic magazines. But it was still a long, long way to Tipperary....

I sent my first drawings to several magazine editors. Here, I thought, lies the sunny future for my talents. But their critical sense was more highly developed than mine, and my cherished work was returned with discouraging regularity, accompanied by the identical form letter: "Thank you for sending us your interesting work. We regret that we cannot use it."

My rosy dreams would have soured completely had I not had a very understanding art teacher, Herr Papst, in high school who lent me support in word and deed. He recognized my talent from the beginning and encouraged my mother to let me be a painter. Papst was Austrian, came from the Sudetenland, and had a university education. After his years as a bohemian student, he found he had to earn a living and got a job with the esteemed court painter Iser in Stettin. Iser had what amounted to a factory for turning out portraits of government officials. He furnished city halls, schools and other public buildings with the urgently needed portraits of senators, deputies, mayors, generals—in other words, all the worthy sons of the community. Papst became one of his assistants. Later, for reasons unknown, he gave up that job and became the second teacher of drawing and gymnastics (the top man being funny old Herr Fitzlaff) at our high school. He was tall and thin, had a wrinkled face, high Slavic cheek bones, and a crew cut, and though he certainly did not look like one, he became my guardian angel.

He encouraged my mother to see him and he gave her new hope
for her wayward son. For wayward I was; I had been thrown out of
school—not only a major disgrace in the eyes of my mother and
sisters, but also a bad omen for the future. And rightly so. Without
that diploma, I would have to serve for two or three years as a
lowly private in the Prussian army, which meant the loss of
valuable time, quite apart from the human drudgery. Important as
that drill might have seemed, in view of future events, those
barrack yard games of discipline seemed an awful waste of two or
three years for a would-be painter. It was socially demeaning too,
being a common soldier. An upper-class person who had that
diploma served only one year, was an officer and a member of the
social élite. The prejudices of the people who mattered were quite
rigid, almost Chinese; that one-year service was the key to being a
reserve officer, and that rank was an absolute requirement for any
sort of career, let alone marriage into a family of wealth and
position. You would simply not be considered a "gentleman" and
get anywhere in life without it.

It is important to remember that Germany still had a class
system at the time. And one could see wonderful examples of what
many a petty-bourgeois family would do to enable their son to get
that diploma—even cutting down on the daughter's dowry—so
that he could do his one-year service and be a reserve officer. There
was actually something quite admirable about it, as it was not
money alone that counted, for according to the older Prussian
hierarchy money had acquired a corrupting influence. Still, that
diploma was an absolute necessity. Without it you could only
become a mason or a blue-collar worker, or little more. Any
"proper" vocations were locked behind a barbed-wire fence of
required diplomas, recommendations, attestations, and difficult,
mystical papers.

On the other hand, my life could not go on forever this way.
Something had to happen, even I could see that. Apparently I was
not really cut out to be a good-for-nothing, though some of those
types are said to have become quite good painters; but I was made
of different stuff. I wanted to be a painter, a real painter. I wanted to
paint great big pictures that would be reproduced in Velhagen &
Klasing's *Monthly Review*. Then even people in Stolp would
notice them and be astounded. My mother would be so proud to
hear people talking about me. These ideas kept me happy and
reconciled with a world that did not seem to see things my way.
Lovely dreams—or would it be better yet for me to become an
illustrator? The *Berliner Illustrierte Zeitung* had just announced

the Menzel prize of 3,000 marks to discover and foster young illustrators. Wow, I said to myself without daring to say it out loud, if only I could win that prize! Maybe after I've learnt some more....

That prize really hooked me. It fed my day dreams. My mother was very skeptical; better be a good worker and make some money, she said. Those silly castles in the air never lead to anything but disappointment and a hangover. Uncle August also had a lot of crazy ideas like that all the time and what did he get out of it? Nothing. Nothing at all. It cost a lot of money, instead of bringing any in. And finally August had to be put in an asylum. "But elegant he was, Georg, and full of great ideas, and a painter—"

My God, a painter—in the eyes of my mother that was a completely breadless occupation with no butter at all. And can you believe it, after all that education? What was the use of it all? Sure, you would hear once in a while about that little shepherd who had made his fortune and become a professor and even got a medal, but those things very rarely happened, that would be like winning the lottery! And from what I heard people say, most artists were quite debauched, lived in garrets with couches and velvet drapes, wore sloppy clothes, were hungry most of the time and owed the baker money. A good-for-nothing existence. They didn't work much either, but preferred to lie around on a bear skin, quite possibly with one of those frivolous models; and they drank, and wasted all the money that their family had saved and worked so hard to provide for their studies. It was nothing but a low life of dissipation at the expense of others.

That was the way my mother saw it, and maybe she was right. Only good old Papst was able to persuade her that it was really only half as bad as she thought. He had good common sense and he reasoned that a fellow could go to seed and be a failure in any occupation; there was no doubt that my talent was far above average; he had come to know me as a person, and had a high opinion of my character; he therefore had no hesitation in advising me to become a painter. "Your son has what it takes and will make his way," said Herr Papst.

Though I was not yet that sure of my ability, his confidence dispelled my mother's doubts. With a heavy heart she agreed to my choice of a career that was as uncertain as a lottery ticket....

I wish I could see my old art teacher again. Perhaps you are still living in that little town in Pomerania, dear friend? I salute you across all that may divide us. Your figure stands at the turning point of my life, and it is with gratitude that I think of you.

THE ROYAL ACADEMY OF ART

So I was to be sent to an academy of art, either in Berlin or Dresden. Herr Papst offered to prepare me for the entrance examination; he knew what was needed, having studied at an academy himself. My career as an artist had begun.

Oh, those misty, romantic illusions in the head of a sixteen-year-old! Exciting and happy days! Papst taught me how to draw plaster busts on blue paper. I used charcoal, finished with black chalk, and eventually learned how to highlight with white chalk. My first model was the life-sized plaster head of a Greek goddess. Next was a portrait bust of Lessing in monochrome—black and white, and grey half-tone—first full face, then in profile. Herr Papst would discuss my work with me, and give me all sorts of useful tips for my future career.

Meanwhile I had written my sister Claire in Berlin to ask her opinion. She was a department store manager, and had mentioned that the painter Hayduk, whose advertising art I greatly admired, worked for them. His ads were very modern and effective; I had made a collection of his clippings from newspapers. So I thought my sister might possibly show Hayduk my stuff and get his opinion. That might be useful. She may actually have done that, but Hayduk was a very busy man, so he probably just said yes, yes, very nice—or words to that effect, the way well-paid, busy men talk.

My sister had always been very fond of me, which may have been why she was not very supportive of my going into art. When I had to leave school so unceremoniously and said I wanted to be an artist, she very emphatically advised me against it. But she never held my obstinate decision against me, was always very kind and helped me whenever she could. When times were difficult, she would send me food packages with all sorts of goodies. So I now sent her another package of my work. She wanted to show it to a Professor Seeger of the academy to get his opinion. I had been drawing diligently, and not only the things for Papst; in view of the tradition of the Berlin Royal Academy, I included a painstaking, minute drawing of a shoe. It was this sample of my art that impressed the professor enough for him to advise me to try the Dresden Academy, since the academy in Berlin was full.

So Dresden it was. I put my best drawings together again, added a polite letter and my resumé, and sent it off with great trepidation. In due course the reply came, telling me where and when to appear for the entrance examination.

I was overjoyed. Swelled with pride, I bragged about it to my friends who were still sweating away at school. I greatly looked forward to this new phase of my life and was in high spirits even though secretly quite worried about the exam. My aunt, the one who worked with my mother at the casino, took me to Dresden where she had some old friends. I was to stay with the Kuhling family in Dresden-Striesen until the outcome of the exam determined my immediate future.

Herr Kuhling was a friendly, worthy gentleman, very tall, usually with a cigar in his mouth. He must have been a sort of civil engineer; at any rate he had a nice apartment with an alcove and a balcony in a suburban house typical of the eighties. Very pleasant, and quite homey.

Equally attractive—and very exciting to me—were his two grownup daughters with their unusually firm bosoms. Those bouncing hemispheres filled me with ideas and wishes that had very little to do with my impending examination. In vain I tried to master my emotions, invoking the spirit of my old benefactor Schönboom. I even contemplated vegetarianism. All in vain. I was possessed by a sensual devil and could think of nothing but those two sisters with their voluptuous globes. How I would have loved to approach them! But I was far too young and much too shy. Just as well, as I would not only have been turned down, but undoubtedly been thrown out of the house by their father. In view of my previous history at school, that would have made a fine start to my career as an artist....No, I could not take a chance on that. And though the erotic devil pursued me for quite a while, my good resolutions prevailed as the time for the crucial examination drew nearer and nearer.

I had to get up early when that fateful day finally came. The

Royal Academy of Art was a beautiful eighteenth-century building on the famous Brühl Terrace. It was a lovely autumn day with a touch of melancholy, the odor of fallen leaves, mist over the river Elbe—just right for my fatalist mood before the crucial examination. Something like a Chekhov story, or being summoned to court.

I was wearing the green hat of a country gentleman, and a fine new suit. There was the shining Elbe with the old Carola Bridge that Kühl so often painted, and across it the new part of Dresden, illuminated by the morning sun. It seemed a pity to have to enter this mighty palace to prove your artistic ability, but that was the way the world was, with all those tests.

Where were the meadows of Stolp and my dear old bicycle? Far, far away. This great, ornate baroque door was my new path. I opened it and entered a cool lobby. One was immediately aware that something was happening today. A crowd of newcomers like myself was assembling before the superintendent's cubicle, trying to get information, while others, who knew where they were going, tried to buy the supplies needed for the test. Some of the candidates were starting to disappear down the hall, carrying paper-covered mats and clutching chalk and eraser in their free hands. Others, presumably older students, were looking at the notices on the board or having conversations with the superintendent. Their paint-spattered smocks gave them the look of old soldiers who had been in the regiment for a long time and knew what was going on.

I got the information I needed and continued down the corridor to the beginners' class. I happened to notice in passing the card of a Professor Richard Müller who, unbeknownst to me, was soon to be my teacher. The beginners' class was a large studio with a sky light; it had presumably been cleared for the exam, as it was fairly empty. There was a big closet full of junk and old smocks in a corner; plaster copies of antique statues on movable trestles had been pushed against the wall; a rather dirty running plaster Greek raised his sword arm toward the newcomer; a few easels with newly papercovered stretchers stood in the background. The result was a grey and rather dusty atmosphere, heightened by the cold, subdued overhead light.

A number of candidates had already assembled when I came in, chattering not only in the local dialect but in every variety of German. I joined a group that was discussing an oil painting brought in by somebody. A bespectacled fellow with a local accent was explaining that it was by Hodler's nephew, who had just been transferred to the painting class of Professor Zwintscher. I had not yet heard of Hodler, let alone seen his work, and was not impressed by his nephew's landscape done with lots of thick green paint. The conversation then moved to Professor Richard Müller, and I learned of his significance as a painter. The same bespectacled young man with his thick Dresden accent was greatly impressed by the horrendous prices Müller's paintings fetched, and told us that his drawings had even been purchased by the National Gallery in London. I suddenly felt very small and thought of the long road of hard work, luck and talent that lay ahead before one could get anywhere near the National Gallery in London....

We were quite a mixture of people, we future artists. There were rich, poor, healthy and even cripples who limped or could use only one arm. While one had a particularly expensive paint box with shiny brass handles and hinges, others simply pulled a piece of chalk out of their pocket. Then there was Naumann-Coschütz, a "simple man of the people" who was born in Coschütz near Dresden and still lived there; he had been a lithographer for many years and had acquired red, inflamed, teary eyes from the constant use of a magnifying glass needed for his detailed drawing. He had worked and saved for many, many years and finally, at the age of thirty-five, achieved his only wish and lifelong ambition of attending the Royal Academy of Art....

Our examiner was a Professor Robert Sterl, a pleasant bachelor with the small eyes of an impressionist used to looking into the sun, and a good-natured, radish-colored face. He looked like a man who talks little, but likes to listen to others over a bottle of red wine. For our test we were to do a life-size drawing of a plaster bust of Emperor Nero. After some pleasantly growled instructions, we were left to our own devices, and pretty soon you could hear nothing but the scratching and wiping of chalk and charcoal on taut paper.

The examination took several days. Professor Sterl would drop in every so often and spend a minute or so giving advice when needed. I threw myself headlong into the work; with much enthusiasm but scant assurance, I sighted and measured like an old academician. My flat charcoal technique seemed to please Professor Sterl; I once heard an approving growl as he was passing. Wonderful! I realized that this pretty much settled the matter, and I would be accepted.

A week later the notice came in writing.

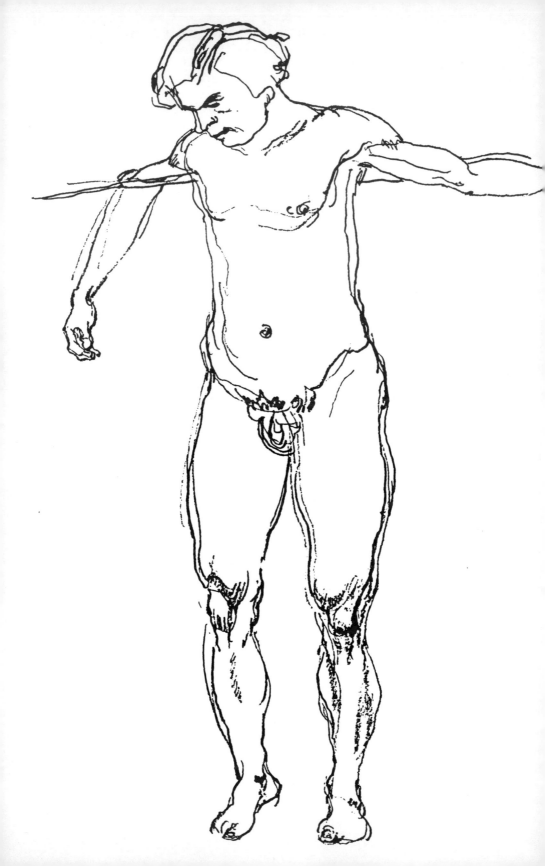

Having settled my immediate future, I left my nice bourgeois family with its two grown daughters, and took a small furnished room with a respectable worker's family. I lived there for about fifteen marks a month, including coffee and rolls for breakfast. There was a small bed by the wall, the usual clothes closet with carved ornaments, a simple couch with crocheted antimacassars, a table that was much too small, a chair, and the tile stove in the corner. I sat here in melancholy loneliness during the first stage of my Dresden life, drew by the light of an oil lamp, or read after my simple supper of wurst with potato salad and Dresden cheese, popularly called corpse's fingers, because that was what it looked like.

I seemed to be in a cocoon, or on the bottom of the ocean, slowly floating I knew not where. But I did think of the future, I recall that distinctly, and that was dark too. As dark as the bottom of the ocean. This unknown current might sweep me upward or drag me further down to the depths; it was all dark, mysterious, and beautiful as a dream. Life had only just begun, the day was young though still dark and misty, and everything lay before me. Who was leading me I did not know. What propelled me was a dark will to succeed—a will still without the destructive force of doubt that was later to breed so much depression. Not until we are beset by the annihilating ambition that drives us to ever greater tasks does doubt take hold of us. At that time, the mountain to be conquered lay straight ahead, its summit in clouds and mist. I was still in the valley, happy and free.

I began by taking my academic instruction very seriously. I was full of good resolutions and serious intentions. I always got up early because I lived quite a distance from school and had to hurry to be at my easel on time. I was in the beginners' class, a leftover from the old academic tradition of Winckelmann and Cornelius; you could also cynically describe it as a retirement home for some of the painting professors. It no longer exists.

Professors Richard Müller, Oskar Schindler and Robert Sterl were our instructors. Müller ruled with military discipline, a maulstick, and a dozen very sharply pointed crayons; Schindler was more civilian and relaxed. We mainly used plaster casts except when we had live models twice a month. Architect Beyrich taught us perspective, and we learned anatomy from courteous Professor Dietrich, who always wore a black tail coat. A smart-looking young landscape painter by the name of Berndt gave us courses in landscape painting; they were optional and attended mostly by students of architecture who went and got drunk afterwards.

Our main work was copying plaster casts in their original size; we had to deliver one every two weeks. Former lithographers were the best workers. They would make exact copies that included every minute accidental scratch or scrape, to the delight of our instructors who themselves were masters of such detail. Whenever we had a head to copy we would literally count the eyebrow hairs; our only, fervent aim was to produce a life-size photograph in chalk. We all had to use that maulstick to prevent our hands from going lame, and our crayons were periodically checked—numbers one to five, sharply pointed. A true symbol of Prussian order!

As we did nothing but copy those boring plaster busts, the work was getting pretty stale. There seemed no purpose to it; nobody bothered to explain the classical beauty of proportion that they represented, so we never got to understand it. Besides, we were living at a time that glorified ugliness and rejected classical proportion. Copying these examples of great Grecian art was nothing but a stupid chore.

Anybody with inherent talent would seek satisfaction elsewhere. We found more stimulation in talking to each other, or in the library and the few modern galleries than in the halls of the great Academy. We novices had a distaste for punctiliousness and too much detail, typical of beginners and rather healthy, I think. Those fussy chores made us disgusted with nature study. We wanted to charge right in and smear paint thickly, as was fashionable at the time.

As for me, I wanted to be a painter. There were pictures in my head that I wanted to paint. They were like those that I had studied at home, all those soldiers and those happy monks drinking golden wine out of shiny glasses; and how natural the bread and cheese, the ham and radishes looked—you could almost bite them! When I confided my enthusiasm to my mother and aunt, they would say, "Yes, my boy, if only you could paint like that! That is real art, to make things look as though they were on the table before you, true to life; but there is a lot for you to learn before you can do that."

Well, that was what I wanted. I wanted to paint such pictures, and needed to learn "composition," something one could only get at an Academy, or so I had read. I wanted to be a genre-painter like Grützner, but also to do historic pictures on the side, mostly hussars. Maybe I could combine the two, for instance, a picture that I would call *A Refreshing Drink:* a hussar, arriving from patrol duty, is about to dismount and is offered a large glass of something

shiny and golden by a beautiful maiden, while a boy holds the
horse's bridle; there is a picturesque inn in the background and
everybody is in the clothes of olden days because they are so much
more artistic than the uninteresting things we wear now.

That was why I had come to the Academy, to learn to paint like
that, so I was very disappointed to hear nothing about composing,
let alone "compositions" of the sort I wanted. On the contrary.

Grosz's Mother

When I told a fellow student that I had come chiefly to study composition, he simply laughed at me. Composition was completely out, was passé; my God, thirty years ago they did that. These days you go out into the country, in bright sunlight at noon if possible, stop somewhere and paint a random piece of landscape, without a sketch, with a spatula and complementary dots. Had I ever looked through a prism? "Well then. Anything else is old stuff and posed. Theater, don't you know...."

With the exception of a few French painters, he said, all painting to date has been nothing but theater, sham. Only in nature, in bright sunlight at noon was it real, and "motifs" stopped existing with the first great French impressionists. In nature there is no such thing as a motif, there is nothing but light and air; modern science, thank God, had proved that. Had I never heard of a certain Monet who painted a haystack three times—the exact same haystack—at six in the morning, at one o'clock noon and in the afternoon at five. "That, you see, is what is happening today. What is composition by comparison?"

I was deflated and annihilated. I stopped my imaginary genre pictures and the hussars. I wondered whether I might not first learn modern painting and then do my hussars in bright sunlight, maybe putting in a haystack somewhere, or at least a bundle of hay next to the horse? In sunlight, of course. Painting nothing but a haystack was going a bit too far for the moment, I was not that modern yet.

I swiped a prism from an old chandelier and squinted through it when nobody was watching me. I was trying to plan my new hussar picture, but my progressive friend and his impressionist theories kept getting in the way. This new theory intrigued me, but when I went out to the Dresden heath with it I got nowhere, slammed my sketchbook shut and left my prism unused in my pocket. How I would have loved to learn composition! I knew that there was—or had been—a composition class at the Academy, there was something to that effect on the schedule: anatomy, perspective, composition—once a month—Professor Raphael Wehle, instructor. But nobody seemed to place any value on this.

I would start early every day and work all morning drawing those famous plaster busts. I worked like a robot, my head floating in a daydream, and those dear old sentimental family pictures paled. One day I was walking down a corridor when I suddenly noticed an old sign: Composition Class. I approached, but the door was closed. I tried to look through the key hole but saw nothing but the customary screen covered with monk's cloth. I tried the handle, but the door did not open. What might be in there? What would a "composition class" look like? I deciphered some faded writing that indicated what day the class would be held, and that costumes could be borrowed.

I decided to join that class, and got there on the dot on the given day. The place seemed bewitched, there was not a sound. Or was there? Didn't I hear some peaceful snoring?

I knocked gently, but nobody responded. I knocked louder. Nothing. So nobody was there. Evidently this class no longer existed, it had become obsolete. I felt the prism in my pocket and left, but decided to return in a half hour, when maybe somebody would be there. I had figured correctly. When I knocked again, I heard shuffling steps, a key turning almost unwillingly in the lock, and there I was facing a morose old man with a slight smell of red wine and cigars: Professor Wehle.

He did not let me in, but blocked the door with his stomach and snarled, "What do you want?" I said: "Excuse me please, professor, if I am disturbing you"—I had the impression that he had been asleep—"but I would like to study composition."

"WHAT? What do you want? You—you want to study? You want to study composition? Who ever put that flea in your ear?—Do you have a light?" He pulled the stub of a cigar from his pocket. Fortunately I had matches, so I could be polite and could quickly light it.

"In whose class are you?" he asked, looking at me somewhat suspiciously from behind his thick glasses. "Well, well, Müller and Schindler." He was apparently under the impression that I had been sent by somebody to play a joke on him. "Well, well, so you want to study composition. Well—" he was playing with an apparently very heavy bunch of keys in his trouser pocket, still standing in front of the door. Suddenly he said, "Well then, come in...."

Behind the screen the room looked like an untidy museum, yet quite pleasant. There were heaps and rolls of old materials that had apparently been used to drape models in the days when one "posed" figures and "composed" pictures. There were model figures standing and lying about and all sorts of paraphernalia—goblets, helmets, weapons—in glass cases. Historic costumes were hanging on a clothes rack, and there was an architect's model of a Dresden bridge on a small table. "So you want to study composition?"

I had of course brought a portfolio with a number of my own experiments: sepia drawings, hussars on bivouac, my young man in Biedermeier clothing leaving home by the old mill in the valley and a dramatic battle scene influenced by Emil Hünten and Professor Carl Röchling. Professor Wehle found my things tolerable and as he now realized that I was not there to make fun of him, he started right off with the instruction I had so longed for.

"Now listen," he said. "As you know, I too am a sort of historic painter, though more on the religious side." (He had acquired world fame with his picture *And They Followed Him.)* "All right, we'll try to find out whether you are right for composition. You do know the Bible, I hope at least, and the Ten Commandments?" I assured him with fake modesty that I knew the Bible well, enjoyed reading it, and so forth. "All right, so for the moment let's stay with the Old Testament. You see, don't you, that those stories are really made for the historic painter. They have everything, simply everything: the splendor of nature, and of people too, animals, sun and storm, good and evil, Herr—what was the name again?—yes, yes of course, Herr Grosz, everything is there, ineffable, inexhaustible in invention...."

Professor Wehle exhaled immense rings of smoke. Then he continued: "And especially today when a bit of sun and a few complementary spots are all—today, Herr—right, Herr Grosz— well, it's good that at least you have not been infected. Well, listen. I'll give you a story from the Old Testament, a terrific affair with lots of figures and animals and all the elements—yes, lightning, thunder and rain—don't you see, rain: one day, two days, whole months of rain, nothing but rain—yes, of course, you understand, it's the Great Flood I'm talking about. You can go and rack your brains, that's something for you to sink your teeth into. No, you just do whatever you want, not too big, ordinary drawing paper is enough. No, no, you go and figure it all out for yourself. No, I cannot tell you that either—fine, if you want to bring Noah's Ark into it, that's all right too; but what matters is the whole, Herr Grosz, the whole relationship, the elements, *the elements,* he repeated, blowing a huge cloud of smoke into the air. "Quite all right to look at the old masters," he added. "Cornelius is good too. You can start in charcoal—take your time—do little sketches until you get the whole thing together—and don't forget the rain—." At that point he had me at the door, gave me my portfolio, and I was dismissed.

So instead of hussars I was suddenly to compose the Great Flood.

Incredible! Bold as beginners are, I started immediately. I filled a whole big page with what was supposedly the summit or summits of Mount Ararat, lots of people struggling to save their lives and lots of animals. Rain was pouring unmercifully in many straight, rather clumsy chalk lines; I used kneaded bread to produce lustre. My inspiration was a flood that I had witnessed in Stolp with a bloated dead dog floating in the water and, oddly, my drowned classmate Kassel, washed up by the Baltic Sea onto the beach on a hot summer's day, and covered with thousands of luminous flies. I also thought of the panoramic pictures of my childhood. I had about three hundred people in my composition; after all, wasn't it all humanity that had perished? I had not yet heard of the laws of wise limitation by which you can, under some circumstances, show more with a single figure than with so many.

That deluge was damn difficult. By the hundredth person I had run out of imagination; my realistic conscience told me that all these people must look a little different; there must have been long ones and short ones, fat and thin and so on. I had trouble with the women—women must have been there too—as I had never drawn a female body. So I drew them almost like men, except that I put a big bosom on each of them. Composing really is not easy, I thought to myself, and made some more rain pour down. A cauliflower in the bright noon sun is really child's play by comparison, once you have learned the method of complementary colors....

This lesson of composition was a disappointment. I saw a hussar riding through all that rain in my deluge, complete with that refreshing drink he was being served. I made hints to Professor Wehle about my favorite painter Grützner and my hussar picture, but he would hear nothing of it. "Grand, exalted thoughts are what is needed, Herr Grosz," he said, "and there are only very few subjects, first of all the Bible and then, much further down the line, the classics of antiquity. It takes an exalted subject to develop an exalted style—or can you imagine our Lord Jesus Christ painted in bright sunlight? Well, then."

Professor Wehle's pronouncements were the reflexes of a period of great German art that was past, no longer comprehensible to me. He still knew something of that former real grandeur of ideas and ambition, but lacked the ability to achieve his intellectual ideals in color and shape. (Exalted ideas alone do not suffice either....)

My attempts at composition went on. Among others, I did a Christ at Gethsemane, but was unhappy because such a noble theme did not really move me sufficiently, and was not compatible with my vulgar favorites like the *Refreshing Drink*. That conflict resulted in caricatures. Professor Wehle's desired "grandeur," his exalted classical and religious ideas were not in me, because they were no longer in my time. My time was that of cheap, pompous enlightenment, with prisms and science, of a silly, socialist belief in saving humanity, of a vulgar worship of ugliness and proletarianism at any cost—and the beginings of the counterculture that would destroy socialism, Christianity and ("if somebody is falling, give him a push") humanity.

◆

The classes of our chief instructor, Professor Müller, were no laughing matter. He was a stickler for discipline and military punctuality; a hard worker himself, he was at his easel from six in the morning till eight at night, using lamps when it got dark. Once when I was late and he was already making the rounds looking at students' work, he snarled at me, "And where have you been? What? Got up too late, what? Out drinking last night, hm? What? What does that mean, missed the streetcar? Man like you, with your ability, should be here by half-past-four in the morning waiting for the Academy door to open! So get working!" He swung his maulstick just the way the high-school teachers in Stolp used to swing their canes, and all I could do was slink behind my easel like a wet poodle.

He certainly could let us have it, and he did with such authority that we could not make fun of it, much as we would have liked to. There was something about him that permitted no opposition: we simply obeyed. Behind his back of course we did make fun of him, but when he would glare at us with his penetrating blue draftsman's eyes, we obeyed in silence.

One of the things that endeared him to us was that he was never the least bit boring. There were stories galore about his highly original statements, and his grim sarcasm disarmed us all. At recess one day I was standing in the corridor munching my sandwich when Müller came out of his studio, the latest bestseller in his hand. Not one to mince words, he said, "Going to shit. Using the time."

He liked to use tough language and swear words when talking to us or the models. Anything physical that attracted his attention was discussed openly in class. One day a certain part of a male model was strikingly thick. As soon as Müller noticed it, he let loose: "What's the matter with you? What have you got there? You sick, huh? Sack like a small loaf of bread! Ought to have a doctor look at it!" All this was blared out like a sergeant in the barracks, so nobody could take offense.

Either because Müller had a streak of sadism or because he demanded so much from himself, he would frequently require very difficult poses of the models. They might have to stand on tip-toe, one leg to the back, one hand forward holding a wooden hoop, to impersonate a hoop-rolling girl. As such poses were enormously hard to maintain, many models, especially the female ones, were afraid to pose in his classes.

One of his favorites was a young Fraülein Wittschass because she was fearless and would bravely stand without moving as long as she possibly could. Even for her, however, the "hoop-rolling maiden" was a bit too much, though she had a tall staff to hold onto and there was a sling from the ceiling to hold up her leg; even this good model had to take breaks to gather strength. Müller would often draw with us, as he needed these complicated poses for his etchings; he hated these constant interruptions. He would really have liked to have petrified the whole pose before he started drawing. And once when the poor girl was exhausted and beseeched him, "Professor, I—I really can't go on," he burst out: "What? what? Don't you know, a model like you, Fraülein Wittschass, should float in the air like an angel, should hold still like an albatross in flight—stay! I must finish drawing the hoop." It did not occur to him that the hoop was not very important and could easily be drawn without the girl.

Everything had to be marked with chalk and measured to the millimeter so that the pose could be exactly the same the next day. Models would stand in the same position for three weeks, and that long a pose made us students become fiends for accuracy. Every day someone would find fault with something, and insist that an arm be further to the right, a foot turned to the outside. Sometimes it took days before the general outlines could be put on paper and the conscientious types were pacified. Viewed in retrospect, it was quixotic, but we actually did lose sleep worrying over missed proportions and professorial disapproval.

A brave joker by the name of Hubert Rüther once amused himself by randomly changing the chalk marks after class, when nobody was looking. When we started to place the model the following day, we wondered for a moment what had happened. We understood. Professor Müller understood too. He did not say a word. But from that day on, he used the fancy poses only in his own personal studio.

The gods had been kind to Professor Müller. From humble circumstances he had worked his way up from his first job as a porcelain painter; by hard work and unrelenting determination he had been promoted to full professor at the Academy at an early age. At the beginning of his career he had been a close friend of the mural painter Sasha Schneider, but later they went different ways. Müller was a strong personality, but he had his faults as a teacher and pedagogue. He was completely set in his own way of absolute accuracy in drawing and denied the validity of any living artist except possibly some of the older ones like Klinger, Greiner and Menzel. Not only was he intolerant, but not very wise, for his damning and scolding antagonized his few gifted students and achieved the exact opposite of what he wanted. He rejected every type of experimentation with the very simplistic maxim: "Draw, man, draw—nothing else matters. The pencil is not dumb!"

One day a young, very elegant Czech Jew called Barkus brought a newly published book about Emil Nolde to class. Nolde was a very controversial figure, quite far to the left at that time, and very wild. He no longer used brushes to paint. He later told me that when inspiration seized him he had thrown away his paintbrushes, dipped his old painting rag in color and, in blissful delirium, wiped it all over the canvas. As seen from the august level of technical tradition, his pictures were formless and primitive, craftsmanship was nonexistent, inner expression was all that mattered, and compared to a Rembrandt or a Raphael, all it amounted to was a brutal mess of color. (The new threat to naughty children was: "If you don't behave, Nolde will come and get you, and smear you all over his canvas.")

We youngsters, inexperienced and somewhat bored by old theories, were excited. Here at last we could cut loose, attack all rules with complementary colors—down with maulsticks and sharpened pencils and crayons! Man, just take a rag, dip it in color without even looking, and go to it! Great stuff! How could we have any discrimination at seventeen, bound as we were to copying plaster? Life was not made of plaster; if anything, was it not more like a rag covered with complementary colors? Just look! So smearing is not a sin? Great! Terrific!

So that elegant, literate Barkus brought to class the catalog of the master smearer and rebel against each and every tradition. We placed it so that Müller would see it right away, and he rose to the bait, delighting the progressives among us with a diatribe against such rot. "What? What's that? Fellow sticks his finger up his arse and smears it on the paper!" (We did not know Freud's explanation of the unconscious at that time.) "What a lummox, sketching like a drunken sow with a dung fork—thinks he's a Rembrandt, huh? Ha, ha, look at that one, uses a horseshoe nail and pretends it's an etching..."

At that point he was thumbing through some of Nolde's etchings that really did look as though they had been done with the broken end of a dung fork. Müller was particularly annoyed that the caption on each sheet included the size, 10:14 for instance. In his opinion, that was the prerogative of "true old" masters, and certainly not of charlatans like Nolde.

My friend Hohmann, son of a cider brewer from Guben, was the cause of another one of Müller's memorable explosions. Hohmann was a bit neurotic and a "born" impressionist; he would never quite finish a drawing but kept on stippling and dotting and drawing little lines all over the paper. Instead of a clearly defined shape, he would produce a sort of nervous rain of dots and lines and dashes. That was not only permitted, but even appreciated, when an impressionist did it. Not so for a Müller student, on the contrary. Müller demanded exact, photographic likeness of the model, finished off to the nth degree. When Hohmann mentioned Van Gogh in one of the general discussions that Müller loved to conduct, a storm of hurricane proportions broke out over the surprised young man and the rest of us: "That Gogh—what a shit—plasters a sunset onto canvas in one afternoon, what's the good of that? It takes me two years to paint a picture and that Gogh smears his shit in half an hour and sells it for 15,000 marks—that crap—." We adored his juicy critiques.

◆

Those were interesting times, just before World War I. There was a certain flowering of the arts, enthusiasm for new ideas, and we beginners were greatly impressed with modern painters from Paris. The first pictures of the cubists looked like pieces of broken glass, and meant a continuation of Cézanne. Futurists painted manifestoes and were preparing a sort of fascist art. Boccioni painted a controversial picture that he called *Laughter.* There was "simultanism" that tried to show everything at once, on different planes. There was a search for movement. Delaunay painted his only famous picture, with a reversed Eiffel tower in the center. Symbolism became famous through Chagall and the legendary Belgian, James Ensor, who depicted people as insects and fleas.

The group of Dresden artists "Die Brücke" (The Bridge) went primitive. They wanted to paint like wild black men, with only the basic four or five prime colors. They were followers of Van Gogh and the former banker Gauguin, both of whom had just become known. This group was the forerunner of what later became known as German expressionism. In Sindelsheim near Munich the "Blue Riders" were busy, with a bright blue horseman as their symbol. Their top men were Klee and the Russian, Kandinsky. Kandinsky was one of the most definite abstract painters; in his first famous pictures there were no longer any objects at all, only colored foam and translucent steam.

Berlin was very friendly to foreigners in those days. French art was imported at high prices; well-known critics (whose names have long been forgotten) got on the bandwagon and sang the praises of everything that came out of the rue de la Boëtie in books, newsprint and magazines. The more influential ones who controlled the market and set the prices disdained German art as barbarian and retarded. Even so, a few German painters rose to fame, and even to money, within Germany.

That was the way it was before World War I. But none of it penetrated the thick walls of the academies, nor the thick heads and spectacles of the tenured professors. You had to find your own way. I am not saying that art can be taught; time and again even the most tolerant and understanding instructor fails to develop a talent and bring it to a certain degree of maturity. What matters in artistic development is simple daily life, with its incalculable highways and byways that are beyond the influence of the instructor. Talented beginners are engaged in heavy fermentation, filled with a "something" that they feel but cannot express. They often cannot imagine what their later accomplishments will be, but are full of will and fired with enthusiasm for their thing. And that is where an understanding instructor can be a sympathetic leader and advisor.

I often ask myself what would have happened if I had learned proper composition and painting—I mean in the quiet, orderly sequence of the good old tradition? If I had become a "natural" painter instead of a freak and a warning example, hated by my fellow men and banished by rulers? Was the whole hideous flood of filthy drawings unnecessary, or was it the expression of an equally filthy and extraordinary period? Why, I ask myself, why is the so-called "normal" artist only understood by the masses—and the "abnormal" one only by a small, conceited, educated group?

Perhaps these are senseless questions. Perhaps art is finished anyhow? Perhaps the Russian exterminators who treat art as a natural function, like digestion, are right? But let us leave this infinite, insoluble problem and return to our subject while we are still in the mood.

BROADENING HORIZONS

Among my Dresden acquaintances there was one peculiar character, a former primary school teacher. He had not been a happy teacher, however, not one who quietly waits for the day when he can retire with a nice pension, he was an unhappy one. He was a restless, rebellious spirit who felt a "higher" calling, much against the wishes of his aged parents. Just where this calling was to lead, he did not know exactly; he was still wavering between poetry and painting. At that particular time he was involved with painting, so he wore his hair long, hanging over his coat collar. In addition, he had a philosophic bent, read Schopenhauer during recess, occasionally played the piano during lunch—either Chopin or his own improvisations—in other words, he knew a little bit about a lot of things and was really a failed teacher and a genial dilettante.

He had written a play with the peculiar title *Jesus Christ in Zeitz*. Zeitz was his home town and I rather suspect that his Jesus, who is arrested upon arrival at the train station because he has no ticket, had some elements of self-portraiture. Apparently our playwright was trying to get rid of his fury and hatred and sought revenge for some wrong done to him in his hometown. So the play aimed to instruct and educate, rather than amuse. "I am related to Ibsen," said my new friend, "my play is a sermon and a chastisement." His Thuringian dialect, however, rather marred the intended effect of the words of Jesus.

I had just come from Berlin and was not feeling at all reverent. I did not laugh out loud, but Berlin was a skeptical, sober city of quick-witted, sharp-tongued people, leading all German cities in sarcasm and insolence. My new friend—what an odd name, by the way: Erwin Liebe!—was he just crazy, a semitalented weirdo? All the same, he was not uninteresting. His drawing did not show much talent; he had chosen to start with portraits and while he wiped his charcoal round and kneaded bread for highlights, he would expound his theories as though explaining the miracle of artistic creation to himself.

I often visited him in his furnished room on spooky, cold Cranach Street, the street I lived on too. The houses there were grey, like old, bleached bones, the rooms had high ceilings and were also cold, despite their red velvet couches with crocheted antimacassars and goldfish bowls. There were no balconies on Cranach Street and it looked so cold that you always expected to find snow in some corner.

So that was where I went to see Erwin. He showed me his many nature studies, mostly portraits; I noticed his preference for young boys, but was too innocent to consider it unusual. He then reached behind a bundle of clothes, brought out a bottle of fake Benedictine, and poured the thick, yellow liquid into coffee cups from which we drank. It tasted like syrup mixed with alcohol and lots of saccharin; the colorful label on the potbellied bottle showed a friendly monk drinking a toast to us.

Erwin thumbed through the manuscript of his *Jesus Christ in Zeitz*, explaining its sense, content and meaning. His glance was unsteady, his nervous, bony musician's fingers fiddled with his long hair. Some of the yellow liquor still hung, unwiped, on his

Saints [1935/36]

lips, but I was too shy to tell him.

Suddenly I became aware of the total messiness of this man: his filthy, spade-shaped fingernails, his frayed cuffs that had once been white, the dandruff on his collar and the blackheads around his nose. I had never known anybody like that. I did not yet know the bohemian coffee house with its remarkable collection of talented and semitalented, the retinue that always follows art, studios, music and poetry. The Janus head had not yet been revealed to me. I still had illusions under my green country-gentleman's hat and had not yet exchanged it for the black beret of the artist. I was still at the beginning of my career, whereas Erwin was almost thirty and ahead of me in many ways.

Despite that sudden passing glimpse of the real Erwin, I was still impressed. Nothing had changed. I had another half cup of liquor which made everything even better and more friendly. We used those hideous cups to drink a toast to the success of his play, which by then seemed great to me. I was easily impressed, as my knowledge of poetry was virtually nonexistent, limited to the verses of Schiller, Goethe and Geibel that we had to memorize in school. Poetry as such had never interested me, so how should I have known any? At home nobody wrote poetry except in the kitchen, where cookbook poetry was composed for the officers. I was thus completely unable to form any judgment of what Erwin was reading to me. Outside of pure, straight action, I understood nothing. If there were any deeper meanings, I did not see them, but nevertheless took the whole thing very seriously. I thought it simply brilliant to have Jesus appear in modern garb, particularly in workman's clothes. "Simply brilliant," I said, and emptied the last drop of yellow liquor. Simply brilliant, that.

Of course I did not know that anything like that had ever been written and tried, nor did I see the kitsch and logical inadequacy of a dilettante's fantasy toying with such powerful themes. Actually I had seen a painting in one of the magazines at home by a fairly well-known painter, retired Captain Fritz von Uhde: Christ in street clothes, in sunlight. And I'd also once seen a French reproduction of a modern-dress Christ pointing down at Paris with a threatening finger.

We got to talking about symbolism—Erwin's play certainly was symbolism of the highest order. He became very loquacious and explained that symbolism was the highest art form of all. He spoke with fiery enthusiasm, illuminated from within: this was his favorite subject and I the innocent listener was a new vessel into which he could pour all his arguments.

"The last, great, final aim of all young, free art is spiritualization! Do you understand that, Georg?" he shouted. "I mean
spiritualization—the absolute spiritualization of all earthly filth
into symbolic mysticism! The symbolic line, Georg: the lotus
blossom...the Holy Grail...and the search with your soul for the
land of the Greeks! And Georg!—the unknown God...."

His words thundered and exploded and I kept on hearing that we
must spiritualize, spiritualize....That thick, yellow, disgustingly
sweet monks' liquor had gone to my head. I would have loved
something to eat, a herring or a fried potato or anything. All I could
do was to keep on saying: "Yes, great, certainly," or "God, Erwin,
that's brilliant!"

As I was very literal-minded at that time and "sane"—more
naive and certainly simpler than later—I was dazzled by this flood
of phrases. It did not matter that I understood only half or none of
their meaning—I spent the next few weeks repeating everything
Liebe had said. I started to insert elaborate and, in my view,
profound words into any casual conversation, words like "spiritualize" or "symbolic." Looking at a rather uninteresting, poorly
drawn life study by one of my fellow students, for instance, I
would say immediately something like, "You see, Lange, you need
to spiritualize that into the symbolic." It must have been very
funny, but of course I did not see that at the time.

The borrowed possession of these seemingly deep magic terms
made me feel quite superior. With no true comprehension of their
meaning, I used phrases whose sense and nonsense I was not to
discover until much later. But it was lovely, and I impressed not
only myself but some of my also-struggling fellow students. My
friend Lange and several others suddenly thought I was "deep" and
"spiritual," when I really could barely play a few chords on that
spiritual guitar, let alone a whole melody.

Fundamentally, and despite the long hair that touched his coat,
Erwin Liebe remained simply the school teacher he had been. But
nevertheless he did influence me then, and I learned from him
what I had to learn, if nothing else—that big words make a big
noise, and that their echo is louder than the echo of small
"nonspiritual" words.

One day when he was expounding his favorite theme of symbolism, the name of Karl May was dropped. I was overjoyed to find
myself on familiar ground where I could participate in the conversation. Karl May was one of the most popular and prolific German

adventure writers. His best known stories were about American
Indians and great, strapping blond trappers who were models of
virtue. In some ways, his novels were like the works of James
Fenimore Cooper, or some of the early Western movies.

His best known heroes were invulnerable Old Shatterhand, who
with one blow of his fist could flatten a horse, and Winnetou, the
noble Red Indian; they were the ideals of the German youth of my
day. There was also the Wonder Horse, Ri, and some very special
guns. I had devoured the Karl May books when I was a kid and
knew them almost by heart. His works, I said to Erwin, are so
wonderfully exciting—written for youngsters, of course—but as
such they are really wonderful, I added naively.

With knotted eyebrows, Erwin gazed at me a bit derisively.
"No," he said, "that is exactly what they are not. What you see is
only the crust, the cover if you will, probably jazzed up by some

clever publisher. No, Georg, that is the usual pitfall. If you can ever learn to look for the spiritual symbolism under the surface, you will come to understand Karl May as quite different, a great symbolist and not merely as an author of children's books."

I was dumbfounded. Nothing like that had ever occurred to me. Try as I might, I could see nothing more in Karl May's works than constantly exciting adventures—in the mountains, in the desert, on the ocean. Wild! So I was still stupid. That Liebe, and all the things he knew! (Or could he be making it up?)

Erwin continued his lecture. As all great world literature, Karl May's books could of course also be read by children. That was merely further proof of their great, naive spirituality—yes, spirituality—but that did not make them children's books. On the contrary, they were really much too difficult for youngsters, and their mystic-symbolic kernel could be deciphered only by deep study of their concealed spiritual-symbolic-ethnic Teutonic ideas. That of course took dedication, plus knowledge of the ideas of Houston Stewart Chamberlain, Langbehn, knowledge of oriental philosophy and theories on race, among other things—because Karl May's work was cosmic, and valid for the whole spiritual West.

"You know," Erwin continued in great animation, "Karl May is about the same to fiction that Nietzsche was to philosophy—no, wait a minute, I said 'about,' but not exactly—you understand, Georg, there is the question of religion; May is more Teutonic, less heathen than Nietzsche, who of course was a mortal enemy of Christianity—but fundamentally the worlds of Karl May and Nietzsche are closely related..."

He became solemn: "Three immortal geniuses—Friedrich Nietzsche, the philosopher, Richard Wagner, the musician, and Karl May, the epic writer of the Teutonic myth." And then he waxed prophetic: "One day, not too late I hope, the true importance of Karl May will be recognized and appreciated!"

I was speechless. There I had been, mistaking the greatest works of epic literature for exciting juvenile fiction. Obviously I also lacked sense for the hidden Rhinegold in this Rhinestream of poetry. So that was it! I was speechless once again, but, as always, fascinated by the fireworks of great names and "profound" words.

Once home, I gave the matter much thought. I had always considered Karl May an excellent writer of thrilling stories. No, never would I have guessed that there was a profound, hidden, cosmic, basic-Teutonic-spiritual-mystic meaning in them. From now on those stories must be looked at quite differently: spirituo-symbolically. They acquired something like a double bottom. So that old trapper, prairie hunter and adventurer Old Shatterhand was really the Teutonic racial theory; he was protector of the weak and innocent; and the man with the iron fist was a sort of Siegfried looking for the Holy Grail or the gold of the Rhine maidens....God! I must go tell Lange immediately; he too has read all of Karl May. So the whole secret Teutonic ideology is hidden in those books! Crazy, all the things that Liebe knows. It was as if Erwin had suddenly pulled a rabbit out of his empty slouch hat.

Liebe showed me a collection of work by Sasha Schneider, a well-known artist and friend of athletes. Professor Schneider came from the Sudetenland. The figures he drew to accompany Karl May's works were practically naked, wearing nothing but leather bands and belts and carrying shining swords: there were distorted faces with glowing eyes, and crawling monsters in chains wallowing on the ground. Of course I preferred the surface world of trappers with rifles and powder horns to this "inner" world of Karl May—but the inner one was more profound, more spiritual, and therefore more valuable, said Erwin, and again I half-believed him.

Old Shatterhand does look like this, he maintained, naked, bearing a sword like a guardian of Paradise; he might also be Ormuzd or Ahriman or Siegfried, God of Light. In any case, those trapper clothes were a disguise, because one dared not show the deepest, most spiritual and holy things to an unbelieving, unwilling populace. That was why Erwin had put his Jesus Christ into blue worker's clothes rather than the robes of sunbeams and celestial light....Would I like to go out to Radebeul with him to call on Karl May some time? He was no longer receiving new people, but Erwin could arrange it. It would be a memorable day for me, and would mean much in my life. Karl May was one of the few really great spiritual men of our times, not only a writer, but also a seer and a prophet....

It was a rainy autumn day when we bought our train tickets to Radebeul at the main Dresden terminal. The rain was noisily splashing at the train window as Yenidze, the cigarette factory built in Turkish style, surfaced. It looked like a fairy palace through the rain, and made me think of Karl May's stories of travel and adventure in the Orient: this is the sort of house he should be living in, I thought, if he is at all like his books. But no, of course not, it's all symbolic, I remembered, and suddenly got a very profane longing for a cup of hot coffee and a buttered roll. Erwin Liebe, sitting next to me, had not uttered a word. Now he said, "We'll be there in a minute. I hope he isn't confined to bed."

We walked through the dripping rain to Karl May's house. It was disappointingly bourgeois, just like all the others in the neighborhood. Not bad, but I had expected something more personal. Perhaps it was different inside? ("You have to look behind things, my friend, to find the truth; this mediocrity is nothing but a mask....") Over the entrance, large letters proclaimed VILLA SHATTERHAND.

Frau May opened the door herself. Portly, though not really fat, she looked more like a middle-class woman than a valkyrie. She had a shawl around her shoulders and there was a pleasant smell of coffee. Good, I thought. Nice and comfortable. There was a fire in the tile stove, too.

She was sorry she would have to disappoint us, she said after a short greeting. Her husband would not be able to see us; he was not feeling at all well, and a pending lawsuit had taken a lot out of him. "So he wants to see as few people as possible," she said.

We were standing in a very bourgeois anteroom with lots of framed photographs on the four walls, apparently from trips to the Orient that Karl May and his wife had taken. Camels, mosques, Moorish houses, date palms. There were African weapons on the walls too, a few Kelims and a beautifully decorated saddle. One had the immediate impression that these were all souvenirs bought in bazaars for pleasure or decoration, the sort of rarities you would find in an urban travel agency; only the sales counter and timetable were missing.

The coffee table in the living room was set with a tablecloth over the red plush cover. It could just as well have been at my aunt's house: bourgeois, homey and comfortable. There was a tall glass cabinet in one corner, and through its immaculate sparkling panes you could see an enormously long rifle with a stock completely studded with silver tacks and notches carved by a knife. I immediately recognized the "Bear Killer," so frequently described in Karl May's stories. Next to it was a smaller, modern carbine, equally well known to readers as the quick-firing Henry repeater, the gun so skillfully handled by Old Shatterhand.

What a pity, I thought, that Karl May cannot come down. What would such an inventive genius look like in person? All I had ever seen was a faded photograph. Is he tall, short, or what? Erwin had talked only of the Master's soul and I—it just occurred to me—had never asked what he looked like. I had automatically assumed him to be something like Old Shatterhand: high and mighty, with a blond mustache and maybe even in cowboy boots.

Frau May came in with a white china coffee pot covered with a knitted cozy, and we soon enjoyed her fragrant coffee and the crisp little rolls, followed by home-baked coffee cake. The scene was pleasantly conventional middle class; the only thing that did not fit the image was Erwin's long hair, everything else exuded an almost somnolent coziness. The photographs and souvenirs seemed to be yellowing, as though the trips that they depicted had been taken half a century ago, or maybe never: as though the mementoes had just always belonged to this house....

Erwin licked his fingers, sticky with honey, and spoke quietly but eagerly with our hostess about the forthcoming lawsuit. I helped myself to another piece of coffee cake and was lost in my own thoughts when I suddenly heard the soft sound of careful steps coming down the stairs as though in felt slippers. There—a small, whitehaired gentleman came toward us.

Here he was, the Master himself. He had reconsidered, and decided to welcome his faithful disciple.

We stood up politely. I was still chewing my cake, but he did not seem to notice. He shook hands with both of us.

"So I hear you are a painter," he said to me. His hand was small and withered, the hand of an old man. Like parchment, I thought. Parchment with brown spots, marbled in blue. I thought of the inventions of this extraordinary writer, imagining himself in the most impossible dangers, with a fist of iron so strong that he could beat down a steer—and here he is nervous and worried, although seemingly calm, as he discusses his lawsuit in soft, bitter words with my friend Liebe.

So this was the real Old Shatterhand. A small, delicate, buttoned-up gentleman with a white mustache and longish, wavy hair, the way it was worn about 1870. His eyes were pale blue mixed with white and teared a little in the corners as though he had come out of the wind. There was nothing of that awe-inspiring blond giant about him, nothing very interesting either. He gave the impression of inner peace, calm and caution, of wanting to sound more quiet than most people, not louder. His delicate leather boots seemed like felt slippers.

I kept on looking at those small, delicate writer's hands of pink parchment. In his wishful thinking those white knuckles drove a nail in one blow through a four-inch oak board...and there was something chilly about him, as though he was standing always in the wind and freezing....

He left fairly soon, almost without a sound, and went upstairs to his study, or possibly straight to bed.

It had become dark. Frau May had lighted a lamp, and suddenly the gaslights outside flared up, so one could see the unfriendly wet and the red, blowing autumn leaves through the cozy, curtained windows. Frau May said if we wanted to get the 6:20, an express from Berlin that stopped in Radebeul, we would have to hurry. We did, running to the station through the quiet rain.

For me, that visit was the end of many illusions. The great man was somehow smaller than I had thought. I was left with the impression of having seen a faded photograph that was then returned to the album. Such visits, of course, are never very satisfying. Everybody is stiff, formal, and on their good behavior. And I was quite young and stupid too, in those days.

Erwin and I slowly drifted apart. I eventually caught on to the emptiness of his grandiloquence. Anyway, he soon left for Munich, and I for Berlin. My new friend Kittelsen came between us too, a cynic with his feet on the ground, and an attitude much more to my liking than Erwin's amateurish talk of spiritual values and symbolism. Our paths never crossed again, and his *Jesus Christ in Zeitz* was never produced. Through Kittelsen I got in touch with truly great modern literature, and after the Goncourt brothers, Flaubert, Zola and such, good old Karl May seemed quite outdated, and remained what he had always been: a writer for boys and girls in their early teens.

It was only later, when I read that May was one of Adolf Hitler's favorite authors, that I remembered that long-ago visit, and I wondered whether he did not, after all, have a wider influence....

Kittelsen also was an unusual person. He had already been to England and he came from very prolific parents; he was the thirteenth son, I think. He had an interesting, stubborn face and, like all Vikings, a predilection for strong spirits. He was somewhat narcissistic and a great dandy. He liked to talk about Aubrey Beardsley and Oscar Wilde, both very influential at the time. His talent lay in similar areas; he also had a mystic vein, as do many Norwegians.

Yes, Kittelsen was very much a Norwegian. When hit by one of his moods—and that happened often—he would go to a bar and comfort himself with a special drink he had concocted, a mixture of beer and brandy. He would keep on drinking until he was seized by howling misery, then run out crying and sobbing and throw his hat away. He lived in a furnished room on Circus Street. His perpetually well-groomed landlady, Frau Dauth, owned a small, snug wine bar with hostesses. When we had one of our late night discussions in his room, we would often hear her coming home slightly high with one of the waitresses, who had a room in her house.

She was said to be the divorced wife of an officer and, as she told us herself, had started this cozy ladies' bar, The Fairy Grotto, merely to forget the pain of her broken marriage. We believed this romantic and sentimental story not only out of politeness, but because she was such a nice landlady. Whenever we stopped by The Fairy Grotto, we were treated like family rather than passing customers. The waitresses were fashionably buxom; that did not at all displease Kittelsen and me. We had a good time there. They were almost like goodnatured aunts, and never tried to sell us expensive drinks—a bottle of port would do. Then they would sit on our laps—about 180 pounds, I would guess—but when you are young, you don't notice things like that.

I saw Kittelsen almost daily. We would go for walks after the Academy, discussing ideas and exchanging opinions, or I would accompany him to the motet in the Frauenkirche. He was very musical; I was less so, but I enjoyed the dusky mood in the lovely church and the soothing sound of singing following our lively discussions.

Kittelsen was very well-read, so it was always stimulating to talk with him. He would call my attention to books such as the work of the demonic satirist Gustav Meyrink, who had just become fashionable. Wild stories were told about him. He was said to have cured his spinal meningitis by gazing at a crystal ball while

taking hypnotizing foot baths; supposedly he could walk on water; it almost goes without saying that he could make himself invisible—Strindberg claimed to have done that too, on the way to his bride. My friend Kittelsen, spellbound by these demonic books, said he could do that too; if and when he wanted to, he could disappear. In my presence he only managed about halfway, there was always a dim remainder of his figure visible (regardless of the amount of brandy and beer consumed).

I was fairly well-read myself. I had read myself "upward," literally, as a subscriber to a clever series of books *Read Upward*, published in Berlin by the newspaper owner August Scherl. Scherl had the droll idea that everybody started with cheap, low tastes and had to be led gradually "upward" to greater intellectual appreciation and enjoyment. He thought, correctly, that you could not start right out with really heavy literature as you would not understand it, be bored, and quickly discard the book. Slowly, quite slowly, you had to read "upward": starting with thrillers dripping with action, excitement and sentiment, by way of Dumas and Walter Scott upward to Hauptmann, Ibsen, Strindberg and Maurice Maeterlinck, then in a sequence that I don't remember on to Tolstoy, Dostoevsky, Zola, Chekhov or Leonid Andreyev, and Sanin. Since the abortive Russian revolution of 1905, the latter was one of the most controversial and best read authors because he dared to write of free love.

This collection was never completed; it stopped with Zola, if I remember correctly. Probably it did not pay. The assumption that the proletariat was starving for culture, or that the thriller-devouring servant girl would read upward to literary heights, was basically wrong. For once a thriller, always a thriller. As for me, I was always attracted to fantastic-demonic writing and therefore read all that I could get my hands on. I read Gustav Meyrink, was delighted with Hanns Heinz Ewers (his *Alraune* was THE book in 1913; everybody talked about it), and devoured Maurice Renard with enthusiasm. I worshipped Barbey d'Aurévilly and collected canes, following his example; I would have loved to wear a top hat and a black-and-purple opera cape too, but the time for that had passed. Many of these authors inspired my work or at least my philosophy of life, if I may call it that. I was fascinated by what was unusual, mysterious, and often consciously crazy. It was beautiful, though probably rather immature, but don't most imaginative young people go through periods like that?

Kittelsen, for instance invented his own technique that started with pen drawings and ended in watercolor and crayon. His dreamy, ornamental scenes in distorted perspective and well-blended color were peopled by peculiar beings, half bird, half spider. He was a rather amateurish genius who wanted to be different at any cost, deliberately morbid. "You see," he used to say, "I am the thirteenth child. Either I'll be a genius, or I'll die young."

We did often have serious disagreements. He was a dreamer, inclined toward the absurd, who cherished his innate contrariness. I, however, my propensity for grotesque satire and fantasy notwithstanding, had a strong sense of reality. I preferred nonornamental Protestantism in contrast to the overdone decoration of the Catholic church. My sense of reality gave me a certain balance. Even when I was attracted by the unreal, my innate skepticism would always bring me back to the seemingly safe banality of daily life; I had an almost sportsmanlike desire to look for the "truth," the actual facts, which would then put me squarely back on the solid ground of "reason" with all my four feet.

I did have my sensitive spots as my friend Kittelsen was to find out. He was teasing me one day at lunch about my "dandyism" and kept on undoing my brand new bow tie. I let him have fun for quite a while, kept my temper, and patiently retied the bow. Finally it was too much—my pride was wounded, the more so especially as other art students at a nearby table also started to make fun of me. With a devil-may-care smile, I asked him to stop, but encouraged by the laughing approval of the others, he continued. I was seized with a veritable Old Testament fury. I took my plate of Italian salad and emptied the entire contents on his head. Hands shaking with rage, I gave his head a powerful massage. It was a real Fratellini clown scene, and now the laughter and approval was on my side. My roguish friend, quite disconcerted by this unexpected shampoo, stepped lively to the men's room.

STARTING
MY OWN LIFE

n reviewing my Dresden years, I can say without resentment that I really did not learn very much. What I did learn during those two years at the Academy, I got from the companionship of friends, and from books and pictures that I came across. It was then that I started sketching nature in the Japanese manner: I would make quick notes in little sketchbooks of people walking, reading the paper, eating in cafés, and of all sorts of things around me.

If I wanted to be an illustrator, I would have to be able to draw just about anything and everything. I had done some sketching when I was a student, but not as systematically nor with a view to the future. I now took my specialization into my own hands, as no such nature studies were offered at the Academy; five-minute life drawing, as I later practiced at Calarossi's in Paris, was something unknown to them. I did a great deal of drawing at home, mostly from memory and usually caricatures. That turned out to be important, as I went from caricatures to the Japanese, from there to Daumier and to Japanese-inspired Toulouse-Lautrec. I soon recognized what I was missing, so I took a closer look at life outside the walls of the Academy with the posed models, and started to take notes on whatever captured my interest—which turned out to be just about all of the swarming, hurrying, whirling life about me, with all its people, animals and things. My drawings improved; they had been suffering from the mistakes of most beginners, substituting a lack of skill in life study with artifice and one-sided stylization.

I was influenced by the *Simplizissimus* artists, Bruno Paul, Klinger, and the illustrator Emil Pretorius, whose longlegged Japanese-style figures I loved. Subconsciously I felt there was something wrong, yet I was pleased with my neat pictures that confirmed my talent and looked as good to me as the beloved examples. The editors I favored with my works were more critical than I, and returned them.

My style gradually changed, I don't know how or why, but I assume it had to do with the mechanics of reproduction. I would draw the contour of a figure and then cover the whole sheet with grey wash. For that I bought a big cake of India ink at the Dresden art store where I had an account, so I did not have to pay cash. Later, probably through Kittelsen's influence, I widened my monochrome style and painted some areas in flat, tasteful colors. I also started to use a thin, pointed drafting pen. Not freely, like Rembrandt; I drew everything in pencil first so as to make sure I would not deviate from the exact outline, and then went over those much

erased lines with my thin pen and India ink.

My work showed all a typical beginner's clumsiness and constraint. I did stumble forward, but it took lots of time and trouble, lots of experience and disappointment before I managed to master the simple tools that have hardly changed since cave drawings. I did feel, however, that I was on the right track (or at least on a side track that would eventually lead me to the right one). I was pretty sure of that. The ambitious dreams of my boyhood—those gigantic oil paintings, scaffoldings and broom-size brushes—had melted into the background. I no longer thought of them. What I did increasingly think about was how to turn my skill in portraying people and things into money. How did one go about getting into that nourishing, crowded feed-trough?

My belief in money was as yet completely wholesome and rural, in full conformity with average popular opinion, unpolluted by the reformed ideas of "superior" people. I was quite unintellectual and unspoiled in that respect. (Even today, money seems to me the symbol of independence, even of freedom. Any idea can have a flaw; a hundred dollar check, however, remains a hundred dollar check. Unfortunately, my trade is not one that makes money....) My best chance seemed to be the humor magazines. So I drew as much as I could, and sent my work to editors.

One day it happened. One of my little drawings, with my signature, had been accepted and was to appear in the next issue of *Ulk*, the comic supplement of the *Berliner Tageblatt*. I was so proud I could hardly stand it. I visualized my future as a well-paid, steady illustrator and would have had "Berliner Tageblatt" printed on my calling card, if I had had one. How lucky I was! There was a check in the mail too, for twelve marks, that filled my greatest desire: a pair of fancy American patent leather shoes.

I had a second wave of pleasure and pride when I saw my drawing actually printed. I would have preferred it a bit bigger, but it was a start anyway, and here I was, in the company of some of my most admired cartoonists: next to August Hayduck, and Feininger, the cubist who was still doing cartoons at that time, and Herbert Schulz-Berlin, an unknown, whom I was still innocent enough to adore. That ridiculously small success had a good effect on me; it encouraged me and made me feel a little more secure. I sent my mother in Stolp a copy of *Ulk*, of course, and bragged a bit about art not being such an unremunerative profession after all, and I was now even wearing patent leather shoes like Sheriff von Schmeling.

How naive I was! I had just turned seventeen when I left the narrow footpath of Pomerania for the broad smooth boulevard of satirical magazine illustration. My knowledge of art was quite unsophisticated, and I had no idea of quality. What I cared about was to use my talent to make money as fast as possible. I entered the arena not as an idealistic sword swallower or fire eater; I simply wanted to entertain the audience, wanted to be nice to them and rid them of their money in a nice way. I kept carefully away from the corner of the snake charmer or the reformer.

Just how and why I became what I am today, I do not know. Perhaps some people are like onions with many skins. When I got to the ticket counter, I think the attendant gave me several tickets at once. When I asked him why I got several when the people both in front and behind me were getting only one, the attendant (whom I heard clearly, but could not see) said, "You will need several, because you will have to make several changes on your way"—and he was right, from a lower to an upper class, and vice versa.

That small success made me work even harder, with the inherited diligence of my basketweaving grandfather. While the birds were singing in the trees and the sun was shining into the window, I would sit and draw upon hundreds of sheets. The subject was practically always the same, two funny-looking people standing opposite each other, for whom I had to think of jokes. Mostly they were not at all funny, but the drawings sold better if they had a caption. It became quite a chore to think of funny things. I am not naturally a witty man, and had not yet started on my journey into loneliness, where I developed composure, real humor and righteous contempt for the masses. I merely had the ticket in my pocket.

I was an ass among asses, but I had a very good time. Influenced by the masters I admired, I had the same experience as everybody with innate talent: I lost the naive originality of my early drawing, but gained in manual versatility. I copied, tried, and experimented so much that there was no Grosz discernible at all any more. One thing seems extraordinary: much as I studied Daumier, Lautrec, Forain and the Japanese, what I produced never showed their influence, but rather resembled their lesser followers. I took the descendants more seriously than the creators.

It was really crazy, all the things one did in those days—was I not equally enthusiastic about August Hayduk, who was quite "chic" then, and did the ads for the big department store, Kaufhaus des Westens? It would have been just about impossible for anybody to detect the later George Grosz in my drawings of that time. Yet, I was quite pleased with myself and my life. My stuff was getting published and would presumably continue to get published. And I was making money, which made me feel superior to my fellow students whose work was not getting printed and who were not making money. I was uplifted, which was probably silly but not unnatural, considering my respect for printed matter. Anything that was printed, particularly in the newspaper, must surely be true. (It did not occur to me that bad people might possibly print lies.) Since I was now in print, even if small print, I thought more highly of myself.

The catchy German marketing slogan "Werbe mit Wahrheit," (advertise truthfully), had not yet been invented; would that not admit the possibility of untruthful advertising? We were still living in the last harmless, simple, happy years before World War I, not yet in the world that Nietzsche had foretold. The supermen, the destructive Machiavellis did exist, but they were still confined to bohemian cafés, studios and the like, or gave vent to their feelings in newspaper columns. The clocks of course were already set. Hitler, Mussolini and Lenin were alive, had their traveling papers, and knew where they had to change trains; but the future was hidden from us simpler mortals. Sporadic screams from oracular priests sounded shrill and unlikely. Human beings are primarily optimistic and want to survive, so they gladly plug their ears with the wax of hope, wait until the last minute, and shun Cassandra.

I was a friendlier person then than I am today, so the world seemed friendlier to me. Now I know that I have lived through the end of a world, and that the last years of that lost world were the least conscious and thus happiest years of my life. The dreams we were then dreaming came from simple idealists. We talked a lot about the future social order as seen by Bebel, the leader of German Social Democracy. If somebody was called a "Red" in those days, it meant he was a Social Democrat, thus not much better than a burglar, arsonist, or rapist. Social Democracy later turned out to be no more than a harmless proletarian insurance company, and Bebel's lovely future state simply a soap bubble. I mention him only because he was so very important to us at that time.

My personal hopes never lay with the masses, even before I got to know the work of Spengler and the beautifully clear Gustave Le Bon. Even my mode of living showed my tendency to disassociate myself. I lived high above everything and everybody in an attic studio, closer to the moon, the stars and the birds than to people, to whom I could always descend if I felt like it. My hopes were based on me alone, not on others. Without being an intellectual egotist, I paid attention only to myself. I wanted to succeed—that was the sum and substance of my philosophy, and probably the creed of most young artists. It goes without saying that I was completely nonpolitical.

It is important to remember that the period I am discussing was still civilized in the eighteenth-century sense, and people did not care about politics the way they do today. The Reichstag—"Dedicated to The German People," or so read the inscription—was popularly called the "gossip shop." The only opposition came from those nasty Social Democrats who kept on criticizing the defense budget. We were living in a quiet, less expensive world that had not smelled blood or seen corpses for almost fifty incredible years of peace and had become so "soft" that people got all excited about the least bit of human injustice. We were nowhere near the bolshevik-fascist contempt for human beings, viewing man as a mere cipher without identity. Nowhere near, but getting closer; still, there were a few years left of "human rights." There was still a trace of the great humanists who lived and worked in Germany in the early nineteenth century, of Goethe, of Weimar as a cultural concept, of the Humboldt brothers, of Hardenberg, Winckelmann, Büchner, of German romanticism—though that irrational movement had seeds that did not germinate until after 1918. Before World War I, German socialism was identical with pacifism and, thank goodness, there were no communists in our country. Rosa Luxemburg, "red Rosa," was merely a socialist organizer; only after the collapse of Germany did she become a communist, and that was after she had voiced her disapproval of some principles to Lenin.

On and off, political rumbles did penetrate the studios of the Academy, but without any after-effect. The socialists were agitating for universal, equal and secret suffrage at the time, instead of the then current class franchise, and I remember a huge demonstration of Dresden workers in front of the royal palace. A lot of workers got as far as the locked iron gates, shouted slogans and sang freedom songs. The Prager Strasse had been cleared by the police, the side streets were filled with cavalry, and some people were hurt. Right next to me a policeman beat up a worker who was walking with his bicycle, and tore his coat; the cop was a fat, red-faced Saxonian. He then made the rest of us run by hitting furiously at us with his flat saber. We fled to a beer cellar, where some of us locked ourselves into the men's room. The police did not pursue us any further, however; they had only wanted to disperse us. So then all of us, demonstrators, curious bystanders and sympathizers took refuge behind our chilled beer mugs and discussed our exciting adventures. Three of my expensive Havana cigars had been crushed and my friend Frankel had his wallet stolen. So we got off easy, unhurt, unjailed and even without having to give them our names.

I must admit that political events of that sort meant nothing more to me and my friends than a welcome sensation. Let's go join them, see what happens, will the army really shoot—? That was our reaction, we were not partisans. We all came from more or less petty bourgeois families and carried no union cards. But emotionally we were certainly on the side of the demonstrators; we future painters and other artists had no taste for the saber-swinging police or the army standing on alert in side streets.

The police saber was certainly still with us, that symbol of authority; it simply replaced the cane of our school days, and you did not argue with it. If authority was not very polite, it was merely because politeness was divided into three levels as was the whole of society, so there was not much left for the second and third levels. But that was all right, that was the way things were. Imperial discipline was still with us and everybody, down to the third class of proletarians, was faithful to Emperor and Flag. (In times of emergency, you were permitted by law to shoot your own father and mother; many a young worker or peasant would have done so without question. That was how much Kaiser Wilhelm expected from his faithful soldiers.)

The full, untouchable grandeur and power of the state was represented by the army and the police. All you had to say to a naughty child was "I'll call the cop if you don't behave." It worked wonders. All the traditional bogeymen had been replaced by Prussian policemen by the time I was a boy; for good measure, parents might also threaten to send you to the fire station. The point was that all civil servants were, and were meant to be, curt, military, impolite and brutally simple, particularly those in uniform. Citizens were not to be spoiled; they were to obey, period. Barracks were barracks, a workman was a workman, a man who took the garbage was a garbageman. The idea of calling him a member of the auxiliary field force of the Sanitation Department

Officialdom [1923]

had not yet arrived.

I have always felt uncomfortable in my dealings with authorities. In thirty years, I have not been able to get rid of that feeling. Every time I enter a police station I start worrying that they'll keep me—are my papers really in order? They never were. Part of the authoritarian system is to find some little thing wrong so that you would be frightened, even though you expected it. Infallibility was always up there, behind the desk, while the rest of humanity down here was fallible.

That Byzantine formalism seems quite harmless and childish by now, compared to the hero worship and human sacrifices that came later. The peace of 1871-1914 also turned out to be but a gentle daydream. The sadistic-masochistic orgy that followed not only confirmed but surpassed all of Spengler and Nietzsche. Geopolitics replaced humanism. The period of enlightenment that had started with the Renaissance went down, and up came the blind, iron ant, and a time totally lacking in concern for human beings, the period of numbers without names, of robots without heads.

TO BERLIN

The Academic Council in Dresden bought two of my drawings, a male nude in chalk and a pen-and-ink drawing, *Yellow Death*; I also got a diploma and a certificate that would enable me to get a stipend at the Berlin Academy; I could not get that in Dresden because I was not a native Saxonian. Besides, my prospects were much better in Berlin; there was where the action was. It was getting to be more and more the center of things, and had surpassed the former art centers of Munich, Düsseldorf, and Dresden. The leaders of modern German painting were living there: Max Liebermann, Lovis Corinth, Max Slevogt, the triumvirate of German impressionism. Berlin was progressive. In addition to Cézanne and Van Gogh, the galleries were dealing in younger French artists like Picasso, Matisse, Derain and others who were just beginning to become known. There were marvelous theaters in Berlin, a gigantic circus, cabarets and night clubs; beer halls the size of railroad terminals, wine palaces four stories high, six-day races, futurist exhibitions, international tango competitions, and a cycle of Strindberg plays in a special theater: this was the Berlin that I was going to.

My friend Herbert Fiedler had gone there ahead of me. He was living in the southern end of town. I looked him up right away, and we decided to get a small apartment together.

Fiedler painted busily, mostly scenes of people working outdoors, railroad workers laying tracks, and that sort of thing. He would go out every morning with his paint box to paint railroad crossings, slum houses, suburban landscapes—quite devoid of any social bias. What he cared about was light and color; the railroad workers could just as well have been potato-digging peasants, or asparagus-cutting women. He was not involved in social controversy. That came later.

We would go outdoors and sketch busily. The outskirts of the city, expanding like an octopus, were what attracted us most. We would draw newly erected buildings while still wet; those bizarre city landscapes where trains teamed on overpasses, garbage dumps crowded garden allotments, and concrete mixers were ready for newly laid streets.

We loved the amusement parks where strange families lived in colorful trailers. There was one painted in the colors of the Spanish flag, labeled "Various Faces of the Tango." The tango was very fashionable at the time; it was performed here by six girls dressed to look like Carmen and a young man in orange—the tango color. I was quite fascinated, made a lot of sketches and painted a picture at home with much orange, green and gold. The Spanish girls were, of course, real Berliners with an uncanny appetite for sausages, herrings and fried potatoes. An enormous amount of beer with raspberry soda was consumed in a neighboring bar; the tango makes you thirsty.

When one of the girls posed for me in my studio, the young man lay in wait for me by the front door. Not with a Spanish dagger, but the brass knuckles he was wearing sufficed to prove that a fellow from the Berlin slums could also have hot Spanish blood. We made up, in spite of my aching jaw, by going up to my room and drinking some real Spanish sherry, left over from my birthday.

We loved the little stand-up bars at the corner where we drank our beer with hod carriers, teamsters and the building super-intendent from next door. We ate pickled herring, and finished with potato schnaps into which you put a piece of rum-soaked sugar. In a more imaginative mood, you would order a "Persico Rose" (rye with a shot of raspberry syrup) or a "Green Minna" (potato schnaps with a shot of green peppermint liqueur).

If you were short of cash, you could always satisfy your hunger at Aschinger's. You would order a plate of pea soup for thirty pfennigs; what you got was not a plate but a small tureen. Better yet was that you could have as much bread and rolls as you wanted. Whenever the basket was empty, the waiter would appear without being called and fill it up again with marvellous little warm rolls, salt sticks, and rye bread with caraway seed. You were not watched and what disappeared into your pockets was not noticed as long as you did it discreetly. Aschinger was a true benefactor for hungry artists.

Then there were the department stores, chiefly Wertheim's in the Leipziger Strasse. At Wertheim's I bought my drawing material, neckties, soap, groceries; at Wertheim's I had a subscription to the

lending library, where I could get all the new books as soon as they appeared; to Wertheim's I'd invite my girl friend for tea. Wertheim's was a world all of its own.

From Wertheim's I usually went to Josty, a famous old café on the Potsdamer Platz. I would sit on the terrace for hours with my sketch book, watch people, or have the waiter bring me the newest magazines (there was a special waiter to do just that), all for the price of a cup of coffee.

I loved the nightlife. Young people are attracted by it like moths to the flame. My friend and I did not have enough money to go to the fancy places, so we had to make do with the smaller nightspots on the edges of town. It was in a café near the Oranienburg Gate that I first heard a jazz band. People called it a noise band. It was not a jazz band in the American sense, but more of a café orchestra gone crazy. Two or three musicians with saws and cow bells would parody the general melody with rhythmic interruptions. The conductor called himself Mister Meschugge and acted like a madman. He would pretend that he had lost control, would break his baton to pieces and smash his violin over the head of a musician. At the end he would grab the bass and use it as a weapon in the ensuing battle, finally throwing the splinters into the audience that screamed with delight and threw them back. Throughout the performance waiters kept on serving the musicians more beer and drinks, increasing the general gaiety. Meschugge would grab instruments from the hands of the musicians, and sing and dance. Suddenly he would jump onto the piano, pretend he was a monkey, scratch himself, grab a large glass of beer to toast the audience, but then, quick as a flash, pour it down one of the trumpets. The audience was convulsed with laughter.

That evening in the café I could not have guessed that we were watching a parody of something that was to become grim reality— a reality in which a different conductor Meschugge would direct a dance of death, beat his musicians with their own instruments until they were senseless, and reap thundering applause. Its ghastly echo can be heard to this day.

The Friedrichstadt was alive with whores. They stood in the doorways like sentinels and whispered their standard: "Want a date, sweetie?" Those were the days of large feather hats and boas, and pushed-up bosoms. A dangling handbag was the sign of their guild. Their best known café was the National on the Friedrich-strasse.

We had read Flaubert and de Maupassant, so this nightlife seemed quite poetic to us. The whore under the street light, her pimp, and free love in general were favored subjects of many a young poet. The whore became sort of a heroine—that too was in the air. We admired Strindberg, Weininger, Wedekind—progressive naturalists, anarchists torturing themselves, death-worshippers and sex-fanatics. It was just before the war.

It was a time of big parties. There were all sorts of masquerades: the ball of German illustrators, a Heinrich Zille Ball, The Masked Ball of the Admiral Palace, artists balls, theater balls and innumerable private affairs. Everybody seemed to be looking for new ideas for parties. Once Pascin came from Paris at the invitation of the Berlin Sezession, where his pictures were being shown, and arranged a Ball of Cannibals. The poster for it showed a wild man gnashing his teeth, dancing, and wearing only a tail coat, and a white tie that had slipped below his waist. The ballroom was cleverly decorated to look like a series of tents. In the center was a huge, red cardboard kettle with skull and bones in which two half naked painters were "cooking;" they demonstrated their agony by drinking wine from a bottle and continually begging for more, which was gladly given to them by amused guests.

The flames under the kettle were not real of course; strips of red paper lighted from below and blown by a fan produced the impression of lively flames. As this was the only light in the room, the illusion of being in the middle of the jungle worked perfectly. Later, when the motor was stopped, you saw almost no light except the glow of hundreds of cigars and cigarettes, like fireflies in Africa. The virgin forest in the West of Berlin.

A fellow I knew had brought along a fresh, still bloody veal bone that he had ordered at his butcher's. He defended the disgusting thing from the cannibals all night, holding it under his arm even when dancing. About four in the morning a few envious revelers decided to slaughter and roast the fellow himself, if he wouldn't give up the bone. There was a big fight that somebody cleverly stopped with snowballs that they got from the courtyard.

In the dull light of dawn the ballroom really looked like a cannibal's camping ground. Some of the tents had collapsed and what appeared to be human limbs hung from the rafters. The cardboard kettle had been trampled and was lying in a reddish puddle of wine and glue that looked truly cannibalistic.

Later in the morning some of the revelers were brought in to the local police station for disturbing the peace and being a public

The Dear Invalid [1915]

nuisance. The fellow with the veal bone was among them, and a society lady with a ring in her nose clad in nothing but a fur coat. A high-ranking police officer who was fond of theater and the arts quelled the proceedings and let them off with a warning. So they went on to the studio of a well-known painter for beer and a hangover breakfast, where the cannibal party continued with a record player. The veal bone had been deposited at the monument for Otto the Lazy, in the Siegesallee.

In between parties there were rumors of war, but they were not taken very seriously. Tension between Germany and France? The usual stuff. Only people who did not enjoy life were hoping for war. I was not one of them.

I was now starting to paint in oil. I had no teacher, I just bought some books and learned as well as I could. I painted from memory, compositions in the style of my drawings, drafting them in India ink on the canvas and then painting over that in oil. The pictures were conceived in line and were more like drawings in color.

I continued to draw for the satirical reviews, but also joined a life class at the School for Arts and Crafts. A certain Hasler, a colleague of mine in Professor Orlik's class, had arranged an afternoon session with nude models. He had classical ambitions and would sit for hours studying Delacroix and Michelangelo. He collected all

the old podiums and boxes he could get hold of and built a struc-
ture that was supposed to look like rocks. He then had two male
models climb that rocky mountain.

My friend Fiedler. had gone to Paris in 1912 and was writing
enthusiastic letters. By the spring of 1913 I had saved a little
money, so I went there too. Paris was quite inexpensive then. I
used to eat in a very cheap restaurant on Boulevard Montparnasse
where the market helpers and chauffeurs went, but the food was
much better than in Berlin. I was continually surprised by what
you got to eat and how it was served. Paris was for me a city where
you could stroll, where rooms extended to the street: you could
practically live on the street. Compared to Berlin, it seemed
southern, almost oriental.

I stayed in Paris for about eight months. I worked very little, and
drew mostly models at the Croquis Calarossi, without correction.
Beside a few friends, nobody knew me. I would have had to stay
longer to get the real feel of the place. But I was not one of those
Germans who went to Paris for ten days and were still there ten
years later.

PRIVATE GROSZ

What is there to say about the First World War in which I was an infantry soldier? Of a war that I never liked from the start and with which I never identified? I was interested in politics, but had grown up in the spirit of humanism. War meant horror, mutilation, annihilation. Did not many wise people feel the same way?

Of course there was some sort of mass enthusiasm in the beginning. And it was real. But the intoxication soon blew over, and what was left was great emptiness. The flowers on the helmets and gun barrels quickly faded. War then meant anything but enthusiasm; it became filth, lice, stupor, disease and mutilation. The heroism of some idealists and their complete devotion to their country did exist, but these virtues had their reverse side too, and they finally came out even. "Enthusiasm is not simply a herring that you can pickle," said the people.

Then, when it all bogged down in defeat a few years later, when everything collapsed, nothing was left for me and most of my friends but disgust and horror. After all, my fate had made an artist of me, not a soldier. The effect the war had on me was totally negative. It had never been the "liberation" felt by some. It is true, of course, that war not only arouses suppressed forces slumbering in us, but also really does liberate some people, be it from a hated environment, the slavery of daily work, or the burden of one's own personality. That is one of the mysteries that will perpetuate wars forever.

I dislike talking about it. I hated to be a mere number; I would have hated it even had I been a high number. I was yelled at so long that I finally had the courage to yell back. I struggled against stinking stupidity and brutality, but I remained in the minority. It came

Pandemonium, August [1914]

down to hand combat, and pure self-defense on my side. I defended no ideals and no belief; I defended *myself*.

Belief? Ha! In what? In German heavy industry, the great profiteers? In our illustrious generals? Our beloved Fatherland? At least I had the courage to voice what so many were thinking. Madness, probably, rather than courage. What I saw filled me with disgust and contempt for people. Everybody around me was afraid; I was afraid too, but not afraid to resist this fear. I could write pages about this much discussed subject, but everything I have to say can be seen in my drawings.

In 1916 I was discharged from military service, but not quite. I was told it was a sort of furlough, and I would be called back again. The Berlin to which I returned was cold and grey. The crowded cafés and bars were in uncanny contrast to our dark, gloomy, unheated living quarters. The same soldiers who had been singing and dancing there and hanging tipsily on the arms of prostitutes in another time could be seen dragging themselves morosely through the streets, still covered with dirt from the trenches, going from one railroad station to the other. How right Swedenborg is, I thought, that heaven and hell are right next to each other in this world! For even if I did not believe in God, I could hardly imagine a world without heaven and hell.

So I was free for the moment.

The catastrophe had begun. The storm of war, so recently praised for its cleansing effect, had broken; the lovely phrases had become

stale-smelling printer's ink on cheap, brownish paper and I lived in my own world, in my studio in Südende, and drew.

I drew drunks, men vomiting, men cursing the moon with clenched fists, a murderer sitting on a packing case with the murdered woman's body inside. I drew wine drinkers, beer drinkers, gin drinkers, and a worried man washing his blood-stained hands.

I drew soldiers in action, using my sketchbooks from the war. I drew lonely little men running crazily through empty streets in flight from unknown horrors. I drew a transverse section of an apartment house: in one window a man attacking his wife with a broom, in another two people making love, in a third a man hanging from the crossbar of a window, surrounded by buzzing flies.

I drew soldiers without noses, war cripples with metal arms like crab claws; two medics strapping a raving private into a horse blanket; a one-armed soldier saluting a bemedaled lady with his remaining hand, as she takes a cookie from a paper bag and puts it on his bed. A colonel with an open fly embracing a fat nurse. An orderly emptying a pail with all sorts of bits of human bodies into a pit. A skeleton in uniform being examined for military fitness....

I wrote, too. My poems were even published. Some appeared in *Neue Jugend*, a new magazine. A longer poem on reddish paper was enclosed, a little later, in my second drawing collection, *Kleine Groszmappe*.

My studio was a piece of my world. It was on the top floor of an apartment house in Stephan Street, Südende, near Berlin. It was furnished with packing cases that I had painted, covered with brown linen, or in other ways made liveable. Empty bottles were lined up along the walls, their labels peeled off and stuck on the wall as decoration. The etched castles of the red wines, the colorful Italian ones with Vesuvius and grapes, and the black port wines with white script gave the impression of large postage stamps. A gaslamp hung from the ceiling, decorated with a huge black spider with wire legs hanging on a thread. It moved and its long legs trembled in the slightest breeze.

I had pasted pieces of a broken mirror at random spots, and enlivened the space by sticking cigar rings and tinsel stars on the furniture, walls and ceiling. There was a desk to the right. There were reproductions and photographs all over: women in tights, old photos from the nineties, a few pictures of men whom I admired, one of Henry Ford, for instance, complete with dedication "To George Grosz the artist from his admirer Henry Ford." (I had written that myself, of course, hoping that Ford wouldn't mind.) My studio was a romantic tent, a tent such as they have in country fairs. I really should have charged admission. My best piece of furniture, the only new one, was an iron bed bought on installment in Wertheim's department store. The little iron stove had to be stoked every morning or else it got very cold, as the wind blew without mercy through cracks round the large studio window. An automatic gas cooking stove with a slot for coins completed the furnishing.

It was here that I painted the big picture that I called *Widmung an Oskar Panizza:* death rides on a black coffin through a crowd of distorted human faces, crowing words or calling out in vain. (The picture belonged to the Wiesbaden collector Kirchhof and hung for a long time on loan in the Wiesbaden Museum's Grosz Room.) In the same studio I painted *The Adventurer,* a picture that later became well known. It was bought by the Stadtmuseum of Dresden, then removed by the Nazis and shown in their exhibition of "Degenerate Art" as a forbidding example. I wonder where it is today?

That breathing spell of 1916-17 was a fertile period in my life, both realistic and romantic. My favorite colors were a deep red and a blackish blue. I felt the floor swaying beneath me, and that showed in my pictures and water colors.

In the old *Café des Westens* I met Theodor Däubler one evening, and he immediately wrote an article about me in the *Weiss Blätter,* an intellectual magazine of pacifist tendency, edited by the German-Alsatian, René Schickele. Even mid-war it printed poems and articles of "enemy" foreigners; we got acquainted with Henri Barbusse and Romain Rolland. The *Weisse Blätter* published one of the best stories of the then still unknown Leonhard Frank *(Der Vater)*, and discovered Franz Kafka *(Die Verwandlung)*. They discovered me too.

Däubler's article—with illustrations—brought me immediate fame, if only in "intellectual" circles. People talked about me. I was a bit surprised, but not unpleasantly so. I now got into circulation. I no longer needed to envy Flaubert's young man in *Education Sentimentale* his social contacts. I was invited. New friends emerged. I met extraordinary people: writers, vegetarian scientists who were interested in astronomy, sculptors with persecution complexes, reformers with hidden vices, a ruined drinker who lived on translations, and painters, musicians and philosophers. What an extraordinarily interesting merry-go-round! There were night people, like moonflowers, like henbane that blooms at night near dungheaps and is poisonous, like moles who live under the earth, some of them invulnerable like salamanders whose tails grow back when cut off.

We all frequented the *Café des Westens*, we sat there in the late afternoon or late at night, and talked. Politically we did not agree. What we had in common—whether of "enlightened" or "religious" persuasion—was our dislike of the ruling military and industrial powers; and we knew as early as 1916 that this war would not end well.

I want to tell about my dear friend Theodor Däubler, nicknamed Fat Theodor. He was a Mediterranean type. He had a beard and a big belly, ate and smoked enormous quantities, and was the author

of the mighty epos *Das Nordlicht*. It was a treat to listen to him. He enjoyed being surrounded by young people, poets and painters; he was the center of a small circle and when he lay on the couch with the tight top button of his pants open, he could really have been a Greek philosopher surrounded by his students. His facial similarity to Zeus would indicate a wise, controlled lifestyle.

Nothing could have been further from the truth. He was constantly rushed and often short of money despite a comfortable monthly retainer from *Insel* publications. The trouble was that money would not stay with him, it ran away, often into murky channels. He also got money from a lady patron, the middle-aged wife of a Dresden mill owner, and that bothered him too, because he was quite unable to muster anything more than platonic affection in return. He was an anxious person who felt persecuted by all sorts of powers. He was ambitious and kept on complaining that he got so little recognition, and was by no means "finished."

I still see him coming out of the kitchen with furious, hungry eyes while his sister was cooking supper. He was holding a big, raw, unpeeled potato in each hand, pacing furiously back and forth, gnawing at them like a rodent and carelessly throwing the peel any old place, into an empty vase, into the stove, or on to the bookshelf. Back and forth, back and forth he went like a prehistoric monster. In between the scraping and chewing he kept on shouting "I am not finished— I am not finished...."

We once had a little dinner party for him and some friends, and my wife made an ample double portion of spaghetti, much more than usual. As Däubler was the guest of honor, the whole dish was first passed to him; but instead of passing it on, he pushed his plate aside, and in no time, with seemingly apocalyptic hunger, ate up the whole dish. There was something volcanic about him when he ate that way; we were watching a natural phenomenon. The spaghetti was then washed down with Chianti; some got caught in his beard, and as he went on talking, squirted off to the right and left. Formidable. It was the very essence of eating, total satiation, that was happening and we watched it in amazement.

Immediately thereafter, he smoked, and he smoked the same way. Puff, puff, the cigar disappeared and he lighted another. Like a chimney.

Later we discovered where Däubler left his cigar butts. He simply tucked them down the side of the easy chairs, under the cushions, where they burned numerous holes. We contemplated fitting the chairs with tin gutters. Finally we accepted them as our due for Däubler's marvelous stories; like the one about red-haired Sollman who died long ago but was somehow still living and had painted all the pictures of the famous Norwegian Edvard Munch; sometimes he was visible, sometimes he stood invisibly behind Munch and guided his brush, which is why the pictures all had the mystical quality admired particularly by Germans.

Däubler had last seen Sollman in Venice. He told Däubler then that he was already over 150 years old: he came from a long-lived family, he said. "Did you ever see him in Berlin?" we inquired. "Yes," said Theodor. "That was quite peculiar. I was sitting in the café. It was very cold—November, I believe—with frost flowers on the window, but not frozen solid; there were spots through which you could see the *Potsdamerstrasse*. Suddenly a street car whizzed by and I see a little man running behind it—no, not running, float-ing—Sollman. Hatless, his red hair like an aureole round his head and, as uncanny as it may sound, with two pairs of butterfly wings on his shoulders! Of course, you will say, it was frost flowers—but I do know what I saw! Just imagine, butterfly wings in November."

He enjoyed reading to us from his *Nordlicht* epic, a cosmological giant work full of secret symbolism and prophecies that only the initiated could comprehend. The only trouble was that he got car-ried away (as easily happens to poets) and never stopped. When his friend, Else Lasker-Schüler, was there, we heard her relaxed snoring, not withstanding the booming voice of the *Nordlicht* poet. That did not bother Däubler, he said that was simply sub-conscious jealousy. (Lasker-Schüler was a poet too, a playful one who had a nickname for everybody; mine was Leatherstocking because at that time I was raving about America.)

One day Däubler introduced me to one of his friends who hap-pened to be in Berlin, a business magnate who purchased raw material, chiefly wool, for the German army command. Däubler said I should come to the Hotel Adlon for dinner that night. Herr Falk loved art, he said, was giving Lehmbruck a monthly retainer and might do the same for me.

There was something quite oriental about Herr Sally Falk. Not only in facial features, but in his behavior toward his wife. He treated her like a rare bird of paradise and kept her literally in a gilded cage, to which he alone had the key. When he was away— and that happened frequently, as he had to travel a lot in his business—he put his little bird on a golden chain. When he was with her, everything round him went into oblivion, he had eyes and ears only for his "Chérie," and we others at the table became

transparent puppets.

He could be charming when he was alone, when he was bored, and when he was through with business. (Though business was never quite over. In the middle of the night, while we were enjoying a bottle of Veuve Cliquot, the telephone might ring: "Herr Falk, Army Headquarters on the wire.") When his wife was not along and he was more bored than usual, he would occasionally listen. As he had become my patron, I would always make use of such occasions to tell him the troubles of struggling artists.

He said he liked the company of artists, because art did not make him jealous. "Once it did," he said. "This art dealer in Heidelberg showed me a Greco. One of the doubtful ones, but the woman in it, in the light—Herr Grosz, she was the image of my wife! Sounds absurd, doesn't it? Well, what should I tell you? I was jealous. Jealous of Greco or whatever student painted her picture. And at that, it was three hundred years ago," he added pensively.

"And then, Herr Falk?" I queried.

"Then? You know what I did? Bought the Greco, of course, yes—and never unpacked it. It is still untouched, in the same case, in my house."

Falk was an autocrat, and made fast decisions. He did not like people to refuse. I was once sitting at the Adlon with him and wanted to leave after coffee. I had an important date with the girl who later became my wife. "You want to go already?" he said. "Yes, I have a date." "Do telephone and stay for a while. I have an idea. Come to my house. I have a few wonderful books I would like to show you—first editions—here," he said, handing me an envelope, "here's a ticket for a first-class sleeping car to Mannheim. You come with me, I can't sleep at night. Need company."

What could I do?

In our world, ruled by the commercial spirit, artists like to dream of patrons, the ideal sponsors of the arts. Today art is merchandise that can be sold with clever promotion exactly like soap, towels or brushes, and the artist has become a sort of manufacturer who must produce new goods with ever-increasing speed for ever-changing show windows. He is allowed no time to develop. He has moved from private to public ownership and takes orders from its representatives, be they businessmen or Worker and Soldier Commissioners. He is a sort of cobbler who makes work boots or pretty slippers to specification. For us artists that was a poor exchange; many of us secretly mourn the passing of those legendary times when there were people who supported an artist (granted, some-

The Glorious Death [1927]

times in near slavery), freeing him from the necessity of making money and worrying about his daily living.

You can play the part of striving artist versus patron in various ways. If you are not well-known yet, you have to get there in any case as quickly as possible; but in addition, your patron must be kept entertained. You have to jump up with a lighter in your hand if your patron smokes, for instance, and that sort of thing. Then there are patrons who like their artist rough. His attraction then is bad manners, dirty fingernails, bad breath and stubbles. Those traits are mostly found in anarchists and the "proud" individualists among us artists. The patron likes them, partly because of their inferiority, partly because he is reminded of his own weaknesses, and partly because some money-makers unconsciously have guilt feelings that are assuaged by a kick in the extension of their backs by a kind of Van Gogh boot.

I did not belong to the "proud" type of artist myself. I was interested in money, and more inclined to toady and to jump up

with a lighter than to do the uncouth, honest "I'll tell you what's what, Herr Falk" act. I knew that the whole thing was only a short lived comedy, and I knew the rules. I might have made more money by clowning. But the crumbs and half-gnawed bones of patronage were not too bad either. After all, there were lots of floors below mine, and many cellars beneath. The patron's table is still well spread; at least there is always a cigar and something to drink. And that is the way it should be.

For reasons that will soon be obvious, I want to dedicate a few lines to a patron of those days. Count Kessler is hardly known any more. He died alone many years ago in Paris, where he had gone to finish his autobiography; he would not stay in Germany as long as the Nazis, whom he hated, were in power. He was perhaps the last real gentleman—one of the very few that I have met on my way through the world.

Count Kessler saw the artist through the eyes of an earlier generation. He belonged to a high-minded aristocracy that has become historical; his attitude was that of those tolerant, artistically minded princes, such as Karl August of Weimar, in whose courts western culture developed along the strict rules of the Greek classics. He saw the artistic genius of man neither as regrettable degeneration, nor as a symptom of infantilism stuck in the phase of self-soiling; nor did he regard a work of art in terms of trade or investment.

He had no "modern" relation to money. He spent lavishly on art that he loved. He never bargained, not even when the price was high. He harbored no resentments, not even for artists who took advantage of his patronage, as happened once in a while. Though an aristocrat who never had to earn his living, he knew there were few artists who could enjoy his generous lifestyle. Artists are defenseless and defenselessness brings prices down. Kessler and I never became personal friends. Our connection was purely the appreciation that this art-loving man had of my pictures. Old-fashioned or even ridiculous as this may sound in our present era of materialism, Count Kessler considered artists superior beings who were important in the life of any cultured nation and must not be allowed to perish. He felt it was his duty to support them—and it so happened that he literally saved my life at the end of the war.

I had to report for active duty again in mid-1917. This time I was to train recruits and guard and transport prisoners of war. But I simply could no longer bear it. One night they found me, almost unconscious, head first in the latrine....

I lay for a fairly long time in the infirmary. All of a sudden, they said I was well. But I wasn't; my nerves were shot; I refused to get up. In fury, I physically attacked the medical sergeant. I will never forget with what lusty enthusiasm seven of my ambulatory "comrades" fell upon me. One of them, a baker in civilian life, jumped with his whole weight onto my cramped legs, happily shouting: "Gotta step on his legs, gotta keep on trampling on his legs, that'll calm him down." It did. But that incident was burned indelibly into my mind; how these harmless, ordinary people beat me up, and how they enjoyed it. There was no personal animosity. It was an unconscious principle: we are not protesting, so you can't protest either. "Let him have it, step on his legs!" Later, we probably continued peacefully to play cards, drink beer, smoke, and tell dirty stories.

That happened in 1917, a time when nobody believed in anything anymore, and we in the infirmary were fed dried vegetables, coffee made of turnips and artificial honey that affected our stomach walls. I had never really believed in the solidarity of the masses and never desired to live with the masses; but then in the war, when I really got to know the so-called masses—! I found soli-

darity only in single cases, from friend to friend. What I did find plenty of, however, was sarcasm and ridicule, fear, oppression, cheating, and slander, and could no longer blame the severe men who ruled and drove these formless masses. The fact that none of this suited me is something else again, and I paid for my personal attitude.

That is all. I no longer have any hope for the underprivileged. I never did participate in the worship of the masses, not even at the time when I toyed with certain political theories. The war was like a mirror, reflecting all virtues and vices. But as an artist tests his drawing in a mirror, the faults stood out more clearly.

One day I was lying in the military infirmary with a heavy head, heavier than usual, and I dreamed of a straw hat and walking stick instead of a helmet and trench spade. I dreamed of a cool corner at Kempinski's and belched a bit, because the artificial honey made my stomach rebel; that luminous greyish-green, when spread on grey wartime bread, reminded me of the background of old Italian paintings. In the bed next to mine was a coachman from Berlin who had lost part of his stomach. "Look," he mumbled, half under the influence of the injections that he was constantly getting. (He

Sketchbook [1915]

Finis [1919]

was as strong as an ox.] "Look, comrade," he said in a Berlin dialect, trying to point to his middle, "funny, comrade," he could not
quite lift his finger high enough, "I was still all in one piece, I
was—where are my legs? I must have left them somewhere—if I
could only remember, comrade, if I could only remember. Now I
have an entrance, but there is no exit, it's gone..." Again he tried
to point to his middle, but could no longer lift his hand. He
groaned, semi-conscious, and went to sleep. That night he died
quietly, without a sound, a shapeless bundle.

The next morning, we were eating our grey-green bread and
honey again, drinking our turnip coffee. Life isn't so bad, after all,
is it? The bed was nice and warm, especially with an ancient
magazine from the collection, *Give books to our brave boys in the
infirmary.* Just don't get ill-humored, don't let the sourpusses
infect you. Not every shot hits...well, yes, the fellow next to me,
he really got it. "No more women for him," said the orderly yester-
day. But the medical corporal corrected him: "So what, he'll get a
brand new wooden dick, made to measure. Man, we've seen better
things than that, we in Gorden. You should have seen that, man,
those Gorden artificial legs are just as good as real ones. Man, in
the obstacle race, in the pole jump, they sometimes did better than
the able-bodied ones!" He spoke in a thick Berlin dialect, telling
stories of his gruesome experiences as a medical soldier, and making them sound funny. "Now nobody looks at us anymore. They
used to decorate us with flowers, man, and now they move away.
'Do you have lice, sir?' Hell, we all had lice, man. The sergeant
was telling us, man, he couldn't sleep in bed with his wife any
more, he lies on the carpet next to the bed. And he was a hardened
type, they say he used to be a football star...."

For me, my art was sort of a safety valve that
let the accumulated hot steam escape. Whenever
I had time, I would vent my anger in drawings. I
sketched what I disliked in my surroundings in
notebooks and on stationery: the brutal faces of
my fellow soldiers, angry war cripples, arrogant
officers, lecherous nurses, etc. My drawings had
no purpose, they were just to show how ridiculous and grotesque the busy, cocksure little ants
were in the world surrounding me.

They said I was to be executed as a deserter.
Fortunately, Count Kessler heard about it. He
intervened for me, with the result that I was

pardoned, and sent to a mental home for war casualties. Just before the end of the war I was discharged for the second time, but with the proviso that I would soon be recalled.

I thought the war would never end. Perhaps it never really did? Peace was proclaimed, but not everybody was drunk and happy. Fundamentally, people had remained the same, with a few differences: the proud German soldier had become a beaten, weary soldier; the people's army had fallen apart just like the uniforms and ammunition pouches made of poor ersatz material. I was not disappointed that this war was lost. I was only disappointed that people had borne and suffered it so long, and that nobody had followed the few voices that were raised against that mass slaughter.

HOME TO BERLIN

I went back to live in Berlin. The city looked like a grey corpse made of stone. There were cracks in all the walls. Plaster and paint were crumbling. The dead, dirty, hollow windows seemed still to be mourning those many for whom they had looked in vain.

Those were wild years. I threw myself madly into life, and teamed up with people who were searching for a way out from this absolute nothingness. We wanted more. Just what this "more" was to be, we could not tell. But my friends and I saw no solution in negativism nor in the fury of having been cheated, nor in the negation of all previous values. We thus, of course, drifted further and further to the left.

In no time I was head over heels in politics. I made speeches, not really from conviction but rather because there were people standing round all day long arguing and my previous experiences had not taught me any better. My speeches were silly repetitions of liberal banalities, but as my words flowed as smoothly as honey, I ended up by believing the nonsense myself, intoxicated by the noise of my own voice. Once I was even hoisted on a man's shoulders, amid shouts of "Long live the proletariat!" As usual, I had been propounding a subject of which I knew nothing: academic freedom. I painted a frighteningly beautiful picture of how henceforth, with the seizure of power by the proletariat, every streetsweeper, every simple worker would be able to attend academies and universities. A privilege, I said with cutting sarcasm, that had heretofore been open only to the sons of the rich—"Long live the proletariat!"

I totally forgot who I was. The "movement" influenced me to such a degree that I considered all art senseless unless it served as a weapon in the political arena. My art was to be gun and sword; I

considered my pencils as nothing but straws unless they served the battle for freedom. What sort of freedom? I never wondered about that.

My feelings were realized in a large, political painting which I called *Germany: a Winter's Tale* after an epic by Heinrich Heine. At the center sat the eternal German bourgeois, fat and frightened, at a slightly unsteady table with the morning paper and a cigar. Below, the three pillars of society: Army, Church, and School (the schoolmaster carrying a cane painted in the national colors). The bourgeois holds tightly to his knife and fork, as the world sways about him. A sailor, symbolizing the revolution, and a prostitute completed my personal image of the times.

In reality, the times were tired and not at all funny. Tired and not at all funny, the soldiers crept back into town, sometimes with a red cockade on their caps.

I remember my old friend and brother-in-law Otto Schmalhausen returning from the Eastern front. I went to meet him at a Berlin railway station. The streets were dark, as the powerhouse was on strike or occupied by Reds. And anyhow, there was an eight o'clock curfew, after which nobody was supposed to be in the street. A feeling of civil war was smoldering in the air. The army

When It Was Over They Played Cards [1916/17]

Germany: a Winter's Tale [1918]

had lost all prestige, but the frightened public assumed that soldiers wearing red cockades belonged somehow to the new powers. Little did they know that the boys merely put those on for self-protection. My brother-in-law, for instance, did so to get home to Berlin without trouble; at many stations there were revolutionary sailors and so-called soldier councils who regarded anybody in regular uniform as an enemy of the revolution.

We went to my studio; Otto was carrying a typical soldier's trunk. We walked happily through the miserable cold streets where plaster had fallen off walls, windows were broken, and iron shutters were let down over store windows. But Otto had a large bottle of Pernod and an excellent sausage in his case, just how he came upon these treasures I will never know, so we were looking forward to a pleasant evening.

We were just turning into Hohenzollerndamm, taking turns with the heavy case, when suddenly a bearded bespectacled man leapt out of a door, raised his hat politely, bowed, and offered his help in carrying. "Please sir, good soldier, sir, before I help you—as I hope you will permit—would you gentlemen do me the favor and the pleasure to come upstairs for a modest supper? And, if I may ask, do you have far to go? If it is a long way, we would gladly put you up for the night; we have a large place and plenty of room. And fortunately, it so happens that we are having veal cutlets tonight—I was able to get them without ration stamps—so please, won't you please do me the honor—?"

A bit amazed, Otto and I looked at each other with amusement. And Otto, who always had excellent manners, impersonated a member of the soldiers council and expressed regret that he could not come, as we had to attend an important meeting of the Workers and Soldiers Council—as for the cutlets, they could be eaten cold—because, as the gentleman undoubtedly knew, there were roaming bands of Reds, so measures had to be taken by us who were standing by the Democratic Republic....

Of course, said the gentleman, and that was why he would like to have soldiers at his house for a few days—for security.

Otto graciously replied that he would gladly stop by in the next few days to see that everything was all right. Equally graciously, he accepted the intimidated citizen's offer of a token of his gratitude—"I'll be right back, gentlemen, with a little snack and a bottle of Chateau Lafitte—quite an exquisite bottle, gentlemen, just right for Officers of the Republic like you...."

More happily than ever we went on to the "urgent council meeting" in my studio. The cutlets and the wine were of course first rate, and we long enjoyed the parting words of the German bourgeois: "Gentlemen soldiers, sirs, now that I have met you I feel that at last we are on our way to peace and order."

In that year, 1919, we walked the unlighted streets hugging the house fronts, and ducking under high archways. Inhabitants, half-crazed with fear, could not stand the confinement of their own four walls, so they went up on the roof to shoot pigeons and people. Their sense of proportion, or size, somehow got misplaced. When one of those roof hunters was picked up and shown a man whom he had hit, he said, "But officer, I thought he was a large pigeon!"

You could buy guns and ammunition everywhere. My cousin, who was discharged a little later, offered me a complete machine gun. He assured me that I could pay for it in installments, and didn't I know anybody who might be interested in two other machine guns and a small field gun? He was thinking of my connections with political parties, of course, which were starting to rise against each other. Later he brought me six Mauser rifles in prime condition—model 98, the ones we soldiers had used—and various other things I wanted. Wild times!

All moral codes were abandoned. A wave of vice, pornography and prostitution enveloped the whole country. *Je m'en fous* was the motto, at last I am going to have a good time. A few young Americans who a few days before had been playing in an army band came to Berlin, and the orchestras playing Vienna waltzes changed overnight into jazz bands. Instead of first and second violinist, you saw grinning banjo and saxophone players. Everybody was happy. Frightfully happy. The war was over!

Now inflation began. Slowly, at first. Comedians in cabarets sang funny songs about the falling currency; between glasses of champagne, patrons would check the rate of exchange of the German mark against the dollar and the pound by telephone. "We're drinking up Grandma's cottage, and her first and second mortgage too!"

Out on the street one group of white-shirted men was marching to the slogan of *"Deutschland, erwache! Jude, verrecke!"* (Wake up, Germany! Jew, drop dead!), while another in equal military formation hailed Moscow. That left smashed heads, broken shins, and some nasty gunshot wounds.

The whole city was dark, cold, and full of rumors. The streets became ravines of manslaughter and cocaine traffic, marked by steel rods and bloody, broken chair legs. Nothing was known for sure, but there were rumors of secret drills of the Black National Defense and a budding Red Army. Furious female "patriots"

attacked my friend Wieland with umbrellas when he ventured into a forest of opinions with his attempt at clarification. A policeman saved him from being lynched by the angry masses, and he had an equally narrow escape from being shot by volunteer troops. He got away with some whip-lashings and kicks. We had to go into hiding, did not sleep at home, where we were known, and waited for better days.

Real or fake war casualties were sitting at every street corner. Some of them sat there dozing until somebody came by, then they would twist their heads and start convulsive shaking. Shakers, we called them. "Look Ma, there's another one of those funny shakers." We had become quite immune to all the weird and disgusting sights. Other invalids would peddle American chocolate that suddenly appeared in quantity. God, how long it was since we had seen chocolate! In the hands of the war cripples it seemed like the olive branch that the dove brought to Noah's Ark. A sign of improvement. "If chocolate is available again...!"

Many of the niceties that we had missed for so long showed up once more. Suddenly all the stores had Libby's condensed milk. "Supposedly all American army surplus. A bigshot bought it all up and is now selling it at double and even three times the price!" And that is the way it was. Fortunes were made overnight. Always overnight. If you looked closely, you could see what was going on. They got started with nothing. As soon as they had something, they sold it for three and four times the original price.

My friend Albert, who had been drafted for the second time when I was, was a dreamer, still believing in fairies and pots of gold. "Tell me," I asked him one day, "how did you get so rich so fast?!" We were smoking expensive cigars with Albert's breakfast drink: Pommery & Greno Extra Brut with porter. Well, he said, as he was morosely traveling in a troop train (sad, because the nice civilian days were over) and deeply dreading what he was going into ("Almost like a prayer to Fate, believe it or not") and absently gazing out the window ("I'm no little kid any more—honestly")— well, there was a fairy gliding along next to the train. ("Quite clearly and distinctly...no...like a white cloud, but transparent.") And she, he continued, had suddenly raised her hand and motioned toward a heap of old, rusting rails and screws. "And that is how I got rich."

His was typical of the sort of careers that were made in those crazy times. Unreal. What I saw and experienced in those days now often seem fantastic dreams. Or is it just the years that hang

Silence! [1935/36]

Friedrichstrasse [1918]

like colored veils between then and now that produce that illusion? Oddly, not everybody was happy about the return of all those goodies. Because not everybody's hand was led by a fairy. Most people could merely observe, and press their noses flat to the windows where everything was displayed. The tastefully arranged still lifes on the shelves aroused your appetite, but you had to hurry. During the very time that you admired the fat turkey, the larded hare, the Prague ham and were wondering which you could afford and while you were just thinking...the prices went up....

You could almost hear it. "Hear it? Hear it?" people said, "that isn't crackling, that's the prices!" It wasn't funny. You decided in a flash and bought; while you were walking through the door, that hare could cost a million or two or more.

It was odd: as prices rose and rose, so did the lust for life. Oh, wasn't life great? New dances everywhere; French champagne flowed freely; in front of every café, hotel, bar, dozens of people were standing as before the castle gates in medieval days, some in picturesque attire, empty hands extended. No Saint Agatha here, however, to comfort poor beggars. No pious young chatelaine carrying food and drink in a wicker basket, and humbly tending sores and ills. Here came—"What else?"—a fat uniformed doorman with a large umbrella to shelter us elegant people from rain, and chase away all the poor and the hungry and whatever loiterers there were: "Get outta here, will ya? Get a move on, or I'll call the cop!"

The cop was the redfaced young man over there in the blue uniform with the funny new helmet, gaitered calves and polished shoes. The cop was there for law and order. He had a secret understanding with those inside and, as his gloved hand was not meant to hit, he had been given an extension in the form of a solid rubber stick. That was something new at the time, and supposedly humane. He could use it to caress too—chiefly dogs, people less. Unfortunately, the truncheon was always hitting toward the same side—the left. Which was, strangely enough, where all those staring people unvisited by fairy godmothers were standing. The blows went to the left, always to the left.

I carefully drew all these things, people, happenings. I spared no one, neither in the fancy restaurants nor on the street. Arrogantly, I considered myself a natural scientist rather than a painter or even a satirist. Actually, however, I was everybody I depicted: the rich, gorging, champagne-guzzling man favored by fate, as well as the one out there holding out his hand in the pouring rain. There were two equal parts of me. In other words, I participated in life....

One might think that the rich and privileged were content with the bounty that God had laid out for them. But many were not; and this discontent was a boon for the jesters and actors among us. Rich and mighty people would approach some of us, my friend Erwin, for instance, and say, "Erwin, couldn't you perform for us? I mean, imitate us; like, for instance, my crooked legs, or the way friend Oscar stuffs himself and then pukes on the carpet, or how Hugo sits in his wine cellar and counts the empties? Take your time, Erwin, and enlist a few of those talented loafers who'll sing for a few pennies, we'll get you a big theater and we'll all be there, you can count on it. We'll enjoy seeing what we're really like, ha ha ha...."

I was neither a talented loafer, nor a circus clown, nor a sidewalk artist (though, between ourselves, I was and still am something of all the above), but I played along. We were well paid. I became almost rich, and Erwin got really rich, merely by making faces at the rich and mighty, and displaying our bare behinds. (Come to think of it, that's the way it was before the fall of Rome.) As Hugo said, "My dear Erwin, for the final curtain we show our bare behinds to the boxes and the orchestra."

This was considered a great blossoming of the arts and the theater. Erwin and I were crowned with laurels, beribboned in different colors; mostly red, sometimes black/red/gold, rarely black/red/white. The wealthy of those days had an open heart for the fine arts, but they were getting weary, and liked to toast their own decline. "Prosit! Filter down to my fat belly..." "Oh, Erwin, say something really disgusting to me, something really insulting!"

"You perjuring, stinking capitalist!"

"Oh—say it again—isn't that sweet! Erwin, here's a blank check. Any amount, any amount...." "Prosit, Herr Grosz, hurrah for the Decline of the Western World!...Yes of course, what else? Wasn't easy, but the author finally agreed. No long dedication, just his name: Oswald Spengler...Herr Grosz, that's like a bible to me. Though I don't get to read much...."

In those incredible days when we were practically all millionaires and billionaires, something unheard of happened: our steadfast, to date unshakable faith in money collapsed, and we all reverted more or less to primitive barter.

Very few men and women, except possibly a few saints, are able to live without food. We normal mortals have to eat, if possible, three times a day. In that respect we are animals; our spirit nourishes only a quarter of us. The hungrier a person gets, the more he dreams, and it is always the same dream: of good, solid food. Medically those daydreams are called hunger syndromes. They are the origin of never-never land, the land of milk and honey, where cool wine flows from mountains made of Swiss cheese, some hills are made of golden butter and others of raisin-filled cake; chickens and suckling pigs run around already roasted, sausages hang from trees and you need only open your mouth to let a cooked pigeon fly in. All of us had these fantasies. On seeing those luscious things in a food store window, we would first wipe our greedy eyes: was the larded hare perhaps a mere mirage, or a cardboard model that our imagination filled with juice? It was like a Breughel picture.

Before continuing my narrative, I must add that the times were medieval because we also had magicians, real, black magicians in possession of knowledge closed to the rest of us. Not only did they rule matter to the degree that they could move objects from one place to another; they could make things that we remembered only by name appear and disappear again with equal speed; things like condensed milk, chocolate or sugar. And they had the classic magicians' power of making both themselves and those lovely, seductive things invisible.

One night, just as the clock was striking twelve, I happened to meet one of those magicians. Offstage he was a cook. The only thing we talked about in those days was food. At breakfast (coffee made of turnips, a greyish-green roll with artificial honey) we talked about lunch, and at lunch (turnip cutlets, mussel pudding, turnip coffee) we talked about supper (mussel sausage, grey-green roll and cold turnip coffee). Simple and unpretentious as our menu was, it did seem to lack some things; which, in turn, stimulated our imagination. So I told my new friend with a good deal of animation how I felt, and how that chemical honey was corroding my intestines. When my stomach joined the discussion in loud, discontented rumbling, he observed quite simply that I was not eating the right sort of food.

As all magicians, he spoke in poetic symbols. He

said that since I was an artist and he liked me, I could be helped. The trouble was my unappeased imagination. Real ham and sausages were simply not the same as painted ones (I had told him of my attempts in that direction) as they did not really satisfy. I still hear the devilish laughter of that magician whom I took to be a cook. "Ha ha, dear man, what is all your art worth if you cannot cut a juicy slice of that ham in red wine that you painted so beautifully?" We had another double brandy. "Look, I'm going to take you to a place where not only ham grows," I was struck by the word "grows"; medieval, I thought. "I'm going to show you—we'll take a taxi—I'll show you a real utopia. Not painted, either," he said with a wink.

It was raining. It was past two o'clock. The sleepy doorman held his umbrella over us, opened the taxi door after receiving the usual millions in paper money, bade us good night, and closed the door. After we started, I vaguely heard the magician say he'd better close the shades. Then I must have dozed off.

I wakened as we stopped at one of those faceless houses in the west of Berlin. No lights—probably one of the usual strikes in the electric or gas works. Not a soul in sight. It was pouring now, but all the brandy that I had consumed kept me warm inside. I had the impression of a completely uninhabited house. Max, my new friend, pulled a huge, old-fashioned key out of his back pocket. A cat with phosphorescent eyes mewed, came closer, suddenly bristled, hissed at us, and disappeared yowling into the dark.

"Damned beast! Here, light one of these matches." He handed me a box of wax matches such as I had not seen for a long time. The flickering light outlined his silhouette as he tried to open the squeaky lock. "Should be oiled," he said.

My God, I though with mixed feelings, this is getting to be like *The Tales of Hoffmann*. I remembered a story that fat Willi, the bowling boy in Stolp, had told me when I was a kid. One night, when only a few brother Masons and the Master were left to finish their bowling, a ball came rolling back that looked like a skull and had a greenish glow. And then, when he nervously went to pick it up, it looked just like the others but was much lighter; and afterwards, fat Willi claimed, there actually was one bowling ball more....Queer that I should remember this, I thought that night; maybe we're on our way to an alley and we will bowl for a ham! My mouth started to water. Oh God, oh dear God in heaven, what I'd give for a big, juicy slice of ham, even without the wine sauce....

The magician had opened the door. "Walk quietly," he said, "nobody must hear us going upstairs; watch those steps, the

carpets have been removed. No, no light, we can see well enough."
Carefully, we went upstairs. I hung tightly to the carved wooden
bannister; the November rain was pounding on the window panes.
I felt as though I were climbing an enchanted mountain. Nice.
Very nice. If this is how magicians live, O.K. A few more steps and
we came to a landing. There was a large, elaborately carved door
with opalescent glass. "Now you can give us some light," said the
magician, "nobody can see us here."

The secrecy did not surprise me at all. The multiplicity of daily
changing laws at that time was such that everybody would break
one or the other unintentionally, or even unknowingly. I supposed
that even a magician might have his reasons. Max had been telling
me of his connections with secret powers. "Well," I said, "if you
can do all that, then you are a magician."

"Of course, of course," he said.

The door seemed to open by itself. My foot hit a barrel. In
fumbling for the light switch on the magician's instructions, I felt
something soft and yielding, like a sack of flour. As soon as the
light was on (despite the strike) I saw where I was.

The large entrance door was covered by three heavy, bluish
sheets of iron-plate, reinforced against intruders by three thick
iron bolts. This was necessary, the magician explained, because his
power over people was limited, and much smaller than over
inanimate objects. This was stated in his contract, he said, giving
me a funny look. Where was I? In one of the old residences of the
elegant west side of Berlin; but that could barely be recognized. I
had been right when I believed my foot hit a barrel, except that it
was not one barrel but a double row of them, and on them, peacefully and comfortably, stood two rows of larger and smaller sacks
of flour and sugar. The other side of the room was stacked with
cases. This magic mountain was very neat; the magician's helpers
had utilized every nook, and stacked the cases by size all the way
up to the ceiling. Prunes, raisins, colorfully printed labels, many in
foreign languages, identified the tasty contents of these boxes and
containers.

"This is lard," said the magician, pointing to a row of sealed
cans, "but I never cook with lard when there is more butter than
one can eat." The door to the next room, called the Berlin Room,
was ajar, so I could see the containers labeled "AA Dairy Butter."
"The other rooms are all filled up. We really don't know where to
put all the stuff. Now that money has become worthless, we're
even using the corridor for storage."

We went through the narrow passage to the Berlin Room. Cases to the right, cases to the left, pails of jam, huge jars of tomatoes, cucumbers and pickles, blue cans of caviar with Russian labels piled to the ceiling, if a ceiling could be seen. Like fruits or stalactites, sausages were suspended, sausage after sausage of every variety, by the hundreds. And not only sausages. Here was a row of beef tongues. Then, bacon sides, lean, fat, the black, smoked bacon from Swabia. And hams of every variety including the oversized cottage-smoked Westphalian. Truly, I could not take my eyes off these treasures, and I quickly touched my nose, which was pleasantly prickling from the smell of smoked ham to find out whether I was not dreaming about all this.

I was not dreaming. I saw several uncut wheels of Swiss cheese standing in a corner. The chandelier was dismounted, there was only one bare light bulb hanging from the ceiling; several antique armchairs, red velvet, with tassels, were standing around for no good reason. They must have been left behind before the magician moved in. The windows, those that were not blocked by cases, sacks, cans or packages, were obscured from view by shades and heavy velvet drapes so that no one could look in. What could have become of the residents of this comfortable bourgeois apartment of the 1880s? Had they been pushed back, foot by foot, by all the cases and sacks and cans and parcels until they were finally squashed? Maybe under that sack over there, or by that enormous red lacquered cheese? Or did they actually starve amidst all this plenty?

We did not starve. The magician showed me all fourteen rooms, baths and kitchen. As I finally sat down on the protruding edge of a case, he disappeared for a moment and returned with an unusually large, brand new knife, shining in the reflected light of the bulb. Then he said: "Whoever comes here has to taste my wonder ham. You are no exception. And once you have tasted it, you will not rest until you possess a whole one—and then several—and finally," his face became weirdly transfigured, "well, well, possibly all the hams in the world!" He looked at me through narrowed eyes and cut off a huge slice.

"That is the penalty for one single mouthful. That's the curse. Pass me that bottle over there—no, more to the right, next to the condensed milk—that's it. This, you see, is the spirit that belongs to the ham: clear, unadulterated juniper gin...."

I brought over the huge crock, complete with spider webs, and put it on the table where two shot glasses were waiting. He filled them both, gave me mine, lifted his to his hooked nose and sniffed it. "Cheers!" he said, raising his glass, "long live the land of milk and honey!"

I saw my friend quite often thereafter, but he would never talk about that night. Maybe there were magicians of greater might than his? Something seemed to bother him. He once confessed that his magnetic power, his ability to command the cases and cans and hams, had considerably diminished. The last time I saw him he was tired and ill-humored, quite unlike his old self, and seemed much more like an ordinary cook. He made me promise faithfully never to tell anybody, not even my wife, of that night in the land of milk and honey.

I kept my promise. This is the first time the story has been told. The cook has been dead for a long time, thirty years have passed, and the hunger fantasies of Berlin have become dim history.

The "Republicomic" Automatons [1920

DADA

Our artistic persuasion at that time was "Dada."

If that expressed anything at all, it was our long fermenting restlessness, discontent and sarcasm. Any national defeat, any change to a new era gives birth to that sort of movement. At a different time in history we might just as well have been flagellants.

Dada, as much as I know, came from Zurich. During the war, a few poets, painters and composers founded the *Cabaret Voltaire*. It was directed by Hugo Ball with the help of Richard Hülsenbeck, Hans Arp, Emmy Hennings and a few other international artists. Their program was not exactly political but rather modernist-futurist. The name Dada was conceived by Ball and Hülsenbeck by opening a French dictionary blindfolded and pointing to a word. The word happened to be dada, meaning hobbyhorse.

Hülsenbeck brought Dada to Berlin, where it immediately became politicized. The atmosphere in Berlin was different. The esthetic side was maintained, but got increasingly dislodged by a sort of anarchistic nihilism whose main protagonist was the writer Franz Jung. Jung was a Rimbaud-like audacious adventurer, not to be deterred by anything. He joined us and because he was so powerful, he immediately became the guiding influence of the whole Dada movement. He drank heavily; he also wrote books in a style that was hard to read. He became very famous for a few weeks when he captured a steamship in the Baltic with the help of a sailor named Knuffgen, had it steered to Leningrad, and presented it to the Russians, at a time when the victory of the Communists seemed imminent and there was no real government in Germany.

Jung had no real occupation; he was always surrounded by a few loyally attached vassals. When drunk, he would shoot his revolver at us like a cowboy in a Western; he made a living writing about the stock exchange; at one time, he published his own journal on the subject of economics. He was one of the most brilliant people I have ever met and one of the most unhappy.

We Dadaists had "meetings" (we used the English word) in which, for a small admission fee, we did nothing but tell people the truth, i.e. insulted them. We spoke without inhibition using plenty of four-letter words. We would say, "You old heap of shit over there—yes, I mean you, you stupid ass," or "Don't you laugh, you moron!" When anybody answered, which of course they did, we would shout the way they did in the army: "Shut up, or I'll give you an ass full" and so on, and so on.

Word spread fast, and soon our meetings and our Sunday morning matinees were sold out to people who were amused and/or angry. Eventually, we had to have police in the hall because of the constant fighting. Later on it got so wild that we had to get a permit from the local police station. We derided everything, respected nothing, spat upon everything: that was Dada. It was not mysticism, not communism, not anarchy. All those movements had some sort of program. We however were complete nihilists; our symbol was nonexistence, a vacuum, a hole.

Intermittently we produced "art." But our procedure was to interrupt the "art act." Hardly had Walter Mehring started to get his typewriter going and produce something, for instance, when Heartfield or Hausmann or I stepped forward and shouted, "Stop! Surely you don't want to show those asses down there what you can do?" Often that sort of thing was planned, but more often it was improvised; as some of us had always been drinking, we were always having rows which happened in public.

Up to then, there had not been any visual Dada "art," that is artistic expression and/or philosophy of the garbage can. The leader of this school was a certain Schwitters from Hanover who would scavenge everything he could find in rubbish heaps, dust bins, or heavens knows where: rusty nails, old rags, toothbrushes without bristles, cigar butts, old bicycle spokes, half an umbrella. He collected everything, arranged the stuff on old boards or canvas into smaller, flat rubbish heaps fastened with wire or string; those he exhibited under the name of "Art of the Rejected," and actually sold some. Many critics who wanted to be in the know took this stuff seriously and gave it good reviews. Only ordinary people who know nothing about art reacted normally and called the Dada art junk and garbage—of which indeed it consisted.

One of the main products of our school was an enormous sculp-

ture representing "The Grandeur and Decline of Germany on
Three Floors," which actually was nothing more than what
happens if you sweep all sorts of refuse into a heap and mix it up at
random. That "monument" was the work of a certain Baader, who
thereby acquired the title of Chief Dada. He had been at one time
wedded to the Earth in some mystical manner, suffered slightly

Dada Montage [1920]
The Kaiser, the Social Democrat Frank and a Lost War

from religious fanaticism and totally from megalomania, a real madman; but in those peculiar days he was hardly different than the rest of us Dadaists, myself included. (Certainly not according to the opinion of the nice staff physician in the Army who examined me and found my drawings "totally insane," at any rate insane enough to have me tested. I made a high score on the insane

Dada on Long Island [1952]

questions!—) Baader had also composed the "Dadacon," the mightiest book of all time, larger than the Bible, that consisted of thousands of large pages of newsprint, put together as photo montage. The purpose of this method was to produce dizziness when you thumbed through the book—"for," said Baader, "only when your head starts to spin can you comprehend the Dadacon."

So that was our Chief Dada, but the rest of us also had titles and functions. I, for instance, was the "Propagandada," as was printed on my cards between my name and in smaller type, "What will I believe tomorrow?" My job was to think up slogans to further the good cause of dadaism. Such as *Dada ist da"* or "Dada wins" or "Dada, Dada above all!" We printed these slogans on little slips of paper, and pretty soon had all the shop windows, café tables, and house doors of Berlin plastered with them. It was quite alarming. The noon paper, *B. Z. am Mittag,* had a whole article about the Dada danger. Upstairs, downstairs, right and left, above and below we stuck our slogans. When a waiter at Kempinski's, the restaurant favored by affluent dadaists, cleared the table, he took along the slogans stuck on the empty plates and bottles and on boxes of Havana cigars. Even on his coat tails you could sometimes see "Dada, kick my arse, I like that."

There was, of course, more to it than just a joke. What mattered was to stir up the deep darkness. We did not know what we were doing; it seemed to us as though we were stirring the mud of a dirty puddle, without any purpose. "Dada is senseless" was also one of our slogans, and that really infuriated people. A new movement must have an objective, they thought. But we said no, look, we're just pushing the mud around. As though that made sense.

Another member of the Dada movement in Germany was my brother-in-law, Schmalhausen. As Dadaoz he became part of Dada history: he also had the title of Dadadiplomat and, as such, was attached to me, the Propagandada. He was a perfectionist by nature: always elegantly dressed, his trousers sharply pressed, wearing a bowler hat, cane and gloves, he brought some worldliness to our enterprise.

Another one who joined us was my good old friend Rudolf Schlichter. He was one of the most erudite painters, with almost encyclopedic knowledge. At that time he had not yet become religious and was full of contradictions. He still thinks his art is that of an outsider, but I disagree. I see his work as the continuation of the romantic German, medieval tradition. In our first international Dada show in 1919 in the Burchardt Gallery in Berlin he was, however, neither a painter nor a graphic artist but rather an ultrarealistic sculptor. His lifesize and completely realistic figure of a general, invisibly suspended from the ceiling, scared the daylights out of the angry visitors.

These peculiar contraptions, posters, and montages had a truly shocking effect on the public and on public opinion. Particularly angry were the modern artists, because nothing was respected or taken seriously. We made fun even of the avantgarde. A charge was brought against the organization: Dr. Burchardt was made to close the show and even had to pay a fine.

We had rich friends, too, who could stand a joke and liked to kid around with us legendary Dadaists. I remember one who had a mansion in the Grunewald and a fabulous, deep wine cellar with miles of barrels and cases of select wines. These subterranean wine streets were named after his Dada buddies (the George Grosz Street, for instance, went between the barrels of sherry), and he would ride around them on his motorcycle with the bright lights on. A specially made giant barrel was called Dada Barrel and contained a marvellous Piesporter which the experts among us praised as a "truly Dadaist little wine."

A certain Dr. Dohman, a dermatologist and thus no Dadaist in the orthodox sense of the word, was our chief composer. His Dada tunes were never put on paper, he merely improvised. He also wrote grotesque poetry under the name of Daimonides and was one of the few Germans who knew how to play jazz piano. One evening I went to the Hotel Adlon with him. In 1919 the Adlon served as headquarters for the American press. They were having a party. The host, whom they called Benny, was sitting cross-legged on the piano and playing "Everybody Shimmies Now" on his violin accompanied by his wife. There were glasses and full ashtrays all over; on the table were Havana cigars, cigarettes, two slender bottles of Rhine wine on ice, a bottle of Black & White scotch, and a bottle of brandy. The huge tin can on the piano was said to contain hard tack. (In Germany we were still on meager rations at that time.) Later that night, taxis were ordered and we all went to a secret nightspot; around four o'clock Benny conducted the band and gave the piano player some instruction in ragtime.

The name of this American was Ben Hecht. He was perhaps the first one to come to Berlin, except for the military commissions. A big American paper was paying him a lot of money to find out on the spot whether we were really as awful as Raemaekers had said, and whether our new republic was really a republic and not just a trick of the German general staff. There were rumors at the time that it was not the real Kaiser who had escaped to Holland but

The Pillars of Society [1924]

rather a double, cleverly chosen by Ludendorff; that Ludendorff, disguised as a miner, was busily plotting the counterrevolution out of a specially equipped bunker; that there were whole infantry regiments that had simply disappeared from the face of the earth at the start of the revolution and had never been seen again; explanations that this disappearance was caused simply by new, heavy land mines that had simply swallowed them up were not believed. People prefer fairy tales and legends. Statistics and easy Marxism furnished by the new government were to no avail; people wanted mystic explanations for what they could not comprehend. But for the moment there was nobody to provide those: the big daydreamers did not come until later. Ben Hecht's job was thus to get to the bottom of this dusk, this obscurity that will always surround my people, the German people, and report simply and clearly what was going on.

We soon became good friends. He was the guest of honor at an important Dada happening: a race between six typewriters and six sewing machines, accompanied by a tournament of insults. As a symbol of his honorary membership he was presented with a beer mug, painted black and half filled with sand. Unfortunately, however, that symbol was grabbed from Ben (who was a mere spectator) in the usual fist fight between Dadaists and the enraged audience, and was shattered. We were unable to replace it; according to the strict rules stated in the Dadacon, that could be done only after the passage of 65 years.

The Dadacon was subsequently offered to Ben for the bargain price of $25,000. He would pay no more than half that, and after much discussion back and forth nothing came of the deal. The Dadacon is said to have finally been buried by the Chief Dada near his house in Lichterfelde-Ost.

Ben Hecht went back to Chicago, wrote successful books, became disgusted with literature, switched to film, and became one of the best paid screenwriters of America, nicknamed the Shakespeare of Hollywood. Whenever we have met, over the years, we exchange a few yarns about Berlin—that mad, corrupt, fantastic Berlin just after the First World War.

We Dadaists became so famous and infamous and aroused so much curiosity that we toured all over Germany. Young people attended our performances, came backstage, and wanted to join us. There were old people too who sympathized with us, invited us to their houses to eat and drink, and the Dada nonsense usually went on until the early morning hours. We soon found out that there were many more unconscious or "secret" Dadaists than one would have believed. One of those was a certain Dr. Stadelmann.

Dr. Stadelmann was a friend of darkness, a friend of night. Where others would say yes, he would say no. He also had his own, highly personal and mystic opinions about people, things, and the world.

In his professional life he was a psychiatrist. He had always been fascinated by abnormality, thus had preferred psychiatry to general medicine. He was very successful, had a good practice and a lovely little private lunatic asylum. He called it "my little bird house." He regarded his patients as precious exotic birds; actually, they were just wealthy neurotics, and their ailments may have been merely imaginary.

Stadelmann was interested in art and literature and had founded a literary club in his home town. He often spoke of white and black magic and the unknown powers between heaven and earth. He was particularly interested in the much discussed research in histology and cellular systems of a Professor Fliess who had written a book about the course of life. Stadelmann himself experimented, and had published a paper on artificially produced tissues. He had set up a sort of homunculus theory, partially proved by his own experiments. It was quite exciting to listen to him.

Dr. Stadelmann was many-sided, very many-sided. Among other things he had constructed a piano for spirits, invented a completely new calendar system and a new mathematical theory. He read medieval writers and studied forgotten old manuscripts and medical tomes. He read only at night, and only by the light of candles. He had removed all electric wiring and all iron gas and water pipes from his study and the adjoining space. Such metals, he wrote in one of his pamphlets, interrupted "sympathetic" currents and waves.

He incessantly practiced his willpower and concentration. He asserted that he had progressed to the point where he could animate nominally lifeless objects, as ancient magicians used to do. He was able to command sewing needles to do his will: one of the most difficult experiments, despite the ridiculous smallness of the thing. It had taken him fifteen years of nightly work to force the needles to obedience. "I know it sounds fantastic," he said, "but there is no such thing as dead matter. There is only incarnation. In all things there is a magic secret. There is a stone of wisdom, and it has a magic key." He could say no more just then, but he was on the way to great discoveries, he added.

Once he showed me a thick manuscript, written by hand on peculiar old paper. It was his work, Stadelmann's secret book of knowledge. The title was *Dr. Stadelmann's Bunch of Keys: Expla-*

nation of Jakob Böhme's Magic Spiral, Paracelsus, Swedenborg and Doctor Faustus! Studies of a Secret Theory of Will." It was from Stadelmann that I learned in detail about megalomania and the concept of superman. He read Nietzsche to me and analyzed Zarathustra. He said that Nietzsche, genius that he was, was nevertheless mentally ill; his last books showed that quite clearly, as did the last of Van Gogh's pictures: "Just look at the recurring spaghetti-shaped spiral lines. A clear symptom." For Stadelmann, art and the impetus for imitation were harmless mental disorders. He considered the painter, any painter, an eternal child that had not gone beyond the anal stage of development. (He was ahead of his time in that too, leaning toward psychoanalysis.)

We had a big Dada evening in his home town. He had primarily, though anonymously, financed the evening because he considered Dada a sort of social mental disease worth studying, and he invited all of us to spend a night with him in his study. "But please don't come before twelve o'clock. The sympathetic waves are much better after midnight," he said, smiling mysteriously.

He lived alone, in a house surrounded by a garden. ("The wind must have access from all sides," he said.) We found him in an almost empty room, leaning against a big, green tile stove. He stroked his greying walrus beard with one hand, gesturing round the room with the other. "I regret that I cannot ask you to sit down. As you see, there are only two chairs, and I need those for my experiment. I have never used them myself to sit on. They are in a way the magic incorporation of years of patience."

He seemed to float away from us to a place where we could not follow. Then, as though he were returning to reality, "So, I am sorry, but you will have to stand. As I intend to prove my magnetic power to you tonight, we must not split our energy by sitting. Sitting, gentlemen, has a noxious effect on the solar plexus"—he made a circular motion round his lower abdomen—"and I need all your energy and concentration for my experiment." And repeating himself, to stress the importance, he concluded with a raised finger and an expression of superior knowledge that we could not share: "Yes, yes, if the solar plexus is crushed in bending—gone are the magnetic rays!"

In addition to the chairs for the experiment, ordinary wooden chairs with cane seats, there was a middle-sized table in the center of the room, covered by a red plush tablecloth, with a lighted tallow candle. That was the only light in the room. It flickered and seemed slightly perfumed; like the votive candles in a Catholic church, I thought. Next to it was a punch bowl of green glass,

decorated with grape vines and leaves. It was a woodruff punch, the spicy fragrance of which I had mistaken for perfume.

The light was mirrored in the glittering ice cubes in the bowl. There were long-stemmed glasses surrounding it, and a silver ladle; cigarettes and black Mexican cigars were in a glass box with an open silver lid. On the box was a cigar-cutter with a handle that in the flickering candle light looked like a mummified child's hand. On the wall across the room there was a framed photograph that at first seemed to be a map or a surrealist picture. It was neither. It was an enlarged, immortalized excretion of ectoplasm.

That photograph, explained Dr. Stadelmann still leaning on the stove, came from his friend Professor Schrenck-Notzing in Munich. No, it was not the famous/infamous medium Eva C, it was a much more interesting case: a lady whom he knew, a young woman of twenty-four, whose name and circumstances, uh, must of course be concealed..."But, uh, well, it was a case of quite extraordinary psychic endowment, if I can call it that, uh, and besides, we have incontestable proof that the young lady is the incarnation of a high Catholic priest who was buried alive by Montezuma in Mexico."

Beneath the ghostly photograph stood a small wooden table with traces of handprints on all four sides. This little table, the doctor explained, was the instrument that helped one to receive communication from the fourth dimension. It was fashioned without nails, always magnetically charged, and often harbored spirits of the deceased. At night when he was working alone, it sometimes flew round the room all by itself.

There were about half a dozen polished crystal balls of various size, lined up on a narrow shelf. Next to them, a gadget used by hunters to attract larks. It consisted of two wooden wings inserted with little pieces of mirror and attached to a roll; a string is wound round the roll. When you pull the string, the wings start turning, so that the pieces of mirror shine in the reflected light. Larks are attracted by this glitter and fly toward it, providing an easy aim for the hunter. Good that I'm not a lark, I thought uneasily.

Stadelmann, still speaking from his stand by the stove, said that he had excellent results on his patients with that gadget. "It produces hypnotic sleep in an instant. Shall I show you? There— look how it whirrs and glimmers? Even the strongest will succumbs."

Like birds, like birds, I thought, it's absolutely eerie! And I remembered a story that he had once told me about a patient, a wealthy former news editor who suddenly started one morning to crow like a rooster. No sound other than "cock-a-doodle-doo" has since come out of the man's mouth; he has to be fed grain that is strewn on the floor of his room; he picks the kernels up with pointed lips resembling a beak, bends his knees, waves his arms, and crows.

Stadelmann certainly had highly personal theories about every-thing. He qualified mental disease, leaning personally toward the theories of medieval doctors and the great Egyptian healers who thought of the tormented head of a supposed madman as the abode of bad spirits, and aimed treatment at their expulsion. From the point of view of today's "enlightened" medicine and research, Dr. Stadelmann's would probably seem straight "superstition." On the other hand, he saw all of us as peculiar, smart, dumb, or absurd birds.

"Do you think of me too as a bird?" I once asked him. "Of course, of course! You are all birds, all of you, all of you," he said with a sinister laugh, at which point his voice cracked and he suddenly looked like a bird himself. I can still hear him: "What of it, what of it, gentlemen, progress? Really, I ask you. A few years from now we'll have the complete middle ages, like the history books, with demons, children's crusades, the evil eye, flagellation, and burning witches. You don't believe that electricity is progress, do you? The old Egyptians knew all about it. No, my friends, we are heading toward a new era, darkened outside, illuminated inside by magic hypnosis."

On another shelf there was a lump of plaster with a dated tag. You could see an impression on it, but it was hard to tell of what—something like a fist that had slipped, maybe. We asked Stadelmann. Secretively he lowered his voice and said he could not tell either, but for him it was the calling card from another world. What we were looking at was the impression of a sound, an invisibly fluttering sound, that had surrounded him for hours late one night while he was sitting with a magic book; and then, it seemed to flutter out of the window. He had the distinct impression that this invisible Something had fluttered out of the ancient folio which he had acquired from a second-hand dealer who, in turn, had got it at an auction; all that was known was that the old volume had lain for years among other junk in a family grave... Well, yes, that lump of clay happened to be lying there. He always had lumps like that ready for his spiritualist seances. And as he heard it flutter over there by the clay (he was sitting at the table), he saw quite clearly how that invisible thing made an impression, quite slowly, as into dough, but it was shapeless. Then it fluttered away and never came back. Only the impression remained, which he had cast in plaster; it had a slightly musty odor, like mushrooms.

"And now, before I show my experiment," he said, still leaning almost motionlessly against the stove, "help yourselves, gentlemen. Fill the glasses, and let's drink before the punch gets warm and the ice melts."

He went to the table, filled his own glass and raised it: "Gentlemen, to the magic keys, to the sidereal powers and magnetic currents, to the eternal, mystic spiral! Cheers, gentlemen." He took a sip and put his glass down. "In wine too there is magic: sun and moon, silver, iron, gold, and all the cosmic elements of the earth." We emptied our glasses.

"Now look carefully," said Stadelmann, "and watch what I am showing you: the result of fifteen years of effort and research in the realm of magic." He took a sewing needle out of his lapel and explained: "You see, this little iron needle is about to be led by my will. I will thread it on the thread that is stretched between the two chairs, and command it by magnetic fixation through hypnosis to do my will. Without being touched by my hands, it will revolve and perform a sort of little giant-swing. On my inner orders it will move from right to left, and reverse. In other words, dead matter will obey my command. This experiment, small as it may seem, is of earth-shaking importance. It is the hard-earned first step ahead;

the first step up toward the unknown God...."

This was the first time he had mentioned God; the word sounded ironic in this setting. "I must ask you, my friends, to concentrate with me. The rays of our collective will help to countermand the eternally hostile materialist cross-currents." He then leaned down and drew a sort of oval circle round the two chairs with a piece of chalk. "Please do not step into this circle; it is a magical precaution; I hope it works," he added, but did not explain how and against what the chalk circle was to be effective.

I don't remember how we got to talk about washing—possibly because of the chalk on his hands. "No," I suddenly heard him say, "a magic person should actually never wash—" He would not do it, certainly not during the last week preceding his experiment. Water, he said, was a hostile and dissolving element that disintegrates magnetism and destroys the spiritual stratum of isolation round the aura. He admitted that it was not appetizing; but the aura of a person was contained in his sweat, his eliminations and exhalation; a well-washed person could never be magical. From the standpoint of modern hygiene, the old saints were all pigs. If, however, they had washed or cut their hair and nails, they would never have accomplished their great, documented wonders. "Another thing, gentlemen, before I begin: please put all metal objects on the table out in the corridor. You can keep only gold on you; all other metal is sidereal and I want to keep any adverse influence away from my needle so that the experiment succeeds."

As soon as we returned from the corridor, he put the thin end of the thread which he had unfastened through the eye of the needle. He moved the needle to the center; it hung there with the point downward while he tied the end back onto the chair. Again he requested complete silence, and tiptoed to get the lark snare from its narrow shelf. Holding it in his left hand, he marched solemnly toward the needle, his eyes fixed upon it; two steps away, he pulled the string hard.

The snare started to whirr. Stadelmann stared fixedly at the needle as it moved slightly in the draft produced by the rotating wings. The whirring and glimmering subsided slowly; so did the movement of the needle. Leaning forward, holding the snare, Stadelmann stared and stared at the needle in front of his nose. It almost seemed as though the whirring of the snare had hypnotized him himself rather than the needle; his ice-green eyes stared fixedly at the unfortunate object that was forlornly hanging there, perhaps ashamed at having so little magic talent.

For about an hour and a half Dr. Stadelmann stared without a motion at his beloved needle. It did not move, it did not budge. We noticed how he was trying to give it orders. Once in a while we could hear him hissing something like "rm—rm—rm...." Apparently he wanted it to revolve. But it would not. It did not move at all. It remained as motionless and rigid as the doctor who was determined to break its will, if indeed it had one.

The scene was quite fantastic and started to become a bit ridiculous. A bluish haze started to fill the oppressive air. We got restless from standing so long in silence. It was simply boring. It was really all nonsense and stupid imagination, fun for half an hour, but our good doctor was in deadly earnest, and after an hour and a half without any result it stopped being amusing.

There was a general clearing of throats and coughing.

Suddenly, Dr. Stadelmann broke up the meeting. With a deep sigh, he closed his eyes and passed his hand over them; he stood still for a few minutes, leaning his head back. Then, as though awakening with the feeling that one of us had secretly laughed, he looked sharply at us. "No! No! I knew it, gentlemen, I should never have started this, not here and not in your presence. Besides, it's full moon—oh yes, full moon and all that plays a big part in magic experiments. And then, if you'll excuse me, gentlemen, there may be one of you—I mean a skeptic—counter-currents— you understand, gentlemen, counter-currents...."

He stopped. We saw that the total concentration of the past hour and a half had exhausted him. He suddenly looked like an old, tired dog with sad lines around his mustache.

He continued as though musing to himself, "Most of the wonderful things happen only when one is quite alone, when nobody is watching." And with a weary smile he added, "Of course, you never encounter genuine fairies when you are with other people... talking about fairies," he suddenly cried, and knocked his head, "what a rotten host I am! Here my house-fairy has baked this marvellous cake—please open that side door—yes, thank you, bring it in!"

And so he ended, stepping to the table, refilling his glass and raising it: "Cheers, my friends, even though my experiment failed, let us not forego the punch—cheers!"

We wholeheartedly agreed.

Noske, Defense Minister of the German Republic [1919]

THE WEIMAR REPUBLIC

We were like sailboats in the wind, with white or black or red sails. Some boats sported pennants with three lightning bolts, or a hammer and sickle, or a swastika on a steel helmet; at a distance, they all looked alike. We had very little control of our boats and had to maneuver cleverly to keep them from capsizing in the storm. Many a boat was floundering keel upwards. The storm raged uninterrupted, but we kept on sailing; we did not understand its melody; our hearing was blunted by continuous commands. All we knew was that there was one wind blowing from the east and another from the west. And that the storm blew all over the earth.

Even the capital of our new German Republic was like a bubbling cauldron. You could not see who was heating the cauldron; you could merely see it merrily bubbling, and you could feel that heat increasing. There were speakers on every street corner and songs of hatred everywhere. Everybody was hated: the Jews, the capitalists, the gentry, the communists, the military, the landlords, the workers, the unemployed, the Black Reichswehr, the control commissions, the politicians, the department stores, and again the Jews. It was a real orgy of incitement, and the Republic was so weak that you hardly noticed it. All this must end with an awful crash.

It was a completely negative world, with gaily colored froth on top that many people mistook for the true, the happy Germany before the eruption of the new barbarism. Foreigners who visited us at that time were easily fooled by the apparent light-hearted, whirring fun on the surface, by the nightlife and the so-called freedom and flowering of the arts. But that was really nothing more than froth. Right under that shortlived, lively surface of the shimmering swamp was fratricide and general discord, and regiments were formed for the final reckoning. Germany seemed to be splitting into two parts that hated each other, as in the saga of the Nibelungs. And we knew all that; or at least we had forebodings.

Postwar Berlin: noise, rumors, shouting, political slogans—what will happen now? Everybody can say whatever he wishes, so everybody talks about riots and strikes, about martial law and impending political takeover. Erzberger, who negotiated and signed the German peace treaty, is assassinated by members of a "patriotic" society. Liebknecht is murdered by a soldier, "Red Rosa" Luxemburg is thrown into a canal. Those in power do nothing. Ebert has his beard trimmed, now looks more like a Chairman of the Board, and dresses accordingly. Privy Councilor Meissner, Master of Ceremonies of the Republic, tries to fill the shoes of his illustrious predecessors and avoid too many proletarian mistakes. Nasty jokes circulate about him. The little man takes his revenge, as he feels no power above him.

Yes, there was freedom of speech. But people had been used to marching for years, so they simply went on marching, be it less straight, less smartly than before. For years they had obeyed orders; now they went on marching, but nobody gave orders...yet. They had to march because they knew they must fall into line. But what they missed was the sharp voice of command. They simply did not know what to do with the freedom for which they had so ardently yearned. Everyone had his own political opinion, a mixture of fear, envy, and hope, but what use was that without leadership? The unions? They sufficed no longer. The grumbling became increasingly threatening, finally dangerous. As no one felt himself guilty—a whole people never does—everyone looked for a scapegoat, and harmless old ditties about Jews suddenly had the odor of a pogrom.

Not only young people marched through the streets. There were many who could not get over the defeat. Others were unable to find their way back into the working world that they had left. That world had disappeared or was disappearing, and actual work was hard to find, even by those who were eager to work. Berlin was full of the unemployed. To pacify them, they were given games instead of work. Out of every 100 unemployed, 80 lived from government unemployment benefits.

Even those frightening figures did not reduce my confidence in broadbased progress at that time. The statistics may even have supported it, as some of my friends were teaching me a realistic

approach. For a while I succumbed to that intellectual megalomania and believed an ill to be cured if I could explain it by statistics. According to that theory, all I had to do was to spread this enlightenment and see to it that all the unenlightened were enlightened. My friends were determined to eradicate everything irrational, mystic, hazy, or sentimental and replace it by their statistical explanations of history and dialectic materialism. They were pure rationalists with unshakable faith in the intelligence of the masses. And they would absolutely deny, by holy Marx, the fact that the masses were more inclined to believe legends than facts and figures.

I pondered a lot about right and wrong at that time. It was in the air. But my conclusions always came out to the detriment of everybody. Classifying people in a black and white way might be an

efficient method of dealing with large masses, but it went against my grain. The larger the group with whom I associated became, the more individualistic I got. I finally came to perceive the world as a natural phenomenon, an eternal coming and going that could not necessarily be explained. I admit that this was not exactly a religious concept, but ever since Nietzsche I suspected "morality." There is neither good nor evil in rain and wind, in volcanic eruptions, or in the snow that bites your legs.

My development has made me quite unfit to be a reformer. A reformer has to believe that man is fundamentally good, as Ernst Toller does, or old Romain Rolland, or my friend Masereel; but something in me refuses. Although still young then, and enthused about an imagined revolution, I was not sufficiently endowed with the mild and noble virtues of faith.

Large gatherings of people always remind me of insects. I am not the first to have noticed that similarity, but it is always scary to observe it over and over again. For instance at official receptions: what a picture of insects swarming all over each other! The ladies' dresses are like the colorful wings of beetles, while the dark coats of men make them dung-beetles. And what insect-like greed they all develop when they see the lavish buffet! Oddly, you yourself are infected, you cannot keep aloof and you become a greedy beetle just like everybody else.

I should really not start this section with such a grotesque comparison, because it contains my remembrance of a reception at the Russian Embassy in Berlin; perhaps the mood should be more respectful.

Receptions at embassies are all alike, and proceed by standard rules. You come in white tie or formal gown, and wear any medals you have in your buttonhole or round your neck. The formal social picture in the lovely old rooms is quite the same whether you are at a bourgeois or a non-bourgeois reception; there was many a raised eyebrow when the hosts were communists. They were sort of expected to behave like communists. A communist in white tie seemed not only to degrade the formal attire but also to be in a double-entendre disguise, because he looked exactly like a capitalist—and was that not rather suspicious?

Nevertheless, this Soviet reception was different from others, and the difference started right out on the street.

In the huge closed portal of the embassy was a small door through which you were admitted. An embassy employee opened it very quickly and closed it as soon as you were inside. It all

The Pimps of Death [1919]

seemed rather secretive. So the doors are not wide open here, you thought....There were also no potted laurel trees flanking the entrance; instead, there were rows of curious people lined up on the sidewalk, held back by policemen if they moved too far forward. As soon as a car arrived, one or two shabbily dressed loiterers would leap to open the car door to earn a few pennies. So you would hurry past the onlookers as quickly as you could. Inside, you ducked a bit; if you were more sensitive than most, you were almost physically bothered by the envy, the disdain, and sometimes the sarcastic admiration in those looks. The speculators did not know that all this was arranged according to rules set by Lenin; they would not have understood even if Machiavelli himself had explained it to them. They saw only the outside: formal gowns, brilliant jewels, silk legs, white chests, uniforms, helmets and silk hats.

While taking off your coat in the quiet of the cloakroom, the words from the sidewalk still sounded in your ears: "Give my love to Comrade Trotsky!" or "Comrade, don't forget to pocket a few of these Soviet crackers!"

Slightly ill-humored from that encounter, you put your coat check in your pocket and mounted the carpeted, wide stairs to the reception rooms. On the wall was an enlarged photo, the well-known picture of Lenin with a cap on his head and his hands in his pockets. You thought of the stupid proletarians downstairs who did not have tail coats; that was obviously why they could not be in as festive a mood as we were on the anniversary of the October Revolution. When you looked again at the picture, it had changed: now it was Lenin in a dress coat, looking like a model in the window of a smart tailor shop.

But it wasn't Lenin at all. We were mixed up. This was the old Bolshevik with a trimmed beard, now disguised as an ambassador, shaking hands. And carried off by the wave of chatting, chewing people, you said to yourself: away with those sentimental thoughts, they don't go with formal clothing.

If all this had impressed me as satirist, which I was more then than today, the painter in me now took over. I forgot the anachronism while admiring the dazzling, colorful picture of the splendidly illuminated rooms. I thought of our great painter, Adolph von Menzel, who had captured similar receptions at the court of Wilhelm I in paintings, often using menus or placecards as his sketch pads. The setting, the decorations, the magnificent rooms were unchanged from the days of the ambassadors of the Czars.

The white, red and gold architecture with the many mirrors, reflecting hundredfold the waves of the passing crowd, had lost nothing of its charm and beauty. It radiated a feeling of elegance mixed with warmth and comfort that spread to the guests, who were flattered by the satisfaction of belonging.

Submerged in the crowd, circulating with filled plate and champagne glass, you surrendered to the loud festive mood. You spoke with acquaintances, and pointed out diplomats, statesmen, and other famous people whom you recognized from the newspaper or magazine pictures. Elderly, elegant servants who looked like sexless, obedient puppets of another age, served with dignity, unimpressed by the changes of time and manners; they hardly registered when the fresh caviar sandwiches were literally grabbed off the newly filled trays. The still life of loaded tables was a treat to eyes and palate. The caviar, especially, attracted people

like swarms of bees.

Next to a table with many colorful bottles and a bowl in which pieces of pineapple and ice cubes were swimming, stood several high-ranking German and Russian officers who drank to each other. They raised their glasses, clicked their heels, and said "Prosit, comrade." It was surprising to see how they resembled each other.

In one of the rooms I bumped into Maximillian Harden. Though still suffering from an attack by members of a patriotic secret organization, he had testified brilliantly, quite in his old style, in my behalf in the *Ecce Homo* trial. Now I found him embittered. His eyes wandered over the crowd as though looking for somebody whom he could not find, and if he found him, could not stand. He had used his pen bravely against the camarilla and the politics of Kaiser Wilhelm II; he did not like the new German Republic either. Of the new Russia, he said with a weary gesture of his hand, "All wrong, all wrong...." This was the last time I saw him.

Arthur Hollitscher, however, the journalist and poet, who was sitting on a couch with some other intellectuals, had just returned from a trip to Russia and was giving an enthusiastic account of the enormous progress "over there." Ten years earlier I had been greatly interested by his book about America; only now, as he waved to me in passing, did I notice that he looked like an old woman. When he laughed, he seemed toothless. (He died later, lonely, in Switzerland.)

For a few minutes the rigid, impenetrable face of General von Seeckt appeared in the crowd. His monocle seemed glued to his face, his grey mustache cut like a brush, his carp mouth arrogantly closed. His incredibly slender waist looked corseted.

In the next corner I ran into our friend Sokoloff, who was performing at the Reinhardt theater, and the poet Tretyakoff. Sokoloff had mysterious power over the circulating waiters, and managed to get a whole tray of fresh caviar sandwiches just for us. He was a great storyteller; we could not stop laughing while he was with us.

Tretyakoff was less fun. He had a cleanshaven head, and the spectacles that he kept on taking off and polishing gave him a professorial look. He drank only seltzer. He used to belong to the Mayakovsky group and was interested in futurism; he now aimed to write in the style of instructions that come with American mail order merchandise that you have to assemble yourself. "Your writing must be such," he said in good German, "that any peasant might be able to assemble a tractor by reading your poem."

Accompanied by a stylish lady, a prototype German walked by, as though painted by certain French caricaturists. A man with the swollen face of a former duelling student, further enlarged to the size of a Chairman of the Board (probably in heavy industry); a red-faced man with thick veins, excessive blood pressure, and small, red, swollen eyes. With his wife Käthe, the Minister for Foreign Affairs Stresemann looked very German indeed.

Madame Lunacharsky, the wife of the Russian Commissar for Cultural Affairs, was gazed at in envious admiration. She was said to be the most elegant woman in the Soviet Union, next to the diplomat and author Alexandra Kollontai, who had once been ambassador to Norway.

I have forgotten, strangely enough, whether or not there was an orchestra. I think there was; anyway, somebody played the *Internationale* and Russian folk music on a piano. But he may just have been one of the guests, some slightly inebriated famous musician or composer. The general animation was such that the music could hardly be heard above the noise of loud conversation.

It was fairly late when we left the hospitable embassy. The same unliveried employee let us out through the little door. The fresh air felt good. The crowd of curious onlookers had long since disbanded. Only the same shabby figures were there to open car doors, but they fled at the approach of a policeman.

It was past midnight, but we did not feel like going home. Instead, we went to one of the late nightclubs for a beer and sausages or hot pea soup, and let the events of the evening march past again....

◆

In Vogtland in central Germany, a Red Army actually was formed. Its leader was a certain Max Hölz. He is one of the few figures who stands out as a romantic picture, colorful and lively, from the grey mire of the so-called German revolution.

Hölz came close to what I would call a folk hero. He was of the Robin Hood type, like the men we admired in our youth: a friend of the underdog, enemy of tyrants, adored by women. As though left over from the early peasant rebellion, he was not a leader in the sense of superman, but rather a simple rebel with a hot temper. He hated cold calculation, theoretical analysis and party politics. He would rather grab his gun, tuck a few grenades into his belt or his boot tops, and lead his men into action, as in medieval times.

Wondrous stories were told about his brave actions. How, for instance, he went alone to encounter a patrol of the Volunteer

Corps and so intimidated the half-dozen heavily armed men that they surrendered and begged for their lives. He was much like the knights of old (unfortunately most of his sort were on the other side) who did not hesitate to mete out punishment, burn down houses and retaliate when they considered it necessary. The cry "Hölz is coming!" would spread, for a time, terror or pleasure—depending; he almost became a legend in his lifetime.

♦

In this Saxon rebellion things happened differently than planned. Hölz was captured. He was to be sentenced to death; but his speech in the trial, to this day the classic speech of a rebel, made such an impression on the judge that he was merely sent to jail. Even in jail, and a Prussian jail is no nursery school, the Hölz legend had an effect. I went to see him once with a mutual friend and was amazed at the respect with which he was treated. Like a gentleman! After passing through many iron gates and locked doors, we approached Hölz in the visitors' cell; immediately a guard appeared, and deferentially asked: "May I bring a stool for Mr. Hölz?"

Extraordinary things also happened when Hölz was pardoned a few years later and released from jail. The Red Rebel came to Berlin and was immediately a social lion. He sent a huge bunch of roses to a rich lady who had invited him to a dinner party. The millionaire's wife, groomed and dressed to show off her beautiful figure, welcomed him: "How happy I am, comrade, that you are now at liberty! Let me put one of these roses in your buttonhole before we go in to dinner...." Hölz leaned down and kissed the crook of her elbow. "No, comrade, please. If my husband sees that...not here... there is a long evening ahead."

And it was a long evening. Later, he wanted the lady to sit on his lap. "Here, come here, little bourgeois baby—give me a kiss!" He asked for more wine and food to drink to the revolution. "Help yourself, comrade, help yourself," he told a friend whom he had brought along, "maybe everything will be ours tomorrow after all."

Hölz loved such things. In that way he was a real folk hero. Dignity, reserve and restraint were not his way. Manners? That was for the rich. Why should he not enjoy life? So there!

Other groups decreed that members should live monastically and have but one love: the Party; only one vice: Marxism; only one model: Russia. The little party bureaucrats hated Hölz, and he fought with the big ones. As he was anything but a shirker, he told truths where they were not wanted. What thoughts he had, or

Civil War [1930]

"lines," as they were called, did not agree with the party lines. This was the time of resolutions, long meetings, theoretical work, not at all passionate Max's style; he would rather have taken a gun and gone after the reaction himself. But Russia decided differently.

Soon Max Hölz was all alone, sitting at the bar telling his stories, like the old soldier of my childhood. He became bitter and quarrelsome. So there was but one way out: send him to Russia for re-education, give him one of those fine-sounding inspector's jobs that were kept for such cases....

"Over there" Max lived a while longer. On and off friends brought back news of him, shaking their heads. One day he fell in the water from a boat, simply into the water from a boat, and drowned...the end of a little German revolutionary soldier.

Worker and People [1921]

RUSSIA IN 1922

In the summer of 1922 I went to Russia. Not straight to Russia, but first to Denmark to meet the writer Martin Anderson Nexö. He was to write a book about Russia, and I was to illustrate it. We two were not at all compatible, and it was not only the difference in our ages that later made us split up. To add spice to our book, we decided to take a route that was then used only by illegals and fugitives: via western Norway-Vardö-Murmansk-Karelia to Leningrad.

Nexö had arranged through Soviet connections to have someone in an official motorboat pick us up in Vardö. Our first disappointment was that of course the boat never came. Day after day we waited. Nexö tried to send telegrams. People were friendly, and assured us that the boat would arrive tomorrow, or certainly before the end of the week. It never came. Finally we hired an ordinary fishing boat that was going up the Kola Fiord anyway, to load hay in a Finnish monastery. It would simply continue, and land us in Murmansk.

The autumn nights were getting chilly when we started. We stocked up thoroughly, as we had heard that there was not much food in Russia, except for cabbage soup. I took two suitcases, not too big, so I could easily carry them. I bought a lot of chocolate, and packages of crackers. We each had a big bottle of schnaps that soon served us well.

The boat was driven by an old-fashioned kerosene motor that stank and smoked. The deck was black and greasy from fish oil. After two days we entered the calmer water of the Kola Fiord. The entrance narrowed so that we could see flat land on both sides. Not a ship in sight. A few hours later we saw the first beacon blinking. We were drawing nearer to Murmansk.

I started to remember stories of the good revolutionary fighters and secret emissaries who had gone this way when the easier land route was closed to them. I though of brave Lefèvre, a French revolutionary, who perished here with his companions in the attempt at illegal entry to Russia. I remembered many a tale I had heard, coupled with the romance of my boyhood books; had I not wanted to experience all those adventures myself? The collision of these dreams of adventure with the icy spray of reality was a bit chilling, but did raise my confidence and courage as I leaned against the mast, shivering with cold. After all, I told myself, after all, we are only doing this for fun! And I swallowed all adverse feelings with a big mouthful of whiskey which, oddly enough, had a medicinal rather than an intoxicating effect: I became stronger and more confident.

Slowly we proceeded up the endless Kola Fiord. Evening turned into night, but it was comparatively light, so that we could distinguish masts and poles and sometimes houses. We perked up, our lethargy vanished. We were able to move now too, did not have to hang on with cramped fingers, could take a few steps, and shake a bit like dogs coming out of the water. Great adventure, after all. It was midnight when we got to the silent harbor and tied up by the other fishing boats. Deep silence. A few frightened night birds rose screeching into the air. Not a soul anywhere. Deserted. A light here and there in the distance, tiny, like stars in the black sky. Remarkably, the darkness seemed darker now that we had landed. Or was that a black premonition of what we were to expect? For this was Russia the mysterious, hated and beloved Russia, that we were entering. The two boatmen paid no further attention to us. As soon as the boat was well moored, they lay down on the narrow, smelly benches in the cabin, threw their old coats over them, and went to sleep. Nexö and I however went ashore. We felt much better, refreshed by the long, quiet sail into port, and the night air. We decided to go exploring. Maybe we'll find somebody, we thought; surely there must be some official whom we can notify of our arrival. We had our carefully wrapped papers and passports and specially stamped entrance permits with us.

We struggled over old railroad tracks—it really was much darker here than on the water—and followed them toward a light that showed through the window of a rough wood cabin. Peering inside, we saw a man asleep at a table. We went round the house, found the door, and knocked. It was three o'clock by my watch. No reply. Martin opened the door. The man, wrapped in a huge fur, jumped up in fright, grabbed his gun from the corner behind him, and pointed it at us amid a torrent of words. We did not understand a single one. He stood motionless, but continued his harangue. Martin and I tried to explain, by pointing to the port, that we had just arrived; then, with our heads in our arms, that we wanted to sleep and eat; but our man, who looked Mongolian, said only "nichevo, nichevo." Eventually he did see that we were harmless, so he pushed us gently out, pointing toward other cabins in the distance, and closed the door. Opening it again, he repeated his direction with his hand and his gun, bolted the door, and extinguished the light. Just as it says in fairy tales, I thought.

We went as directed, falling over railway ties and what seemed to be wire that got entangled in my coat. We stumbled on, saw a lot of railway cars without wheels that looked like houses and were overgrown with grass and shrubs. Not a soul. We decided to go back and spend the night on the pier or on deck. We had trouble getting back; we had not realized how far we had gone. We finally found our boat, lay close together on deck under old sails and sacks, and waited silently for morning. I sucked my pipe. Healthy snoring was heard from below.

Somehow we must have dozed off; toward morning we were wakened by calls and conversation. We had not taken our clothes off for three days, had no water to wash in, no way to clean our teeth, and were rather weary. But the fresh hot coffee made by the boatsmen, plus chocolate and crackers from my suitcase, livened us up. Meanwhile, lots of Russians had arrived on the pier, gesticulating, talking, and pointing down at us.

Only then did we see where we were. It must have been part of a fishing port, as there were many regular fishing boats alongside. But the whole place seemed unreal. It seemed untidy, begun but not finished. It looked as though a large, new port had been planned, but then in the middle of the work the idea was dropped and everything simply abandoned. There were half-submerged boats, some upside down in the water; a half-finished jetty; sacks of hardened concrete; bent and rusted pieces of iron. A bellbuoy was resting on its side, as was the crane that should have placed it. We saw a submarine upside-down, like a big fish, full of barnacles and seaweed, the paint flaked off. Wooden ships, loaded with stones were stranded in putrid water; empty kerosene barrels piled high; whole rows of railway cars, mostly without wheels, with people living in them. It was like a gigantic junk heap. In the background, slightly uphill, we could see cabins and wooden buildings; there were people in brownish, shirt-like clothes, many barefoot, others obviously former soldiers in their worn uniforms. Everything grey, brownish-black. Here and there a small, stunted birch.

We went back ashore again, but there was no one in the gaping crowd who understood us. The people seemed of many different races, and very poor. Somewhat like yellowish ants, startled out of the earth. Eerie. Not exactly an inspiring picture, but this was daytime, and we would soon be continuing our trip to Leningrad and Moscow. Or so we thought. We walked through the inquisitive, squirming crowd, but had gone barely a few steps before three men approached us. Two of them looked like commissars; they were wearing good leather jackets, high boots, military caps with hammer and sickle, and carried briefcases. The one in front, a short, dark-eyed sailor with a ferocious look, was strapped into a heavy, black, cartridge bandoleer. He was holding a large army revolver—aimed at us. He seemed furious; paying no attention to our imploring gestures, he poked his gun into our ribs and angrily ordered us to get back on our boat. Nexö, who could usually assert his authority, was furious. To no avail our gestures and explanations: back we went into the boat to wait for whatever would develop.

Our sailor posted himself before the boat, his huge revolver still aimed at us. Soon the two other men in their handsome jackets came below, paid no attention to us, but talked with our boatsmen. The conversation seemed negative. Meanwhile, the sailor kept the curious mob at bay, brandishing his shooting iron. We sat and waited till the two commissars came to us. The only word we understood was "interpreter." Then they pointed at our suitcases that had been brought onto the deck, and, pointing at the sailor, made clear to us that we were not to touch them, but to sit still where we were. That we did. Our Black Sea sailor marched proudly back and forth, revolver in hand, as though we were precious prey or even spies, landed here under the cover of night. Maybe we were a valuable catch; granted, there were all sorts of disguised agents around at that time, and Sawinkow himself was still at large, conspiring against the hated Bolsheviks.

In Russia you have to wait, and wait. A new group came in the late afternoon, including a woman who spoke Danish and English. We were thoroughly cross-examined and questioned; every letter, every note, simply everything was confiscated. The suitcases were opened, thoroughly searched and we had to remain on board. The interpreter indicated that our papers needed thorough verification. Possibly the counsel in Oslo who had issued our entry permits would have to be contacted by telegram. That might mean that we would have to stay on our boat for two or three more days.

Guarded, of course. She explained, her brow earnestly knitted over her humorless eyes, that we were very careless to rent a fishing boat without procuring the proper entry permits for the fishermen. We assured her that we had been promised a boat from Murmansk; that we had truly waited in vain for almost two months; that it would probably have taken another three or four months to get the necessary papers; that we really and truly were not anarchists, nor disguised Sawinkow people, nor agents of any bourgeois country. The answer was simply that we had to wait for the results of the queries from Oslo and, if necessary, from Berlin. Our political innocence and loyalty could be proven only by verification of our papers and confirmation of our statements.

"Verification of our papers," I thought out loud, "well, that could take a long time!"

"Yes," said the lady emphatically. "When your papers are verified, not before." Our careless arrival without the permission of the Murmansk Workers' and Soldiers' Council was an insult to the right of hospitality of Russian Workers and Peasants. We would be lucky if they let us go; recently five spies from a capitalist country had been executed; they too were disguised as writers and had perfect papers....

The Workers and Peasants crowded the pier and stared at us; their representatives gave us a little scare with their pedantic, disciplinary speeches. They accepted the pieces of chocolate and soap we offered with proletarian pride but without a smile. When Nexö made one last attempt to get permission for us at least to wait on the pier where we could walk up and down, we were told that in the land of the Workers and Peasants there was law and order; it was not like the mess in capitalist countries where there was chaos and no Workers' and Soldiers' Councils to protect the people from spies and sabotage. With that, our upright interpreter climbed off the boat, and disappeared with the three Peoples' Representatives. The sailor was still above, and seemed to look angrily at the chocolate. So I put it away.

The air was thick. Our good boatsmen had not counted on this, they had expected to return early in the morning. Now it had changed, and all of us were like prisoners on the little boat. Up there on the pier the curious crowd was suddenly penetrated by an old, ragged woman with a scarf over her head; her hair, like many others, had either been cropped, or had fallen out from some disease. She pushed through the crowd, calling and chattering, and held a wicker basket down toward us, filled with red berries and rather unappetizing greenish-grey cake which she wanted to sell. As my money had been confiscated, I looked for something to give the witch, just to get rid of her. I found some chocolate—the commissar had broken most of it, looking for hidden documents—and I gave her a piece.

She seized it eagerly with her gnarled, dirty hand, put down her basket, and started to turn it with both hands. She thought it was soap. I made negative signs, took another piece of chocolate and bit off a little piece. She understood, and started to suck it with her toothless mouth, eagerly watched by the surrounding workers and peasants. I can still see the barefooted, yellowish fellow with his thin beard, freckles, and sly eyes suddenly grabbing the chocolate from her. He gave it a lick, then it traveled on from mouth to mouth like a popsicle, amid the screeches of the old hag who felt cheated. Funny, I thought, just like a movie I once saw, but that took place in deepest Africa, some sort of expedition. Who knows how long it had been since these people last tasted chocolate or sugar? It was tragicomical, like a natural phenomenon. I was reminded, too, of some Russian prisoners of war in that terrible winter of 1917-18 when we were totally reduced to ersatz, dried vegetables and blue potatoes; at least that was all there was for us common soldiers. I still see them, those Russian prisoners with their rusty tin cans crowding round a garbage can and fishing around in the fermenting, maggot-infested brew, eating and drinking: so fierce was their hunger.

So my first impression was hunger—direct, physical hunger. In America, thank goodness, they do not know that direct, growling hunger that gnaws at your intestines and dulls your brain. In Europe we did all get an idea of it in the war. "See," said the German farmers, "see, never throw bread away. Daily bread is blessed and therefore holy. But if you don't know that and disrespect it and throw it in the garbage can—then George, the big locust will come, and eat up everything, simply everything—it picks the kernels out of the corn, eats the grass, eats the bark off the trees, makes the cattle starve. Then, when nothing is left, then people get so hungry they eat each other up. You see, that huge locust is everyplace where people make war; it follows the armies through the countries and breeds little locusts who eat and eat until there is nothing left but shorn trees and the naked, crusted earth...."

Yes, up there there are locusts too, I mused, maybe this is real locust country, maybe these yellowish, barefooted insects will

suddenly scrape their wings together and take off, following the smell of chocolate....My God! I thought, and felt my pocket come alive, as though creeping with locusts.

The two of us sat there by the hatchway, taciturn and pensive. We were in a bad mood, dirty, hungry and thirsty. The two fishermen were furious at having to stay here and the possibility of being jailed for a few days or even having their boat confiscated (that sort of thing did happen) did not help matters. The day was grey and cold; a pale sun shone soberly, as though not sure that it had permission from the Workers' and Soldiers' Council.

At last, several hours later, our interpreter came back. "You certainly have been lucky that things worked so well," she called to us, "you can now come with us to the local Soviet." We went to a simply furnished office in one of the barracks. Here I got my first whiff of the way Russia smells. It is hard to describe: a mixture of stale beer, chewed sunflower seeds and wet boots. Here there was also the pleasant smell of fresh firewood. The room was stuffy; no wonder, the storm windows were sealed, having only a small square of the upper window frame that could be opened. We were questioned once more, then given a sort of pass, and were free.

As we were leaving, a smiling young man in a long black coat with a velvet collar appeared, his shaved head covered by a blue cap without insignia. He called himself an engineer. He seemed to have been selected for us because he spoke both Danish and German, was to be a sort of mentor and guide, and was to check on our possible doubts about the progress and liberation of the proletariat. His method was to pretend he shared our opinions, as he assumed we would disapprove of much that we saw.

We did, of course, but not nearly as much as he expected. What he did was to start all his statements disparagingly. For instance, we were passing a group of soldiers standing round a big heap of smoked fish and a heap of greyish-green bread, both piled onto the bare ground. Supervised by a soldier of higher rank with a Tartar helmet and boots, they each took a piece of fish and a piece of bread with their bare hands. Our new friend took this opportunity to pretend we were his close friends, and so he confided to us in a low voice: "You see the salmon over there, comrades—look, half of it is so badly smoked that it is starting to spoil. That's what the new order is like, comrades, it's all on paper. We have such good fish, it's incompetence, comrades!" I retorted, "But comrade, the soldiers don't seem to mind, they look content and happy." To which he said, "Oh, well, those aren't real soldiers, those are exiles who are helping in the fishery. They are here by way of punishment, so of course they get the rotten stuff. You wouldn't think," he looked round as though he were being very daring, "you wouldn't think the commissars over there...?" he indicated the barracks with his thumb over his shoulder. "They, they get the very best, nothing like that fish would ever appear on their table. They, they have everything!" We noticed that our new friend himself looked well nourished. He had fat cheeks and even a little paunch. His coat and suit were new, and his boots of excellent leather. Even his nails were fairly clean, indicating the use of soap, and he was shaved.

Nexö and I immediately had the same idea: this comrade is testing us, trying to provoke us to criticize and grumble. The liberated workers and peasants have chosen severe masters who cannot bear criticism. So I did not rise to our friend's remarks, but parried with clichés—give us time, we don't understand the language, etc. "The language?" he snarled with scorn. "Why do you need language when a heap of rotten fish stinks to high heaven? Language? Just use your eyes, for goodness sakes—people in their bare feet while the commissars are shod in the finest leather, not just one pair, several...." When it got to be too much for me I started making speeches about their having gained the highest, most valuable, holiest of goods: freedom and the dignity of man. In view of the enormous poverty, dirt, and miserable looking people, I began to feel quite uneasy about my beautiful phrases about human dignity and freedom. But I spoke them anyhow, the way one uses magic formulas and prayers, to restore dwindling confidence. Besides, we were so familiar with all these silly, hackneyed phrases from our political friends, had in fact repeated and used them so often ourselves, that we almost believed them.

It occurred to us that our mentor, our new friend, might be honest and used cleverly by the commissars in the leather jackets. He might have been caught criticizing the Soviets. As Lenin's followers often had Machiavellian minds, they said to our man: "Look, friend, we intended to shoot you, as you really do not fit into the new Soviet happiness and the laborious proletarian construction, but we changed our minds. You enjoy grumbling and whining and criticizing. So instead of a bullet we are giving you a job where you can grumble and criticize to your heart's content. You accompany foreign comrades, and report everything they say. Now run along, go with the two newcomers, do all your complaining, and see whether one or both of them follows suit." But we were as smart as they, because this game of agent provocateur, most masterly practiced by the Russians, was played in Germany too, and the radical parties were teeming with such figures.

We were taken to our rooms in the wooden barracks built by the British for that abortive international military invasion in 1918. Martin and I shared the only bed there was, my feet at his head and vice versa. We kept our underwear on, used a fairly new Russian army coat as a cover, and were tired enough from all our hardships to sleep peacefully and soundly. As there was no heat, our new friend had brought us a bottle of vodka, but no glasses. When I asked politely, I did not want to criticize, whether we could have a water glass or something, he said pointedly: "They, they over there, the comrade commissars, they have glasses; they have more than they can smash into the mirror! But I'll find you some, comrades."

Now I was certain that we were being tested. I knew for sure that our mentor kept lots of glasses in his room next door to ours, that he was testing our power of resistance, and that he himself really was one of the comrades whom he pretended to resent. That cheered me up. Nexö was slower than I because his beliefs were stronger; he doubted my opinion, thought he was a "real" counter-revolutionary, but decided nevertheless to remain careful. Nexö belonged to the former generation, which meant that he was an idealist. He would and could not believe that such Machiavellian tricks would be used on non-comrades. "Then where would truth be?" he asked me more acidly than usual.

Truth, my dear Martin, is a bourgeois prejudice, according to Lenin, and is thus definitely abolished for believing comrades.

The next day we visited the town, which was mainly a line of uncoupled railway cars, in which Soviet people of all races were living. I noticed Chinese features, and oddly enough some heads that looked negroid. Everything was extraordinarily primitive. There were chicken coops under the cars, small black pigs running all over, and a strong smell of cabbage. I tried not to look too closely but rather to get a positive artistic image. I also accepted the invitation of some half-Chinese to share their simple meal. I could not refuse, as I would have insulted these simple, ant-like people, our guide whispered to me.

We had greenish-yellow, unappetizing little pancakes, similar to the ones of the old witch on the pier. I swallowed one with great effort, and managed to sneak into a corner and spit the next one out. It was terrible. It took me months to get rid of the rancid taste of this greenish-yellow, fatty offal.

It took a long time to answer all the questions and follow all the instructions and get all the permits and tickets for the continuation of our trip. This new country and this new "optimistic" proletarian movement harbored deep suspicion. Not only were the remaining counter-revolutionaries suspect; sensibly, the lower classes who had just been liberated and armed were not trusted either. To counter the feeling of threat, stamped papers were issued as amulets of power. There was no telling at that time to what degree all these papers, numbers, passes, pursuits, certificates of honesty and trust were expressions of fear, or the slow beginnings of the subsequently famed proletarian law and order. In any case, they were a nuisance for the traveler, even if possibly important.

The station was already quite Asiatic. By that I mean the way whole families squatted there for days, like dirty bundles. Patiently they would sit in front of the terminal, insensitive and hardened against bad weather, dirt and vermin. There was nothing touching about this picture, it was simply a piece of nature, beyond good and evil. The people of this icy steppe were in no way comparable to West European peasants or proletarians in such circumstances. They belonged to the lowest ranks of society, and traveled in a different class. Because, as higher functionaries explained to me, it would be quite impossible to travel in the same car; I readily believed that, but it cut me to the quick. It was understandable, yes, but contrary to all our aspirations of equality.

I admit that it was difficult to find anything positive in Russia in 1922. It was only a few years after the long war that had left all the places we saw in dreadful destruction. The Murmansk railroad that we were using had only been completed during the war. German prisoners of war had worked on it, and allegedly there was one buried under every railway tie. At every depot there was a huge pile of wood, fuel for the steam engine. The Russians got out at every stop to fill their kettles with boiling water for tea which they then brewed in their compartments. No Russian traveled without a kettle, and the hot water was free. Peasants were waiting for the train at every stop, hoping to barter their wares with foreigners who often used this route, for tobacco, for instance, or chocolate, or maybe even a cake of soap; there was a shortage of everything. What they offered were cold roasted chickens, some sort of cake, mushrooms, and if I remember correctly, occasionally, fruit. Their clothes were fairly clean, made mostly of khaki cloth of which a huge supply had been captured from the army of invasion, and distributed to the people; once in a great while we saw a white, embroidered linen blouse, reminding us of long-forgotten Russian pictures. Footwear ranged from good high leather boots to slippers woven of raffia and tied on with string. Best dressed were the various commissars and functionaries. The women wore scarves over their heads; I was told that they had either shorn or lost their hair from typhoid fever, which was also why nobody drank unboiled water.

Firing the engine with wood caused a steady stream of glowing sparks out of the smokestack. When the wind was on the same side as our window, we had to keep it closed to prevent the sparks from blowing in and burning holes in everything. That was unpleasant because the air in our compartment, which we shared with two Leningrad-bound Russians, was like that in steerage on a ship. The greyish-green bread and occasional berries also added unpleasantly to internal vapors, so that the place got to smell like a stable. The toilet at the end of the car had not been cleaned for a very, very long time; the seat was unusable.

The sparsely inhabited landscape was beautiful. Wide forests interspersed with lakes and little islands, pine trees, firs and spruce all the way to the water's edge. Unfortunately, my mind was so set on pure politics that I did not appreciate the beauty of the glistening, cool lakes, the slender evergreens, the graceful birches that are so typical of the Russian landscape.

Then we got to Kem—or was it Kandalaksha?—the reader will have to forgive me for my inexactitude, as I cannot check the notes and diaries I kept on the trip. In any case, it was an important town in Karelia, possibly the capital. Gulling was the name of the governor. I do not know whether he is still alive; at that time people did not die quite as quickly as they did later. We were invited to his house. Another Finnish revolutionary was there, with a British wife. She owned something very valuable, a box of sugar, and we were especially honored by getting a whole lump of sugar each for our tea.

Life at the governor's house was simple, but they were content and optimistic. When Gulling had any spare time, he liked to browse in a fairly new, very thick Sears and Roebuck catalog left with him by a friend. As he lovingly leafed through it, he said to Martin and me, pointing to the catalogue: "One day, we will produce all of that and even more!" It was quite touching to witness the governor's eye traveling the promised land of plenty—via a Sears and Roebuck catalogue. Next to the writings of Lenin and Marx, this product of the hated bourgeois-capitalist system was his bible.

We saw many interesting things and met all sorts of people. The townspeople sat round their samovars in their wooden houses, guns within easy reach. In a way, Karelia was pioneer country. But the foreigners I met there in 1922 were certainly not all pioneers. Many seemed to have been misfits in their capitalist homelands. Some of the other engineers, surveyors, writers, organizers and advisors seemed not to be in the wild north by choice, but were possibly gently pushed here, out of Moscow or Leningrad. Revolutions attract not only healthy, highly estimable and talented people, but also those known in bourgeois life as so-called reformers, eccentrics, harmless lunatics, and permanent planners and inventors. Soviet Russia had no use for those. The fact that some of the best people failed, or were swallowed up by power politics, is another story.

Some of the important people I met went down in that battle, among others Grigori Sinoviev, who at one time was the absolute ruler of Leningrad. He was a man of medium height, slightly overweight. As was true of almost all the upper commissars, he gave the impression of too much work and too little exercise in fresh air. He was pale and seemed to have a bad heart. Those were the days of the thousand officers that worked all day and all night; most Russians enjoyed night work. Sinoviev was friendly and spoke

German very well. He invited us several times, and we saw Leningrad and the surrounding countryside in his car. I regret that I have nothing personal to report about him, but somehow all the people's representatives and functionaries seemed quite colorless. Most of them had no private lives, and their conversations with foreigners were always geared toward the foreigners. Many seemed like living, red-bound pamphlets, and were proud of it. As the emphasis was on the masses, they actually tried to repress whatever individuality they had; what they would have liked best was to have grey cardboard disks for faces, with red numbers instead of names.

One day a small group of foreign writers and artists was brought together to discuss the possibility of a rapprochement of Soviet writers and literary sympathizers from Western countries. While we were waiting for Sinoviev, his secretary by the name of Tivel entertained us. He was a charming, small man who looked like a parrot, wearing an exotic Caucasian uniform, quite refreshing to us Westerners after all those khaki shirts. He must really have been a parrot in an earlier incarnation, as he hopped around with the versatility of a bird, jumping from bench to bench, onto the table, up on the window sill. The similarity increased as he nibbled on sunflower seeds. He never kept quiet, chirping in every language of the world, just like a smart parrot.

His job was subsequent interpretation of the short speech his boss would make. Sinoviev spoke with a high voice that sounded as though squeezed between two wet towels. What he said, however, was crystal clear, intellectual, and sometimes a bit condescending. (We Western sympathizers could not really be counted on; he never said that, but we felt his thoughts.) He submitted a large-scale proposition: all literary efforts were to concentrate on a super-colossal magazine. As he did not take us completely seriously, he did not mind bragging and exaggerating a bit. Headquarters were to be in Paris and Berlin. The very make up, presentation, printing, and illustrations were to demonstrate the "enormous importance of the cultural front of the U.S.S.R." The very best and greatest minds would join the cultural front of the Union of Workers and Peasants immediately, or in a short while, when disillusioned by the cultural decline of their own countries. The editorial staff must be set up and authorized immediately and given money; much money, as the magazine was to combine everything that up to now had been sketchy and dispersed. We should discuss the matter among ourselves; his secretary Tivel was at our complete disposal. He, Sinoviev, now had to excuse himself, he had to attend a meeting of the Leningrad Workers' and Soldiers' Council, the car was waiting, "Long Live the Soviet Union and the World Revolution!" "World Revolution!" crowed parrot Tivel from the window sill, while the door closed behind the People's Representative.

There were about eight of us, writers and artists from various capitalist countries. Arthur Holitscher was elected secretary for Germany, because he was old and dignified, and because he believed practically everything he was told. (He became quite bitter and disillusioned later, when he learned the truth.) Martin Anderson Nexö was the obvious representative for Denmark. He was not quite so credulous, but was a born administrator. Max Eastman was with us too; I was struck by his beautiful American boots with red rubber soles. I don't know much about him because he hardly participated in our hot-headed discussions, being buried in an English-Russian dictionary. Did he know more than we did? He was very good looking, with his white hair and open smile, a pleasant contrast to some of the fanatic true-believers' faces among us.

As the reader has guessed, this whole super-colossal project was nothing but a Potemkin village, a hoax, possibly just something to keep us busy. Because, as the "artists" among us soon noticed, the Workers and Peasants had absolutely no use for any sort of "individualistic" art. What they wanted was purely practical stuff; their first choice would have been to import a dozen American commercial artists to illustrate their slogans with useful, attractive pictures.

Leningrad seemed very "Russian" in the sense of the writers whom we had all read. I saw the houses here that that great humorist Dostoevsky had described. They combined that same inexorable, rather melancholic sense of humor with past elegance and grandeur. I was staying with a certain Rotkegel, a former German revolutionary sailor. He was forced to leave home when Social Democrat Noske teamed up with the very reactionary Free Corps to re-establish law and order; in addition to his revolutionary energy, he had organizational ability, so he had found an administrative job here in Leningrad. He lived in one of those big, elegant, former upperclass apartments. The splendor, though faded and a bit moth-eaten, still showed: a man-sized gilded French mirror, which someone had shot at, leaving cracks like a spider web, a gilded dressing table with brushes and combs engraved with coats of arms; silver-capped bottles and flasks; dusty velvet frames with signed photos; costly silk curtains in 18th century patterns, slowly disintegrating. Rotkegel lay comfortably in the large, French, double bed and had his breakfast brought to him on a silver tray, while he studied the progress of the world revolution in *Pravda*. Snow flakes blew by the window, a nice fire heated the huge tile stove, and a spot of vodka in the morning wasn't so bad either.

Of course not all proletarians lived so comfortably; you had to have special merit. There were restaurants. There was beer, in peculiar long bottles. You could get delicate crayfish, good soups including different sorts of borscht with sour cream, meat, fish, vegetables or cucumbers. Excellent were the pickled wild mushrooms and the many varieties of caviar; you could see shashlik, pieces of mutton and kidneys, the national dish of the Caucasians, turning on a spit. There were many foreigners in the restaurants, but also well-fed men in leather jackets who could afford good and plentiful food.

Once we went to a hotel, just after the end of the so-called "new economic policy" had been announced. We were sitting under old, dusty, artificial palms around a table covered to the floor with old damask, waiting for dinner. Suddenly I noticed a small brown spot with legs crawling on the far edge of the table cloth; it was taking a leisurely walk across the table. None of us said a word. Our host, a Russian of some importance, said nothing either. We seemed almost to have made a silent pact to ignore this crawling spot that was nothing but a little bedbug. We often noticed this indifference toward vermin, as though to say, "What's the use—nitchevo— even if we kill this one, there are millions more, more and more. Let it go."

At that time there was a movement in art called constructivism. The name was probably chosen to indicate that its adherents believed in construction rather than destruction. There was a strong input of mechanical civilization, and a preference for the looks of an electrical turbine to the looks of a landscape. Human beings were eliminated from their pictures or, if used, they were transformed into a wheel, a cylinder, or an obedient puppet, subject to the machine.

Constructivism had many followers in Russia. Their leader was a certain Tatlin, a peculiar Russian child of nature. Tatlin came from a wealthy family and had traveled in Germany before the First World War. At that time he had been a member of a famous balalaika band and choir which had played before Kaiser Wilhelm at court. He then became a painter and also studied at a school of technology. He got known when he exhibited his big project for a monument in Moscow. That is, he himself would never have called it a monument, that word was too old-fashioned and romantic, he called it the "Tower of the Third International." The model of this whole powerful construction was about ten feet high, consisting of all sorts of rods and bars put together at odd angles. The Tower of the Third International did not reach straight up toward heaven; oh, no, it leaned toward the left, a direction seen as symbolic by enthusiastic critics. According to the pamphlet given to the visitors, this slanting Tower of the Third International would be three times as high as the Woolworth Building, at that time the highest skyscraper in the United States. But it would not stand still, it would be in constant interior motion, part of it rotating from right to left, the other in the opposite direction; these movements were to symbolize the permanent powers of the revolution. The top would be decorated with a hammer and sickle of glass, a compromise from the pure orthodoxy of constructivism.

People were excited. My God, said our modern critics, tremendous, those Russians, terrific. Only one person poured cold water into the wine of general enthusiasm. That was Leon Trotsky, at that time the strongest and most popular leader after Lenin (who had no interest in art except for propaganda). Trotsky had a sharp mind and could occasionally be cuttingly sarcastic. He looked at the "Tower of the Third International" and asked why the thing was turning, and if so, why always in circles around itself? That question could not be answered to Trotsky's satisfaction. Thus, the gigantic project fell into oblivion, as did all of constructivism. Tatlin dropped completely out of sight. Other constructivists emigrated, if they could, and went first to Berlin, then to Paris or London. Meanwhile, the masses were victorious, inasmuch as their opinion counted more than before, and old, embittered painters who had been regarded as petit bourgeois were recalled from banishment. They now turned out to be better illustrators than all the modern hotheads and intellectuals.

I went to see Tatlin once more. He lived in a small, old, dilapidated apartment. Some of the chickens that he kept slept in his bed. They laid eggs in one corner. We drank tea, and Tatlin chatted about Berlin, Wertheim's department store, and his performance at court. There was a completely rusted wire mattress leaning on the wall behind him with a few sleeping chickens

sitting on it, their heads tucked under their wings. They furnished
the perfect frame to dear Tatlin as he started to play his homemade
balalaika. Darkness appeared through the curtainless window;
most panes had been replaced with little squares of wood. We
suddenly seemed surrounded by the melancholy humor of a book
by Gogol. Tatlin was no longer the ultramodern constructivist; he
was a piece of genuine, old Russia. I never saw him again, nor did I
ever hear of him or the formerly much-discussed "Tatlinism." He
is said to have died alone, and forgotten.

I remember Lenin well. He was suddenly standing among those
of us who had been carefully selected and examined and provided
with special passes to assemble in one of the red reception rooms of
the Kremlin. He was not very tall, looked slightly Tartar, and was
actually not very impressive. He gave the impression of having
always been the way he was now, never different. There was
nothing awesome or fearsome about him; rather, there seemed to
be an inexplicable sort of twinkle in his eye which the eyes of
Tartars often have, without meaning to smile.

He was accompanied by some secretaries; he shook our hands; I
noticed Bucharin and Radek. It was all very fast and informal.
Lenin was supposed to speak. Standing next to me was the
American correspondent Albert Rhys Williams, a nice man who
told me confidentially that Lenin, whose speech was in German,
was apt to lose his thread or miss a word because of his illness. We
were standing fairly far from Lenin, but could occasionally hear
somebody prompting him with a word or a date.

I was a bit depressed. Because of Williams' words, I saw only a
sick man up there who would lose his train of thought every so
often. Oddly enough he made me think of an aunt of mine who had
a brain tumor and would suddenly have similar symptoms. That
sort of thing did rather spoil the image. Lenin's condition
deteriorated soon thereafter, and he was not to recover. As soon as
he had finished his speech, which was about an hour long, if I
remember correctly, he received an enthusiastic ovation. He left
the platform immediately, helped by his doctor. He is said to have
appreciated my work, especially *The Face of the Ruling Class.*
Apparently it seemed to him another means of dissolving the
much hated capitalism. As so many people, he was mistaken in
the effect of such caricatures in the new medieval period that we
are now entering. The days of the caricature as an instrument for
progress are past. If one wants to agitate, a photo with appropriate
caption would serve the purpose better.

Leon Trotsky's appearance came much closer to the concept of a dictator. When I heard him speak, he was wearing a simply cut uniform of the khaki cloth of the Red Army without medals. He stood absolutely straight while speaking; brilliant speaker that he was, he was aware of the importance of posture. In contrast to Lenin, he had a military appearance and underlined his words with crisp gestures. He spoke Russian and had his words translated immediately.

Radek invited me to the Kremlin. He was clever and knew how "artists" were to be treated. Thus, I saw several of my works lying on his desk as though he had just perused them. I was to have the impression that he leafed through them at least once or twice a day. He gave me compliments which I received with humble gratitude. He was a big man at that time, and we artists, ambitious as we are, immediately soften up in the presence of power, regardless of whether this power is red or any other color, as long as its benevolent rays shine upon us.

I brought with me a tin of good English tobacco, as he was fond of his pipe. His eyes looked dull behind enormously thick eyeglasses, his whiskers were in the style of 1825. On the whole he looked like a peculiar new sort of owl. His study in the Kremlin was filled with books, magazines, newspapers and pamphlets from every country in the world. He nibbled at them periodically like a big beetle, and digested them into feature articles and polemics.

On a trip to Leningrad in a special train, I met Lunacharsky, then commissar for education and culture. The train was pretentious and brand new. The engine had a hammer-and-sickle emblem on the front, illuminated by a floodlight. The cars were all new, everything was first-class and very clean; there were paper flowers on the little tables by the windows. I shared a compartment with Arthur Holitscher, who had written several good books about Russia, and was one of the few important bourgeois writers who championed the Soviet Union. We were permitted a courtesy call on Lunacharsky in his compartment at midnight. I could not take my eyes off his tiny feet in their delicate little black shoes with patent leather toes. Beside him was a typical Russian commissar, a real blue-collar type whose feet disappeared in the coarse, thick military felt boots so often seen in Russia. The contrast between these two types of footwear seemed to me symbolic.

Lunacharsky, who leaned toward the West in cultural matters, tried to bridge the gap. He made me think of Dostoevsky and the scorn that he heaped on the Western-oriented Turgenev in one of his books. Lunacharsky was a highly cultivated man; wherever he could, he tried to preserve old Russian cultural values. That was not easy, as a certain nihilistic element wanted to have a clean slate and destroy all traditional values.

We talked about the *Proletkult*, a new organization formed with the purpose of developing a new proletarian culture from the bottom up. The name was badly chosen: there could be no such thing as a proletarian culture without totally falsifying the word. If a proletarian became cultured, he was simply no longer a proletarian in the sense that the word has been used up to now, because the word itself means something lower, uneducated, ordinary in contrast to the educated. The *Proletkult* soon collapsed, because talent in cultural realms such as poetry, painting and music simply cannot be based on class, economics, or environment. An artist, poet, or painter must have talent, today as ever, and one is born with that, a gift of the muses, and not the consequence of social environment or unused folk energy.

My visit was coming to a close. When I got the required papers, I took a small steamship from Leningrad to Stettin. The sea was rough. I shared a cabin with a Count Zeppelin, one of those extraordinary agents who were then constantly traveling between Russia and Germany. He said he had sold airplane engines to Russia. He was an extraordinarily reactionary gentleman.

My trip was not a success. The planned book did not materialize. I was not disappointed, but not exactly elated about what I had seen. The mote in my eye with which I saw Western capitalist countries was still there, and Russia did not remove it. It was no place for me and the likes of me, I felt that clearly. And as I was not a proletarian, I could not be "liberated." I can be suppressed, my work can be prohibited, I can be starved and physically punished, but my spirit cannot be suppressed. My ideas cannot be sent to concentration camp, nor can the pictures in my head, and that eliminates me as a follower of any liberator of the masses. I have a deep suspicion and no love at all for the politics of supermen.

FRIENDS AND OTHER FACES

I returned to the city that would be my home for the next decade. For me, Berlin in the twenties was fertile and very fascinating. I was more sociable then than now, and always eager for interesting new acquaintances, unfamiliar places and unusual adventures. I had met Eva through Professor Orlik at the Academy for Applied Art, fell in love with her, and married her. That was in 1920; we both believed in hospitality, so our house often looked like the waiting room of a railroad station. My mother used to say, "Food and drink keeps body and soul together," and that became my motto.

I was always meeting new people who became friends for a while, but many have escaped my memory. You do not get close to everybody you meet; how few are really worthwhile? Lots of people are mere shadows, dissolving in mist. Some seem to be made of gelatin, quivering back and forth on merest impact; others consist of clay, soften in the rain and melt into the soil; and even the few, carved by the great maker of hardwood, turn out to be wormy inside.

◆

With Pascin in Paris: Lights, the hum of voices, summer evening on the "Boul'Mich" and Boulevard Montparnasse, foreigners of all nationalities in the sidewalk cafés, carpet merchants...this is 1924. The trees are so green they seem painted, as green as the crème de menthe. People from all parts of the world pushing and shoving...many Americans. An American art student sitting at the Bar du Dingo, his long-unused sketchbook under his arm, a whole bottle of Benedictine at his lips. Could he have been a cowboy? The sound of jazz in all the bars. The band of *Le Jockey* is composed of the entire crew from a stranded ship...There I see Pascin again.

Pushing my way through the dancing couples, I happen to glance

toward the music. A small man dressed in black, his bowler hat
askew, is playing percussion. But he is merely toying with the
drums, swinging his arms like a drunken doll (any minute one will
burst, sawdust or cotton will fall out!), all in the haze of heavy
cigarette smoke.

The little man was blissful. Stupefied. He wanted to be stupefied, wanted to escape from something, of his own free will. He

flung himself into this stupor—did he know that the world had
started to darken? Was this the dance of death, the death of the
butterfly world? All those dear little butterflies, the fat death's
head moths, the yellow brimstone butterflies—are they having
their final fling, attracted by the bright lights of Montparnasse?

The drinks glittered brightly, the women smelled like flowers in
full bloom—or slightly decaying? But weren't they magnificent,
friend Pascin, as they walked around half naked? Weren't they?
Was that not the way you pictured them, time and time again?
Weren't your pictures done with butterfly dust? (But you did have
a sarcastic sting too, you who could look like a strange beetle yourself!) Didn't you live the very life of a fluttering butterfly? Yes, this
was your real home, not the America that you loved so much.

Your tireless hand drew hundreds of sketches, but you cared
little about them. You shed them everywhere, on the tables and
chairs of your studio in the Boulevard Montparnasse, almost like
sediment, dusty and unused, like a bird sheds its feathers. I can
still see you at the old Café du Dôme in 1913 when you drew little
pictures on scraps of newspapers, colored them reddish with a wet
match, and blew smoke into them. Nice little obscene things,
done with such uncanny skill that we gasped in admiration: what a
master! There was Professor Orlick who had been my teacher; the

painter Levy, nicknamed Levy of the Dôme, the Franco-German with the paternal bass voice, and the Bavarian, Paul Thesing, who would tap the cobblestones with his cane like a saber-rattling student, because he was looking for a fight and needed someone to fight with, and the sculptor, Ernesto di Fiori, and the Swede, Niels de Dardel. Sometimes Matisse came there too, looking like a German professor.

But that was a long time ago, and Montparnasse had not yet been "discovered." Then you went to America. Just after the Great War it may have been more fun and perhaps a bit wilder, but we had all changed. Often you would suddenly be seized by a mysterious longing; we would hear that you had gone to Italy to rediscover Raphael....

The last time I saw you was one of those evenings when we went from one night spot to the next until dawn, collected more and more friends and hangers-on as we went, and you paid for everything. You threw money away like dirty rags, but somehow it followed you and there was always more in your pocket. You simply could not get rid of it. I was sitting next to you; our heads were swimming in music and alcohol; in your low voice you revealed to me, just this once, what it was like inside you. And soon thereafter, you slit your wrists as though you were just cutting off the dirty ends of your cuffs....

I met Walter Mehring through Theodor Däubler; one day he brought him to my studio in south Berlin that looked like a romantic sort of cave. We liked each other right away, Walter and I. He was the son of one of the *Berliner Tageblatt* editors, from whom he had inherited wit, sarcasm, and "Berlinism." He was somewhat under the influence of futuristic poetry when I first met him, but even then he had his own line and his own talent for timing and dramatic movement. He was a sort of Berliner Francois Villon with a dash of Heinrich Heine...something like "beer with a shot" as they would have said in Berlin.

But Walter did not live in the shadow of Notre Dame, but rather in the shadow of the Gedächtniskirche and the ostentatious, tasteless residences of the Kurfürstendamm. In the little theaters there he would perform his poems and chansons; he wrote a special one, *Hoopla Wir Leben*, for the Piscator-directed performance of the Ernst Toller drama that created a sensation and shocked both conservatives and liberals.

He was copied a lot and undersold both in price and quality. Walter Mehring had added something to the chanson, something coming from modern poetry, as he really was a poet. A dormant form was brought to light again through him and raised to new heights in German poetry. His biggest hit remained *A Seamens' Song*. It was sung everywhere. Many a night we would sit in night-spots and bawl

> Wir haben die ganze Welt gesehn,
> Von Boston bis Trapezunt;
> Wir sahen Walküren, wir sahen Feen—
> Die Welt ist überall rund—!

Right. The world is round. Thus, Walter kept going in his little boat of songs, always nearly capsizing. He went to France, which he loved more than any country and finally had to leave; he went to fabled Hollywood, but that was not for him. And then he went to Manhattan and lived for years in one of the big, cold houses on Riverside Drive that were so different and yet somewhat similar to the Kurfürstendamm of the distant, the lost Berlin of 1923....

Another friend of mine was Bert Brecht, known in Germany and even abroad for his chansons and minstrel-style ballads. They really were little masterpieces, though they did not get the acclaim of his *Three-Penny Opera* inspired both by Villon and the old, English *Beggar's Opera*, with a score by Kurt Weill. (For a while, you would hear those songs wherever you went in the evening.)

Brecht was an interesting person. He came from a wealthy family, and started out as an expressionist dramatist. His plays *Baal* and *Drums in the Night* were favorably reviewed by young critics. He did not take his ballads seriously, but sang them to friends and accompanied himself on the guitar. He did not stay with expressionism, but moved on to enlightenment, statistics and socialism in order to transpose what he had learned into "teaching dramatics." He became a follower of Pestalozzi, and had his books printed like textbooks to make them look sensible and objective. "I am writing schoolbooks," he once said to me, "that's what we need today." His poetry also focused increasingly on education and purpose; in certain circles you no longer simply accepted what a person had to say or to paint. "Before you take that medicine, let us examine what is in it and what social purpose it has."

Brecht was interested in English writers and Chinese philosophers. He read Swift, Butler and Wells, and also Kipling. Whatever he wrote showed someone's influence. He openly maintained the opinion that it was alright to use existing material,

quoting Shakespeare among others. Some critics and sentimental colleagues resented that, but Brecht did not care; he was an intelligent person who knew exactly what he was doing. He also sought the company of people from different walks of life, as for instance the prizefighter Samson-Körner; they refreshed him and gave his thoughts a non-literary originality.

He had a large map on the wall of his room, as he did not wish to be limited to the confines of Berlin. He loved the Moscow Underground, and was very proud that *Pravda* published a poem of his on page one. He was not mildly melancholic as are most lyricists, and not at all passive. His spoken words were always original and sometimes better than what he wrote; and though he was anything but colorless, he loved grey, not the opaque but the sober, unromantic grey of the theoretician, the explainer, the schoolmaster. He would undoubtedly have preferred to have an electric calculator instead of a heart, and the spokes of a car wheel instead of legs.

He had his own style of clothing. Like a person who has a lot to do with machines and likes to lie under cars with an oil can in his hand, he used to wear a leather tie (without grease spots). Instead of ordinary waistcoats, he had vests made with cloth sleeves added. His suits were "American," with padded shoulders and wedge-shaped trousers, a style no longer worn in America (but in Germany it made you look American). He never wore a hat, but often a leather cap, and a leather coat when it was cold. But for his monk's face and the hair combed onto his forehead he would have looked like a chauffeur with a dash of Russian Commissar.

Brecht was an excellent driver, but one of the fastest and most careless I have known. In Langeland, Denmark, where I visited him in the thirties, he was driving an ancient Ford with a hand crank; and if it started at all, it would sputter and shake you to pieces. But it seemed to like Brecht, and obeyed him despite its decrepitude. When I arrived, he was standing in his workclothes and leather cap next to that poor, tottering Ford. I laughed out loud. It was like an act in a cabaret: "Bert and His Funny Car," accompanied by a street organ.

I like to remember those times long ago and our unforgettable talks in the woods of Langeland. The world was still at peace, though there was lightning on the horizon. I went back to America. Bert came later as a refugee, by way of Russia. He tried to settle in Hollywood, but did not manage to find a suitable job. After the war he returned to Germany, with an American prize for literature in his pocket as well as the thanks from the investigating committee for his readiness to swear that he had never been a Communist....

◆

My first publisher was Wieland. He had been my friend before, and remained my friend in spite of being my publisher. He was a short man, as was his brother John Heartfield, the "Dadamotor" in the Dada movement. He had delicate features and wore his hair forward when we first met. That gave him a somewhat precious look; but when he used to run after the streetcar with his books under his arm (we were still going to school) and jump onto the back of the rapidly moving vehicle, he seemed to me the very image of youthful strength. It was a matter of course for him to stand up for his friends. If ever anybody said anything nasty about them, there would be a fight. Else Lasker-Schüler nicknamed him "Roland." When a well-known writer once made fun of her, Wieland-Roland threw him out of the *Café des Westens*.

During the First World War, interrupted frequently by being called in by the military, Wieland published a literary magazine, *Die Neue Jugend*. He published poems by his friends, his own poetry, poems and full-page drawings of mine. He loved my work and perhaps saw more in it than I did myself, as he was beginning to move toward politics. He ran the magazine all by himself. He

got the money for it and was always on his feet, at the printer's, the binder's—changes were frequent when credit and kindheartedness were exhausted. The main collaborators were Däubler, Lasker-Schüler, the painters Dawringhausen and Mense, and I, Dr. Friedländer, who wrote satires under the name of Mynona, and occasionally Blüher, the leader of the youth movement, and the pacifist Kurt Hiller, who leaned toward so-called "Activism of the Spirit."

When Wieland had to go back to the Army once again, a new man joined the staff: the poet and powerhouse Franz Jung. *Die Neue Jugend* got another face and became very aggressive. The new format appeared to be inspired by American newspapers; Heartfield developed a new, very amusing style in using collage and bold typography. He stuck black index fingers between random upper and lower case letters, two large, crossed bones, a small coffin, a provokingly smiling woman's face behind a mask, part of an accordion, a tin soldier. There was meaning to all this that frightened the unpracticed eye and went beyond simple collage. The spirit of the age; how dismembered our world was!

We laughed very little, and cried only secretly. Our expression was a challenging grin. Jung would write articles full of anarchist vitriol. I wrote an essay, "Can You Ride a Bicycle?", and reviewed cabaret performances (cabarets were very popular then). Our editorial conferences were influenced by hard liquor, and very stormy. Occasionally Jung would shoot his revolver over someone's head at the wall or the book case.

Wieland, however, was really an optimist. He saw beyond his own person; in his imagination, he saw masses endowed with his own faith and nobility. He turned increasingly to politics and away from poetry, left Dada, and started the publishing house Malik-Verlag, named after a novel by Lasker-Schüler, where he published almost all my early drawings and caricatures as well as the works of Leonhard Frank, Upton Sinclair, Maxim Gorky and Tolstoy. I am sorry to say that following the custom of the time he made deletions in many of his authors, among them Goethe and Tolstoy. I never liked that; I wanted to read whatever a writer had to say, even if it disagreed with the "line" of the publisher. The *Rote Malikbücher* appeared there too, a collection of freedom songs of all times and countries.

All that stopped of course when Hitler came to power. Wieland became a refugee as did a hundred thousand others. The great German publisher kept alive in America by selling stamps. But

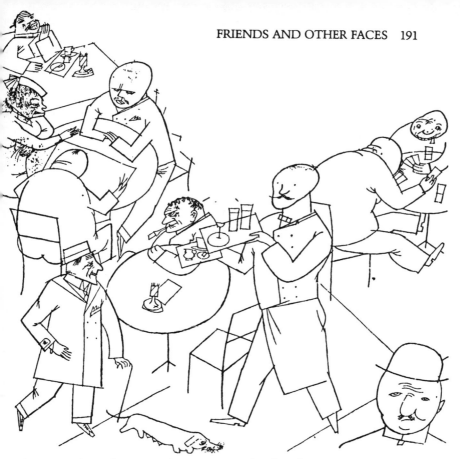

this story has a happy ending: He went back to become a university professor....

Eduard Fuchs was quite a different type. He had something of the beetle about him, the sort of beetle that is always dragging something around. He was a collector who had several thousand sheets of caricatures, among them the largest Daumier collection in Europe. Fuchs collected all sorts of things, good and bad, but his great love was Daumier.

He would stand before a small Daumier sketch and ask (in his South German accent): "Do you know where Daumier started? Well—you don't know—you couldn't know..." and he would look closely at the sketch, from bottom to top, and put his finger on a few indistinct lines. "Look here, Herr Grosz, look here! Daumier began with the nose, he did, Daumier always began with the nose!" he almost screamed as though I were hard of hearing "always at the nose he began!" And he beamed at me, triumphant at his discovery.

He had poor eyesight which sometimes led to funny situations. He once showed my friend Fiedler and me his Thomas Rowlandson collection. The sheets had been taken out of their special case and put in order for us to look at. Fiedler and I came upon a quite unmistakable Rowlandson scene on a swing. Fuchs leaned over the picture, put it close to his eyes, and started to lecture: "This here," he proclaimed with dignity, as though to an innocent audience, "this is a very erotic picture, it is...Close the door! It's not for women!" In complete earnest, he discussed its date and some academic details. It really was funny.

Eduard was nicknamed "Morality Fox" because of his *Sittengeschichte* that was forever being reprinted. It was for this that he collected all those pictures, adding a text with all sorts of quotations from biographies, poems, memoirs, and books on philosophy and medicine. He set out to prove that all art stemmed from eroticism. If, for instance, Daumier started all his drawings at the nose, "Well, that's a symbol...it is," he maintained. He did not subscribe to the later psychoanalytic school that explained almost everything in terms of sex drive; rather, he interspersed his explanations with social significance, as though he were a Social Democrat who believed in progress. A peculiar mixture!

For him, nudity, sensuality and erotic impulses were things of beauty. He had no objection, at least not in his books, to Greek paganism or pre-Christian Rome with its phallic culture. The trouble was that his books were received quite differently than he presumably intended—though that is not quite certain either; I, for one, could not help thinking that he must have had as much fun with his books as his readers did. In any case, his works had an enormous success, chiefly because of the pictorial material and the supplementary volumes that discussed the subject even more fully and contained really erotic pictures from all cultural periods of Western Europe, including contemporary photographs.

Fuchs had carefully collected all this material over the years, and kept it in his house, built by a modern architect. It was like a museum; even in the bathroom there were pictures, etchings, drawings, one next to the other, from floor to ceiling—and sometimes even on the ceiling itself. The whole place was wired with an alarm system, as these were truly unique treasures.

Eduard Fuchs was one of the very few really original people of our times. I am glad to have known him.

There are different sorts of patrons of the arts. I have mentioned my friend Falk who made vast sums on war and ugliness, and invested them in beauty, who let us artists have what he took from the Army, and in whose house a commanding general and I, a private on furlough, vomited together into the toilet bowl. And then there are born patrons of the arts...one of those was Lix....

I met Dr. Felix Weil through out mutual friend, Mark Neven Dumont, who came to me one day with a highly tempting proposal: "Böff," he said (that was my nickname), "how about coming to Italy with me for a few weeks, Eva and you?" "That would be magnificent," I said, "but how? I'm a bit short just now; you know how it is, new apartment and all, so...." "If that's all that is bothering you, don't worry," he replied. "I'll just tell Lix, and that will settle it. He's enormously rich, wheat from Brazil, you know, and he knows your work." "Go ahead and try," I said, "but don't be too sure, Mark. Nice of you to think of us anyway."

A few days later, however, there came a registered letter: two tickets to Portofino on the Italian Riviera, sleeping car for Eva and me, a check for travel expenses, and a few friendly lines. Quite *comme il faut*, I thought, when I also heard that Dr. Weil had rented the famous Castello Brown in Portofino for himself and his friends.

Food was still rationed in Germany, and we were hungry. The hot casserole in Zurich and the real coffee and cream puffs seemed like gifts from heaven. We were happy. The drive over the Corniche was unforgettable. We had had an excellent dinner in Genoa, and then an old-fashioned horse carriage drove us in the Italian dusk through the almost theatrical scenery. A huge iron gate was opened, a liveried servant took our luggage. Then our host greeted us.

He was a tall young man, younger than we had thought. We liked him at first sight; he spoke pleasantly about our friend Fuchs and his research and was enthusiastic about the prospect of endowing a University for Social Research in Frankfurt, his home town. But Lix was not merely a bookworm interested in social questions and economics—this side of him was as strange to me as all those statistical and speculative questions that I do not wish to understand—he also had a boyish, playful side. We would swim and row together, have fun throwing each other in the water and fighting with soaked baskets from Chianti bottles. I can still see him standing on his little balcony high above us as we were swimming toward a buoy in the transparent, blue Mediterranean, and shouting warnings to us about supposed sharks—and those meals served in grand style in the old refectory of Castello Brown! Open windows and doors—moonshine, warm, unreal dream nights.

Lix did give the city of Frankfurt its University, and founded an institute for social sciences in New York, with a branch in California. He continued to help me whenever my path as an artist became rocky. I painted a life-sized portrait of him that now hangs in his New York apartment.

We still get together once in a while with him and his wife, Helen. They always have interesting people at their house, and interesting conversation. Lix no longer looks as boyish as he did in Portofino. He has grown a mustache and a Vandyke beard, and looks a bit like a mundane Greco. Recently he has put on a little weight round the middle. But don't we all, if we're not careful?....

◆

Alfred Flechtheim was my dealer and also my friend, quite an abnormal relationship. But as a cat and a dog will sometimes get along, nature made an exception in our case too, and we really liked each other.

Flechtheim was really a fossil. That is, he was one of the last survivors of a generation of art dealers who regarded art not only as merchandise; they acted more as patrons than as merchants. There were types like that in Europe at the time when princes were no longer buying living art and the rich bourgeoisie, including dealers, took their place.

Flechtheim was a dealer, lover, patron, collector of art, and a gambler. He was a "man about town," knew everybody and was accepted everywhere; he published a magazine, the *Querschnitt*; he was a world traveler, a gourmet and gourmand, a connoisseur of wine; he promoted prize fighting, new in Germany, and commissioned me to paint Max Schmeling with his blue champion's belt.

Alfred came from wealth and was destined to take over the family wheat business. In 1905 on his Paris honeymoon, he once told me, he spent all of his bride's dowry on modern French art and came home penniless. His in-laws were aghast. What he brought back was a heap of incomprehensible cubist pictures that he claimed to be not only beautiful but even valuable. His keen nose, big as it was keen, had not deceived him. Within a few years, his French moderns were worth two and three times the invested dowry.

In contrast to some similar types, Alfred was not a miser. His apartment was almost an intimate extension of his gallery; the walls were literally covered from top to bottom with pictures, mostly French moderns that he liked best. (There were a few

Germans there too, but they seemed like stepchildren, comparing poorly with the French.) He was very hospitable and gave famous dinner parties. You would always meet interesting people there and even if you did not care for them, you would certainly enjoy the food and drink. Flechtheim's preference for ultramodern art contrasted with his "classic" table, where calories and vitamins did not count; his food was in the best tradition of old Rhenish fare.

It was in that pleasant house that one evening I met Joseph von Sternberg, nicknamed "Svengali Joe." He had discovered Marlene Dietrich and brought her to worldwide fame. The nickname came from a sarcastic Berlin critic who maintained that Sternberg had mesmerized this unknown little actress and formed her into his dreamed ideal. His influence was supposedly so great that she never could, or never wanted to, free herself of it. She remained enchanted, the living reality of Sternberg's imagination. His Beatrice, if I may be permitted to compare a Hollywood director with a God-given poet.

Later, when Svengali Joe was no longer working with her, many knights, princes and movie people tried to deliver Dietrich from his spell, but nobody succeeded. The fairy with those lovely legs (that were a little piece of Sternberg's dream) had to remain the same for the rest of her life, at least in the movies. And I imagine Svengali sitting in his glass house behind carefully draped windows, in the center of a magic circle, a life-sized picture of his dream before him, conjuring the dark forces to make the dream remain forever his own, impervious to alteration.

Sternberg was never without a cane, that last remnant of the eighteenth century sword. Quite out of style in America, a cane was still the symbol of a gentleman in Germany, along with gloves and a leather brief case; it made you look like a former duelling student, a big executive, or a mountain climber—someone of importance. For Sternberg, that simple cane was more than adherence to a European style. It was his fetish, a magic stick that brought good luck when he held it and bad luck if ever left at home or forgotten. There was a story that this peculiar cane had once made itself invisible while Sternberg was shooting a picture and could not be found anywhere, despite desperate searching. Sure enough: the picture was a flop. Later, the cane reappeared.

"No, I am not superstitious," said Joe once when we talked about it, "at least not in the ordinary sense. But see here, this stick can do things that you cannot explain. After all, it may have been a sawed-off branch that actually was a wishing rod without anybody knowing it. Let's drop the subject; too much talk could spoil the secret."

I went to see him at the UFA studio in Babelsberg near Berlin, where he was shooting *The Blue Angel*. He was having rushes shown to some friends; then he took us to another room where his assistant was cutting some strips. He had brought the assistant with him from Hollywood. Both of them were wearing berets and thick woolen scarves, as though they were freezing. They paid no attention whatever to us. Like a magician and his helper in a fairy tale, I thought. They were communicating in an incomprehensible whistling language, sounding like birds. The whole room and everything in it suddenly took on an exotic hothouse atmosphere.

A friend who was with me, a college professor who had a side interest in the migration of souls, contended later that the assistant must have been a canary in some earlier transmigration. Being an enlightened person, I took that as sheer nonsense. But when I thought of that soft whistling sound, and oddly, I remembered it quite often, I started to wonder, with an eerie feeling, whether the professor might not have been right.

Well, as I said, I first met Sternberg at Flechtheim's. His German was better than my English; in fact it was so good that I had the impression that he must have lived for a while near Vienna. As I knew little about his films, I had taken the precaution of having a knowledgeable friend brief me. So we said nice things, and immediately took a liking to each other; I, because he knew my *Ecce Homo* and admired my drawing, and he, because I had something to say about the "artistic" way he directed his films. We sat down to dinner, expressing our mutual admiration. In the back of my mind was the hope that he might buy something from me, for he collected art. And even in this respect he was different: he

The Ball [1928]

collected German art. That was quite unusual; people with money who followed the fad of collecting went chiefly for the French.

It was one of the always lovely evenings at the Flechtheim's. Salmon with a wonderful, properly chilled Moselle, a Rhine wine, and a Bordeaux with the roast. Figurines by Renée Sintenis decorated the table. Old silver and crystal reflected the candlelight on the damask cloth. Everything was first-rate, but nothing rigid or boring. The wine soon gave rise to lively conversation. But our friend Sternberg sat forlornly between two ladies who obviously had no idea who he was; they probably thought he was an absent-minded young artist or musician, with his sloppy clothes, loose collar and soft mustache. At the Flechtheims, you never knew what sort of people you would meet.

I was sitting across the table, and noticed how it irked him not to be recognized and appreciated. I could almost feel him waiting for an opportunity to make himself known. It soon came. The man opposite him, the sculptor Rudolf Belling, known for his money-grubbing greed, asked him a financial question. In a loud voice so that everybody would hear, he replied, "I, dear Rudolf? Oh no, I don't really make that much. Certainly not more than three times the salary of the President of the United States."

Everbody heard him. The waitress, about to fill the glasses, just gaped in awe, and almost spilled the wine. While Sternberg seemed to concentrate on his dessert, we all stared at him in surprise and amazement. The greedy sculptor kept on opening and shutting his mouth like a fish, and you could practically hear him thinking "three times as much...three times as much...." Sternberg's neighbors started to realize what they had been missing, and my own neighbor, an uninteresting banker's wife, poked me and whispered, "What did he say? Three times as much as the President? But with what? I assumed he was some sort of artist?"

Svengali Joe had suddenly become interesting. He had really scored, with that business about the President. Very clever. Now everyone was wondering how much the President of the United States actually did make. There were some big moneymakers at that table, but they would rather have bitten off their tongues than admit their annual earnings. Let alone to mention their President.

Even at Play [1931]

A FAIRY STORY

Once upon a time there was a man named Schulze. As he lived in Germany, where many people are named Schulze, he called himself Schulze-Leipzig, for Leipzig was where he was born. He had some artistic talent, that is, he could draw a little, so he became a commercial artist. At a big school in his home town he learned all sorts of useful things: wood carving, book design, painting lamp shades, and drawing vignettes to decorate books. Since he had designed them he occasionally read the books for which he had produced headings or arranged typography.

It so happened that Germany was at that time the country with the greatest amount of liberty in the world, and liberty always has something to do with books—you can hardly imagine liberty without books. Well, in short, our man got to be particularly fond of reading books about liberty. He would put down his tools and glow with enthusiasm over the fiery verses of poets who sang of freedom, and their fiery manifestoes. Or he would sit up all night, buried in the strict, dogmatic theses of the high and highest priests of dialectic materialism about the progress that had been predicted for a hundred years, and was now about to begin. He always carried a pamphlet by one particularly important pioneer of progress which he would open and quote when arguing with unenlightened friends or doubters.

Liberty, and what a splendidly, warmer, better tomorrow! Everybody was discussing how wonderful it would be when this new day dawned. That new day had actually dawned once before, and was said to have freed many people, but now had lost its glitter. Now you could often see columns of young people singing and marching through the streets with high hopes for the future. As Schulze came from a freedom-loving family (his father had belonged to the soldiers' council in the last war) he was naturally moved by the music. He played the fiddle nicely, so he joined one of the groups that sang those pretty freedom songs, shouldering their walking sticks, and marching through the streets in military formation.

After people had marched for some years and had been singing and dreaming in groups or alone about liberty and progress, they suddenly got tired of those eternal freedom songs. Then overnight some so-called leaders appeared with insight into human nature, and started people singing the exact opposite. And most of the groups and clubs never noticed the difference; somehow, those other words fitted the tunes just as well. Only the marching and the heavy stick that was carried on the shoulder remained the same.

This is actually where our story begins. Schulze was, unfortunately for him, one of those who liked the tunes as much as ever, but not the new words. He could not stand them. Possibly he had inherited rebelliousness from his father (that soldiers' council!). "Schulze," said his former female marching companion, "Schulze, don't make yourself miserable with your opposition." Schulze got lonelier and lonelier. He went for walks in the woods and cultivated his deep inner resentment. He doubted something, but did not know exactly what. He became increasingly individualistic and subscribed to a magazine called *Action* that advocated the world-wide abolition of muzzles for dogs. He became compulsive and cranky.

It so happened that at that time there was nothing you could buy, not even with a million marks. Supposedly there was a man somewhere, in the Rhineland, they whispered, who was so powerful that he could buy everything, simply everything; in some mysterious way he got hold of even the smallest piece of soap. This man supposedly had subterranean corridors and storerooms as high as a house, in which he kept miles of soap, barrels of the best butter, acres of bread, hundreds of thousands of sacks of sugar, coffee, and tea and American condensed milk. People said the man (whose name nobody knew) was fabulously rich, and if you were fabulously rich, all that sugar and coffee came to you without your doing anything about it. But there were also erudite men with spectacles, some of them in the government, who spent day and night with statistics and calculations to prove that things could not go on this way. According to a secret law of economic ebb and flow, understood only by them, soap, sugar, flour, butter and condensed milk would come to the unwashed, starved, thirsty consumer, if he would only be patient and wait a while.

It was a time when lots of people moved to the country. There there were fields where you could grow carrots and sugar beets and the best of all fruits, the potato. Those who moved out there told themselves, "While I am waiting for good times to come back, I'll be independent and grow my own carrots. I'll make carrot coffee out of them, and sugar beets are like cutlets, and everybody knows that there are a hundred ways to prepare potatoes, so I'll have lots of choice; and when I have tried the hundred ways, I can start all over again. That way I'll have a wholesome change of diet."

Our young hero Schulze also had these thoughts. He took his last savings, which unfortunately amounted only to a few million, but luck was on his side. While brushing an old suit that his sister had sent him from California (he was until his horrible end a clean and orderly character) a 25-cent piece fell out of a pocket. Hurray! Schulze was a rich man. He quickly went to change this currency, first buying a middle-sized laundry basket; he received so much paper money that it would not have fit in a normal suit case. With the congratulations of the bank teller, he loaded the basket on a wheelbarrow, and left his home town in good cheer to move to the country. In an additional trunk he had all his books. As many commercial artists who had not changed their profession had perished from malnutrition, our man Schulze figured correctly, "I'll take all my books along, maybe I can trade with a farmer now and then." One traded all sorts of things in those days, sometimes you could even get eggs or potatoes. Hungry as everyone was all the time, he had visions of a huge, fresh-fried farm breakfast of at least six or eight eggs and three pounds of fried potatoes.

When he got out to the country, everything was nice and green, the birds were singing in the trees, the small paths were prettily laid with gay red bricks, and the cottages were neat and clean; in the windows were neatly painted tin cans with blooming flowers; checkered sheets and blue workclothes flapped on the wash lines; and chickens ran round clucking and pecking. He liked everything. Born in an inland region, he had decided on a small, pretty Baltic village. He was wealthy now, thanks to the 25 American cents of which he had prudently changed only 15 cents. The remaining ten cents were carefully knotted in his handkerchief in case he needed a few billions more, so he was safe. Next day he went to look for a house, and for several billion bought just what he wanted from an aged peasant who was hard of hearing and lived in another world. It was a nice little Baltic cottage surrounded by large trees, with an overgrown vegetable garden.

He bought it as it was, with old, carved, decorated beams, bent and stained by the sea breezes. He was particularly pleased by an old-fashioned door knocker; as an artist, he liked ornamented things. In that, he differed from the local peasants, who wanted everything polished and new, despite the efforts of some gentlemen who had started a "Foundation for the Preservation of Old Cottages and Antique Costumes." They tried, in vain, to improve the taste of the villagers, who wanted only to copy what was urban and new.

Things proceeded along unwavering lines. Fate still favored Schulze. He worked in his garden; his paunch, acquired through his former sedentary occupation, disappeared; his skin tanned, his eyes became alert so that he could see in the dark, like a cat; he had a good crop of carrots, lettuce, strawberries and potatoes in his garden, currants on the bushes, and the chickens thrived in their fenced coops. A hammock, strung between two fine cherry trees, was ready for a nap in the open. All was peaceful, and the city faded like the color of a cheap shirt. Astutely, he had acquired antique furniture from old people's backrooms and attics. His books stood on shelves, and new ones were added. He had built a studio in a sunny room in the attic, painted it pale blue, and arranged his tools neatly along the wall and on the solid old table.

Schulze was happy and content; although something of a rebel, he was by nature cheerful and an optimist. If he had had the gift of telling the future, as some people do, he would have paled with horror; but as he was a thoroughly enlightened person, he believed neither in cards nor in tea leaves. Unfortunately, he did not believe in God either. On the contrary, his tendency toward enlightenment and free-thinking seemed to have increased by being in God's free nature, in his garden and on the ocean. One wonders whether there may have been something in the salt water or the hen's eggs, some phosphorus or iodine or other salt or vitamin that has a special effect upon rebellious glands? Schulze himself may have asked that question. As any enlightened person, he used to claim that human beings consisted of salt, water, albumin and a sort of electrical glue, which was why a decomposing corpse had that sweetish smell of glue. Because of all his reading, Schulze had become quite an educated man. He also knew that there was something like complexes and repressions which, when properly brought to the surface, could be first recognized and then explained and cleared up; then the cure came easily and almost by itself. He believed in a soul as little as in God; the concept of man as a machine came closest to his modern, progressive view of the world. Untrammeled by prejudice you should look east, he said, and see how the peasants in Russia were almost literally transformed into machine parts by the benevolent influence of enlightenment from above. Surely that was a great further development of Darwinian theory, and fitted into the current cultural scheme.

Schulze gave the word "culture" special emphasis and said he was greatly moved by what he saw as human expediency. In this "greatest experiment of world history" even expressions of tenderness and love were derived from the function of the machine. Thus he had heard from a man who had been all the way down in Magnitogorsk that in situations where one used to say things like "sweetie-pie" or "honey child" or "my darling baby," they would now say "you polished screw driver" or "my strong steam plow"! He mentioned a new school for authors where this was taught, and spoke of a scene from a novel in which a former farmer who had become one of the champion industrial workers was on his deathbed; his one remaining worry was a malfunctioning crane; "Comrade, how—how—how is the crane? Has it been repaired?" Breathlessly, his son leaps into the room, shouting, "Father, father, our crane is working!" Transfigured, the old man closes his eyes: "It's working again...now I can die in peace."

I am quoting this in such detail not only because such ideas made up Schulze's inner life (pardon the word, my friend Schulze; Schulze you would merely have scoffed: inner life? soul? Nonsense!—a lot of hot air, that's all!) but also because many people shared such ideas. That novel was a document of the times; its popularity was significant.

Schulze did get to know the village peasants. But it soon became obvious that many of them who seemed like peasants were really not peasants at all, but fugitives from city life as he was, or retired sea captains who rented their cottages for the summer. Schulze got acquainted with a fat physician, an alcoholic, who held his office hours in the village pub with the help of slightly too much red wine. When he got drunk, he lay down in the sawdust of the sawmill next door and slept until sober. Puffing the sawdust from his nose, he looked at a distance like a stranded whale.

Sitting one evening with the doctor in the pub under the oil lamp (there was no electricity), Schulze listened to gruesome stories of a member of the secret patriotic club who was agitating underground at that time in Baltic villages. They were sitting in the back room on the cozy oil cloth settee and eating the local specialty, warm smoked flounder with salt and delicious dark country bread. According to custom, the flounders were eaten with fingers straight from the paper, and accompanied by strong potato liquor that was pleasantly warming and went pleasantly to your head. Through the half open door they heard how the French had spat at our agitator, had used his mouth as an ashtray, and finally brutally beaten his backside. After finishing his fiery account, the agitator bared his back; the pharmacist's wife started to cry quietly and was joined by several other women. Schulze explained to me later that there had simply been a frantic agitation against Poland and France, and that he had thanked his God that he and his friend, the doctor, had not been Poles or Frenchmen.

As you may have guessed, the doctor was unhappily married. While he was sitting comfortably in the back room with his red wine or schnaps, his slightly lame wife (also a physician) would appear. Dressed in black from head to foot, she would wander through the room without a word and without looking at anybody, like a Greek ghost or a figure in an Ibsen play, and then disappear. She came every afternoon at exactly six-thirty. She was so punctual that Schulze would set his watch by her arrival. The fat doctor did not say a word; immediately after her passage he ordered a wine glass full of potato schnaps, emptied it in one gulp with closed eyes, shook himself, and said, "Brrr."

So the summer passed, and all was well. Oh Schulze, Schulze, if only you had known what your future had in store for you, you would have returned to Leipzig the very same day!

Occasionally he went out and drew a few landscapes. I still have one of his woodcuts, *Fishing Boat in the Wind.* He did some drawings of fishermen landing their salmon nets, and helped them with the work. To order, he would copy old family portraits, and paint "portraits" of ships in a near-by harbor, not quite to order. He would neatly paint those Danish or Norwegian ketches or schooners and offer the finished little pictures to the captains for Danish or Norwegian money. They liked to take the pictures home for souvenirs, and that gave him a supply of a few Danish or

Norwegian kroner. Since there was still that legendary Croesus in the West who would soon own all of Germany, Schulze got many pounds of German paper money for every penny of foreign currency.

On and off some odd people called "breakers" would come to these parts. They bought stranded ships, had them taken apart by hired help, and made money out of the old wood, iron, brass and so on. When the wrecking was completed, they would give a huge party to which everybody was invited. They were adventurous, jolly types. Director Schrage was one of them. When Schrage was displeased, he would rip the large tablecloth with all the glasses, plates and wine bottles off the table, jump laughing loudly onto a chair, and shout: "I'm just telling you, Schrage can do everything! Anything! Not only wreck ships." Then the waitresses and the innkeeper had to put everything together again, bring clean tablecloths and fresh food, and it would start all over again. That could happen several times an evening. As he paid in foreign exchange, he could do whatever he wanted; he was well-served and greatly liked. Schulze was of another opinion. "You see, my friend, that alone is reason enough to abolish money; it can buy any nonsense and every debauchery and degrade man to the level of undignified imp," he said, showing his tactful, sensitive nature. When the party was over, however, Mr. Schrage ordered his carriage, whipped the horses, and drove at a wild pace along the Baltic beach with three or four drinking companions and women of easy virtue, sometimes going right into the waves for fun until everybody was soaked.

As we have seen, Schulze was no Schrage. His liking for the fat doctor was not only through the wine bottle but rather because of a kind of mutual discussion of ideas. He had heard that the doctor belonged to one of the ubiquitous secret societies that were having military exercises and target practice at a hidden estate, for the purpose of liberating Germany from the chains of tyranny, Jewish moneyed interests, and the dictates of the Treaty of Versailles. The club had the strange name of Schlagetot, Strike-Dead, after a member who had been shot in a secret sabotage raid during the Ruhr occupation; which was of course the subject of much discussion. The good-natured fat doctor was not at all a fanatic; but he had to participate, or else the influential estate owner who was the chief of the Schlagetot movement would not have sent him any patients. No patients, no red wine.

Occasionally Schulze would accompany the doctor when he

The Unavoidable Chain of Crisis [1931/32]

went to see his patients. And he saw a degree of misery and demoralization that one can usually find only in the very poorest quarters of large cities. He saw the ugly little two-family houses and would often talk with the people who were hardly better than old-time serfs. Though hardly a few miles away from the Baltic, many of them had never seen the sea, so burdened were they with toil. There would be a Bible and an obsolete agricultural calendar on the window sill; in an old cigar box, a dry ink well and a rusty pen that had obviously not been used for years. Schulze considered this still life typical of the educational level of these exploited people; pen and ink were telling symbols.

Foreclosure [1931]

The old rebel in Schulze gradually redoubled. In summer a lot of people came for their vacation, among them many from so-called intellectual professions; and as equals tend to attract each other and as Schulze too was a sort of intellectual, he soon moved in different circles. There were social reformers who were nudists, went round in very short shorts, wore no hats and ate nuts out of little bags they had crocheted themselves. There were former submarine captains with socialist tendencies who painted secretly; young musicians who adored Hindemith; hot-blooded lyric poets; members of a modern-art club who used drugs. Further down the beach, a progressive young lady practiced physical culture in the nude with her pupils. At night people met and had discussions, or went to the village pub, where a salvaged British mine, painted black, white and red, stood as a sign in front of the door.

It happened that one day a young publisher from Hanover came to this Baltic village. He published mainly so-called "lasting" literature and took great pride in a new edition of Goethe, abridged by a professor of the dialectic persuasion after the mode of the latest enlightened economic theories. Apart from his idealism, this young publisher had a good head for business and was always on the lookout for ways to sell his books. His slogan was "I will not be satisfied until not only every German worker, but every German man, every German woman, every German child owns a book of mine." He missed no chance of introducing his books to any prospective buyer.

A new kind of bookshop became fashionable at that time, small, intimate places where you could browse to your heart's content. The young booksellers who ran such shops were pleasant, polite people who often had come from other professions. You could chat with them, and sometimes they would even offer you tea or cigarettes in a back room. The bookshops had ingenious names, almost like old-fashioned inns. "Book-Spectacles," for instance, or "Gilt Edge Shop," or simply "The Binding."

Our young, enterprising publisher had something like that in mind as he came along the village road. He was a man who made his own luck, and tended to admire himself. As soon as he had checked his own reflection in the window of the bookshop, he proudly noted the books he had published. "Look, here's another one of my Red Rucksack series, another step to the sun, to progress! Just look at the cover, that's a collage of old magazine pictures by Schulze, the commercial artist. I think it's good—do you like it?"

He published under the name of Red Rucksack because he had started from scratch, delivering his books to customers by bicycle out of a red pack. He had a one-track mind, as do most people with original ideas. Everywhere and anywhere, in forests, on the seashore, in the mountains, he envisioned bookshops and store windows with his books. Here again was just the right window, up on the path that went along the dunes. It was a completely empty window that had once belonged to one of those little souvenir shops: boxes of shells, seals balancing crystal balls on their noses, candy for good children, tin pails decorated with crabs and harbor views, pin cushions in the shape of lifesavers—all those things that you buy to remind yourself of that lovely vacation. Just how the sight of a few empty wooden cases, some dirty wood shavings, and a bundle of tied *Pomeranian News* behind the window reminded him suddenly of Schulze, we will never know. It may have been the combination of newspapers and wood shavings of which Schulze (he was always avant-garde) had made a collage for the cover of a Red Rucksack book about the capitalist lumber industry. My God! thought our publisher, that Schulze now lives right here in this very village! In his mind's eye he could already see that little shop cleaned up and the window filled with Red Rucksack books. Since he remembered Schulze as an enlightened, progressive person, he decided to look him up.

Ehrenfried, that was the publisher's name, was a man of action and quick decision. No sooner said than done! He hoped also to get all sorts of information: what ideas people here had, what was going on in the country, and whether anybody was familiar with Red Rucksack publications. His ideas gave wings to his steps; he got Schulze's address in the pub, and soon he was hammering the old knocker on the cottage door.

Schulze was at home, working, but was delighted to meet the publisher. He had heard a lot about him and had occasionally worked for him. They drank coffee and rye schnaps and discussed the project. Schulze thought the idea was marvelous. You could kill two birds with one stone; you would enlighten the somewhat backward population, and at the same time make a little profit. Ehrenfried promised to deliver everything on credit; Schulze was not to worry, not in the least; the time to settle accounts always came soon enough.

So the little shop on the dunes was rented and painted bright red. Red was not only the color of boiled lobsters but also the color of enlightenment and of fire. Schulze himself painted "Red Rucksack

Bookshop" in beautiful black and red letters on the door, and under it "Hermann Berthold Schulze-Leipzig, Proprietor." This was the beginning of a chain of events, loosely connected, that ended in destruction; we will probably never comprehend the secret forces, hidden in increasing darkness, that caused it. Up to now we have seen Schulze shine in the light of science and enlightenment. Bright, but diffused, like a modern impressionist painting—in the sunlight of modern times. From here on his figure appears at the center of a mysterious chiaroscuro horror picture of night and destruction. Unfathomable black shadows alternate with glaring lights. It seemed as though a secret power had fired a curse from somewhere haphazardly into blue darkness and it had hit our own Hermann Berthold Schulze-Leipzig like a bolt of lightning. But let us not anticipate....

So, in addition to being a commercial artist, Schulze was now a book dealer. His own pretty woodcuts and etchings were displayed in the window beside the rows of Red Rucksack books, that emitted so many rays of progress. The book in the place of honor was the world-famed *All Quiet on the Western Front* framed by black, white and gold ribbons and little flags.

Civilization Marches On [1935]

First, a big stone came through the window. Then Schulze found a piece of gas pipe with a note "For you, my little friend, if you won't listen" left by an unknown hand on his shop table. For a few days nothing happened, then the gas went off one evening, and next morning as he stopped out of his door he found a heap of excrement as though two or three large dogs had defecated there.

Many people whom Schulze had known well pretended not to recognize him when they met on the street. On the birthday of the German Republic he was the only one who had the boldness to hoist the black-red-gold flag; through the open window, he happened to hear a wild looking, bearded man, dressed in hunter's green, with a gun over his shoulder, say: "By my beard, I swear by my beard that man will take this dirty rag down with his own hands!" What could he have meant?

When Schulze went out at night or walked home through the dunes, he thought he heard steps and voices behind him. Once one of his friends at a dark streetcorner looked nervously around as they met and suggested in a whisper that he take leave and go on a vacation to rest; he had heard that Schulze was sick and suffering from hallucinations. Next morning his store window was smeared with a stinking brown mess, as was the doorknob. When he had painstakingly removed most of it with dune grass and leaves and wanted to open the door, the knob broke and when he leaned down to pick it up, he heard sneering laughter. He rose quickly and looked round, but could see no one.

Schulze went down to the beach, lay down, and covered his body with the newspaper that he had brought, as the sun was hot. He was wakened roughly by a large man in bathing trunks who pushed his belly with a thick bamboo stick and shouted angrily, "You there! Will you kindly get up and sing with us?"

The singers were marching along the beach, led by a man as large as the one who had hoisted Schulze's paper, the *Berlin Progressive*, on his bamboo stick.

"Why, look at this one," he said, while further stroking Schulze's sore lumbar region, "covering his face with the *Progressive*—how about that? Want to provoke us, what? Well, we'll show you all right. Covers himself with the *Progressive* just when the music is coming. Really, that's the limit. You go home, I'm just telling you, and thank your lucky stars that you got off so easy."

Schulze did not "get off easy." One of his ribs had been broken, he was shaken, and his head was swimming. But it made him even less inclined to leave. The bad thing was that he had a tendency toward martyrdom, the very sort of martyr virtue that makes other people humiliate and attack you.

It got worse and worse. If, for example, he built a castle in the sand (he loved doing that as he really was a child at heart), the next morning the sand would stink, and so would the water in the moat. Unfortunately, he stinks, that Schulze, he heard a female voice say, but again there was nobody to be seen. Suspiciously, Schulze sniffed himself. He did not stink.

Schulze sat down on a chair. The back gave way, he fell backwards and broke his arm. The Doctor was visibly frightened when Schulze came in. He bolted the door, listened at the window, closed the curtains, and lowered his voice: "For God's sake, don't tell anybody that you have been here!" he said, and added pleadingly: "And do go to Leipzig for a while. I mean well..."

Schulze stayed.

A black-haired female friend who was living with him walked along the gabled roof at night. It seems she was a witch who cast a spell upon the chickens and cows and infected the pigs with red plague. Schulze knew nothing about all this until one of the few remaining good friends told him. The friend assured him politely that he did not believe it, though actually things of that sort were not unknown. The fact was that the villagers were talking about it; they had told the clergyman and the gamekeeper, and the gamekeeper had said that he still had a few real silver bullets inherited from his grandfather.

Schulze stayed.

He started to worry, but still he stayed. He began to drink a little more, sometimes even in the morning. A few friends had apparently remained faithful: a ruined teacher who could hypnotize chickens and, when inebriated, recite Heine by heart; a former submarine captain who did not smoke and painted; two black-haired female students of dance who supported themselves with rhythm classes; a materialistically enlightened, unemployed editor who owned a letter by Romain Rolland. With these, Schulze celebrated his birthday. The phonograph was still working, thank God, and he still had a few unbroken records. So they ate, drank schnaps and danced to the music of a very popular band. The teacher recited his Heine after he had had enough to drink, and told stories about his successful hypnotic experiments with chickens. The editor, a rather nervous person, thought he had heard somebody behind the house, but he hadn't. Everybody stayed rather late and had a good time.

Who Said Peace? [1930]

Next morning Schulze wanted to lie down in the hammock. Bang! he found himself lying on a heap of broken glass, covered with a brown, stinking mess. It must have been carefully concealed with grass, as he had not noticed anything; as to the smell, dung was still used as fertilizer everywhere in those days.

He went back into the house to take off his soiled trousers; hardly had he let them down when there was a sharp knock at the front door: "Herr Schulze, in the name of the law, open the door immediately, or I must arrest you!" Schulze, furious about his fall, went pale and opened the door. Before him stood a country policeman and two gamekeepers with their bicycles; all were carrying revolvers.

"You are to come with us immediately, to the office of the District President. If you resist, I will have to handcuff you or use my revolver, so you had better come quietly. Damn, what a stench!" said one of the gamekeepers. "No wonder, in the house of such a traitor," added the other.

As an avid reader, Schulze knew exactly what to say in such historic moments of humiliation: "I am ready, gentlemen. I submit."

"You just shut up and come along," said the policeman.

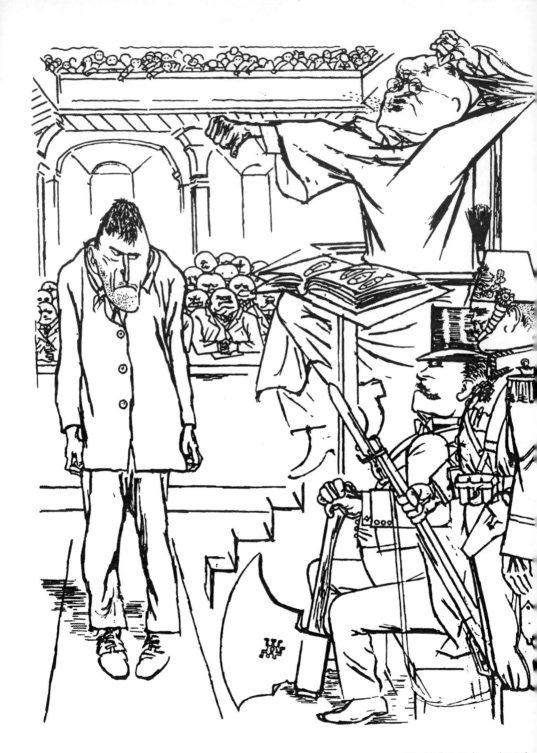

He Didn't Believe [1935]

The District President, a moderately enlightened and moderately progressive man, close to the government in power, raised his eyebrows and his index finger: "Why Schulze, Schulze, what is this I hear? You are bringing not only yourself and me but our whole good village into disrepute. Don't you understand that what you are up to is treason—yes, Herr Schulze, I repeat: treason—and that the penalty is prison? Well, sit down, and we will take down your deposition. You will tell the truth, Herr Schulze, the whole, clear, Prussian truth; I can get tough too, Herr Schulze, and you know you do not have many friends left. Dühling, take down the statement. Well, Herr Schulze, you had a little—hm, what should I call it, a little...."

"Permit me, Herr District President, it was a birthday party. It was my 25th birthday, and so—"

"I am doing the talking, Herr Schulze. You will speak only when you are asked. All right, so we will call it a birthday party. Were there not some girls present?"

"You mean the two dancers from the local dancing school?"

"Oh, I see. So they were *dancers*. Very interesting. So you are 25? Well, I must say, in my time we did not have dancers at our birthday parties. Have you taken that down, Dühling—about the dancers? Herr Schulze, I hear you also had phonograph music? Gamekeeper Nietracht, who bicycled by your house, said it sounded Russian. What do you say to that, Herr Schulze?"

"It cannot have been Russian, Herr District President, because I don't have any Russian records...."

"But you do have Russian books, hm? You won't deny that, will you?"

"The record that we played, Herr District President, is by the famous American band called the Revellers—they are very well known and everybody is playing them now..."

"First of all, Herr Schulze, it is open to doubt whether this sort of—well, alright—music is very well known; I, for one, do not know it. And we will not discuss who the 'everyone' is who is playing this degenerate Negro music. Very odd, Mr. Schulze, that a German man would be thinking of nothing else these days than to listen to American Negro music on his birthday. Besides, did not your friend, Editor Wirnitz, sing the *Internationale*, and recite Russian poetry?"

"Herr District President, it was the poem about the captured grenadiers and the emperor—"

"Oh, by the Jew Heine. Well, that says enough. That should be the last time for him too. We have had an eye on Wirnitz for quite a while..."

The evidence was taken down and signed, and for the time being, Schulze was dismissed.

It might have been better, had they locked him up right away. From then on, everything he did had a double meaning. If he played an American hit behind closed shutters, the whole village heard about it, and the jazz rhythm became provocative, foreign and alien to the ears of the villagers. Everything was changing demonically. Schulze seemed to age overnight. He was only twenty-five, but his temples started to grey. Every day brought unforeseen little disasters. Plaster peeled off the walls, glue no longer held things together, pictures fell down, tables and chairs started to wobble, bread molded soon after it was cut. His house suddenly got damp, the floor started to sag, forming little green pools where frogs croaked at night.

The little shop on the dunes had been given up long ago, and nailed shut by the proprietor. One Sunday, the lovely bindings of the Red Rucksack books started to fade and became a dull pinkish-green. Some of them burst like poisonous mushrooms when Schulze wanted to thumb through them. Once, the heavy oaken door crashed down on his head, the hinges completely corroded by rust. The oil lamp would not light any more; the oil was like thin, smelly water. His chickens stopped laying, and some were found with nooses round their necks, as though they had committed suicide. The orchard was bare of fruit. When Schulze tried to dig up his potatoes, he held nothing but faded tops in his hand; the potatoes seemed to have been cut off with a knife, and the stalks carefully replanted.

One noon a piece of his roof fell in. A foreign ship's carpenter who knew nothing of the secrets of the village and was thus immune to the Evil Eye (he had good Norwegian currency, too) looked at the mess. "But those beams were as good as new!" he told the wearily resigned Schulze. "Good, thick oak beams, they were good for another 300 years. Do you know that somebody sawed through three of them, Herr Schulze? Or do you believe in the saw-beetle they tell me about in the village, who will slowly but surely chew up your house?"

The carpenter with his brown beard looked almost like a biblical figure. In a kindly way, he said to Schulze, "Look here, Schulze, just leave everything, pack what you need, and come aboard my ship. I'll see you through, and you can start over again in my country. Tomorrow evening we're weighing anchor." And he added, "When the saw-beetle is in a house, Herr Schulze, it's high time to get out. I once knew a captain who had saw-beetle, I mean the ship did, and it fell away under his feet, simply fell away; the planks came apart like matches. I wish you luck, Herr Schulze," he said.

The kind harbinger departed. The ship left without Schulze.

It rained next morning; there was a sweet smell of wet leaves in the air, almost like in a churchyard; no birds were singing. Schulze got up early and went out to the moors. This was a wild-life sanctuary, so the undergrowth was thick and luxuriant, as in primeval times. Schulze suddenly felt as though he had lived there for ever and ever, maybe always, as in a dream. The mist hung low. The Revellers were playing. A bicycle passed him, threatening, ghostlike, silent. Schulze walked and walked.

He was never found.

Later, a child found a little wooden boat with these words roughly scratched on its side, apparently with a pocket knife: TOO MUCH.

Couldn't Get Anything Out of Him [1935]

Horseman of the Apocalypse [1936

A CHANGE OF AIR

I am often asked: "Mr. Grosz, how could you tell what was going to happen? How did you know enough to leave Nazi Germany at the right time? Did you have inside information, or a foreboding? Had you consulted a fortune teller or had your cards read? Did you get hold of the secret predictions of Nostradamus? How did you guess the right time to leave, just six weeks before the gates were closed, the Reichstag burned, and all the marked people, of whom you were one....''

What happened to those people? They were seized by the mob then in power, jailed, tortured, and often even slaughtered to the greater glory of the God of the People, whose anonymity increased his power. For the sacrificial offerings, though rather differently interpreted, had become beloved and needed symbols to the masses of their own submissiveness. The gratifications of fear, of abuse, of being debased and dominated seized almost everybody as the new day dawned.

I was not seized. I am not a part of the masses. With considerable effort I had fought my way out of the amorphous, unsubstantial heap to which I once belonged. Thus the story of why I left Germany just in time begins with a dream in which a higher power, an unknown clock-maker, gave me a sign. Or is this just plain nonsense, nothing but bubbling glue, or a story that you tell over a glass of beer at the pub?

This was my dream:

I turn into a side street. It goes downhill, not steeply, but noticeably nevertheless, enough so you shift your weight. The street narrows and gets darker, as though shaded by a large hand or a cloud—no—it seems as though there were suddenly an elevated railway behind me; it was whizzing and roaring—of course, that's what makes the street so dark.

But when I look back, there was a clock there—there is no railroad at all. The houses, all without balconies, are at an angle. What I mean is that you can't see the sky—no moon, no stars, nothing. Well, maybe the houses are unusually high—alright. The light is cold, white with Prussian blue. Definitely cold shades, going toward green. Incidentally, it must have been raining here, or maybe the street had just been washed: it is slippery under foot. You slide a bit. Clay? Possibly a clay factory and its waste water. Actually, it's quite sticky, you can hardly lift your feet; shocking, why do the authorities permit that sort of thing?

In passing, I notice a window to the left at street level. Through the frame I notice a sort of feminine shape in a yellowish light. Her chemise is white, threaded with old-fashioned blue ribbon, I cannot see it very clearly. It is a picture without sharp lines, without contours, like an intentionally blurred oil painting. Maybe some careless person wiped his suit on it without noticing, or maybe the painter was dissatisfied with his painting. I keep on going....

God, how that clay sticks to my shoes! It takes an effort, I really have to pull to move my feet....Well, here at last is the door, one of the doors I mean, as there are several. I can count a dozen, but back there are even more. Looks like the street stops here, and ends in doors. But thank goodness they are not house doors, they are ordinary room doors that should be open anyway. I have no key. Who could have given me a key anyhow? Quite apart from the fact that I don't know anybody here and there is nobody around whom I could ask for a key except for that blurred woman.

Anyway, I do not want to behave obtrusively here, and I am actually still on the street; here is the gutter. I open the door and am in a sort of passage between two large display windows. Evidently there must have been stores here. In one of the windows, I mean behind it, there is an old woman lying in a bed, knitting an enormous stocking. Her son, or even her husband, must be a giant, eight or ten meters high. Possibly he works in the circus. But the thick wool stocking (of rabbit fur) falls apart at the bottom, where everything becomes shady and undiscernible anyhow. The stitches that she has just knitted come undone by themselves and rise transparently, like bubbles in water.

I can now also see that the room, if you can call that display window a room, seems to be damp. There are drops of water on the glass, like spectacles which have steamed up. The old woman's bed takes up the whole room. It is simply enormous. Maybe the

giant sleeps in it. There is mildew on the walls, lots of it. I now see
that even the sheets are mildewed, those spots could not be anything else, greenish and brownish spots. Of course, water is
dripping from the ceiling into an old enamel pot that I had not
noticed before. What an unhealthy place to live in! They must be
poor people, I think, and are used to that sort of thing.

Strangely enough the old lady has not noticed me yet, so I had
better go on. But suddenly I can't find the door that I came in by.
Serves me right for not paying attention, I think; so I will simply
follow my nose. Shouldn't I have looked behind me? Nonsense.
What for? This door leads out to the corridor. I read a sign: Curt
Hodapp, brush maker. Very familiar. Of course, he was a classmate
of mine in high school. How extraordinary that he should be living
here.

The door does lead to a dark corridor. So don't stand still, I say to
myself, just walk on quietly...did I open the right door? No time
for further consideration now, but why didn't I notice the doors
before? That shows what poor observers we are. The street must be
at a lower level than ordinary ones; more like a cellar. But it cannot
be the bottom either, because there must be other empty spaces
beneath me, as my steps sound so peculiarly hollow. At the end of
this narrow passage there is a little light—maybe that leads
outdoors, I think, out—right, the passage goes up a bit. A cellar,
after all.

Could those be barrels, on both sides? Could be. Possibly a wine
cellar. But then, when I think of that poor old lady down there in
her damp, mildewed bed—ugly things are so easily remembered.
No, I cannot imagine that this is a wine cellar. So those must be
buckets, large buckets that are stored here. And it is because of the
humidity that those buckets don't collapse. That's exactly it.

The main thing is to get out of here. I seem to have lost my sense
of distance, and there is a déjà vu that I cannot explain. Rather
mysterious everything, and the bad lighting contributes to that;
actually, there is no lighting at all except for that little light back
there. If only I had a flashlight! My footsteps make a lot of noise,
the stone floor and the narrow cellar corridor throw an echo.
Rather comforting, makes me feel less lonely.

There seem to be no people at all here. Maybe it is Sunday, and
they are all outside at the football game. Nevertheless, I cannot get
rid of the suspicion that I am being followed, or watched from
behind those buckets, always from the same distance...I do think
they are empty wine barrels though, simply because I like that

idea. When I am outside and get used to the light, I notice a square court paved with headstones, with long grass growing between. Anybody here? No, nobody. High walls all around, with windows and shutters, but closed from outside. Now I suddenly become aware of the stale smell. So this must be a drying-house for fish.

Could it be...No...Hold it! Right! That is Sturm's storehouse. It's Sturm's storehouse. But that is long, long ago when I was a little boy. I try to open one of the shutters, the bolt gives way,.and a fairly big, pale, yellowish dried fish falls out at me. But oogh—it's still alive! I can see it move, even though its shiny skeleton is visible through its leathery skin. Must be an optical illusion. But the stench of the fish is becoming unbearable. And it is suddenly getting warm.

Only then do I notice a spiral staircase like a lookout tower over there in the corner. A small gentleman in a black cloth suit with braid on his trousers and jacket and a bowler hat is jumping up those steps like a monkey. He keeps on waving to me. "Come along," I hear him call, "for God's sake come before the stench gets even worse...." He keeps on going higher and getting smaller, in grotesque perspective distortion, waving his white-gloved hands. More shutters are opening, and more dried fish falling out and around me, like autumn leaves, I think, though something is wrong with that comparison, like autumn leaves. They fall past me, and down on to me. Now the falling fish are brushing against my shoulders, one of them breaks apart in falling, a fishy piece of backbone sticks to my suit. More and more shutters open, and it is literally raining fish from all four corners of the yard—absurd.

Now it is getting too much even for me. The dried carcasses are up to my knees; the storehouse must have been overstocked once again. They must simply have poured the fish in from the top, quite senselessly, as into a crate, and now the shutters simply cannot stand the pressure any more. The police should be informed about that storehouse agent. I am practically wading in dried fish corpses. The smell tickles my nose, I have to sneeze, what a mess, that storehouse is. And how I must smell! Careful now.

I climb the spiral staircase, following the little man in black. Only then do I notice that the storehouse must have been buried like a sunken fortress (or how else could I be climbing up to street level?). Buried against air attacks, I tell myself, or because of the stench. No time for such questions; hardly do I raise my head above the last step when pieces of coal come flying. Oh, I think, so they are expecting me. But the reception seems a bit impolite; isn't

The White General [1922/23]

it amazing that they are throwing coal at me, I say to myself. But then it occurs to me that all this might have some double meaning. Perhaps these lumps of coal have some significance. I notice, too, that they are not actually aimed at me. Of course that disappoints me a little: doesn't that mean that I am not really so important? I get even more confused when I miss my newly bought hat. I had it on when I climbed the steps. Odd, the spiral staircase has gone too! So it must have been an elevator, not a spiral staircase—images are changing so fast—where can that damned hat be? My shoes stick to the floor like hot rubber; so soft, I can hardly move ahead.

Now what is going on? That bearded man over there, for God's sake, that really is the limit—he is throwing big lumps of coal at me! Really wild, where on earth does he get them? They come flying in a big curve, as from a sling, and the man laughs as he throws, and looks just like Lenin. Or is it Eduard Fuchs, the Daumier expert, who wrote that famous history of sexual behavior? ("You know, Daumier, Daumier, well yes, Daumier always started at the nose, ha ha, yes, he really did always start at the nose.") I was just about to call him, "Listen," I want to say, "listen, Eduard, stop that, stop throwing coal at me"—but at that moment Eduard's features change and it is no longer Fuchs but my friend Kurt Birr, and Kurt calls to me, loudly and clearly, I still hear it: "Why don't you go to America?"....

I wake up, and tell the whole dumb dream to my wife. Hardly are we at the breakfast table when a messenger brings a telegram from America! It is an invitation from the Art Students League to teach summer school at their institute in New York. Does that mean that I had a sort of premonition in that dream? Where did the voice come from? It was the first communication that I had. Was somebody warning me? Certainly not the secretary of the Art Students League, as the meaning of the story was quite unknown to her. But who?

Today I know that some power wanted to preserve me. What for, I could not say. Perhaps as a witness? Anyway, that is how I came to America.

NEW YORK IN JUNE

When I was nine, I was so enamored with Cooper's Leatherstocking that I copied *The Last of the Mohicans* in full, in my very best handwriting. A friend had lent me the book, and unfortunately I had to return it to him. But I loved those Indian stories so much that I wanted to have them for myself, to read whenever I wished, so I had to copy them. I used to sit on the balcony that was poised like a birdcage on the corner of the ugly tenement house in which we lived in Berlin. Street, coal depot and school disappeared beneath me; I was far, far away with the Indians, with noble old Chingachgook and his son and heir Uncas. I saw brave Major Hayward, the simple-minded preacher and Mabel and Cora threatened by the painted Iroquois; I had a powderhorn on my hip, a hunting knife in my belt, and a long Kentucky rifle, carefully protected against dampness, rested in my hand. That book by James Fenimore Cooper was the first piece of America that I locked in my heart.

But there was a large, rather faded photograph on the wall that I loved too. It was a mighty steamer sailing to New York; with clouds coming out of its smoke stacks, it was just passing Red Hook lighthouse. An uncle of mine had allegedly left that picture behind. I was never able to get any further information about him. When I asked, there was embarrassed silence, but I was led to believe that some uncle did sail to America on that ship. It was nice and mysterious to imagine one of those tiny dots being an uncle on his way to America.

America was still the land of freedom in the early years of the twentieth century. That was where one went if home was too restrictive, or if one wanted to evade conscription, or if one was the eleventh or thirteenth son. That was where whole groups of people went, chiefly Poles and Jews whose life was made unpleasant in Russia and who wanted to escape the constant pogroms. And then there were people with personal reasons: unhappy love, accidental shooting, ruined nobles and officers who were transported because they dishonored the family or the regiment through debts or women or duels. Any family conversation about an emigrated member immediately evoked the question "what had he done?" In some cases of course there were purely romantic reasons, or people who wanted to escape the confining, provincial circumstances of the patronizing bureaucracy to which we Germans had been subjected for centuries and still were.

The other attraction of America was "Americanism," a much used and much discussed word for an advancement in technical civilization that was permeating the world under American leadership. "Efficiency," "advertising and selling," "service," the famous "keep smiling," and the whole modern system of work in which the process is broken down into single, calculated operations, the systems of Taylor, Ford, and others, all of that came from America. American news items, reprinted in the German press, were always sensational. Whenever you read anything unbelievable, where did it happen? Always in America, the land of unlimited opportunities. Where else were there those fabulous riches? Where else could you start as a shoeshine or news boy or dishwasher no matter where you came from, and end as a multimillionaire, whether you wanted to or not? Did not even careful old Goethe pontificate from his Olympian heights, "Amerika, du hast es besser"? The wildest tales came from America. Supposedly, they had plums as big as plates, that were bred to open by themselves and spit out their pit if you pronounced a certain word. And shortly thereafter we read about a Californian gardener called Luther Burbank who allegedly developed a strain of plums that had no pits at all! What sort of a crazy country could that be where such things were possible?

From America came letters to my mother offering her a bargain membership in a universal mystic community. For a mere $12 she would have immediate happiness, success in all her plans, and, thus, wealth into ripe old age. Because, said this amazing letter,  paradise is here on earth, Master Knowles has the key to it and can thus secure admission for my mother at the ridiculously low fee ("only $12—and please send it today, so that you may start tomorrow in happiness"). It was truly an amazing country that combined commercialism, mysticism, and real technical progress.

We heard not only of the brothers Orville and Wilbur Wright, the fathers of modern aeronautics, but also of the newest fads and crazes of the USA: of teddy bears, of Billiken, the guardian spirit of drivers, and of the newest games. All of a sudden, we were all playing Diabolo; two sticks, one in each hand, had string stretched between them, on which one balanced and threw and caught a top shaped like an hour glass humming the tune of the day: "Since my old man caught the latest craze of D-I-A-B-Olo."

We gaped at American tourists who dared to go out on the street without hats. We were amazed at their clothes, those huge padded shoulders, those tapered pants, those shoes that turned in with a sort of bump at the toes. In the *Kaufhaus des Westens* one could buy imported American suits. I treated myself to one and felt quite American with my huge wide shoulders, my leather belt, and the tapered pants that got so narrow at the bottom. In the Cinepalast on the Nollendorfer Square that belonged to an Italian-American syndicate, I had my first look before the war at ragtime singers and dancers, the predecessors of today's jazz musicians.

Cocktails were beginning to get known, and every international hotel had, of course, an "American Bar" where "American drinks" were served. Six-day bike races originated, I believe, in Chicago, but soon took over the whole world, making other types of races obsolete. The better cinemas showed mostly American movies. We loved the early Vitagraph cowboy pictures; how we laughed at funny, fat John Bunny and his capers! Even though we did see a lot of French things, for instance the Pathé films with Max Linder and little Fritz Abélard, nothing was as exciting and as fitting for our juvenile imagination as the films that came from America. No wonder many of us hoped some day to see that wonderful country.

Also, almost every German family had some near or distant relative in America. How often had I heard parents say: "Oh, your grandfather's brother went over there. He wrote a few times, but then we never heard from him again." That was typical. Sometimes somebody came back, but usually only for a short visit; it was always sensational if that American appeared in a small town where everybody knew him. He would shell out too, and quickly spend whatever he had saved there and brought over in traveler's checks. All his things were admired: that brand-new trunk with all the labels, that beautiful blue suit, his patent leather shoes, his pipe and his cuff links with real stones. Then John (formerly called Hans) would take his hand out of his trouser pocket, roll some

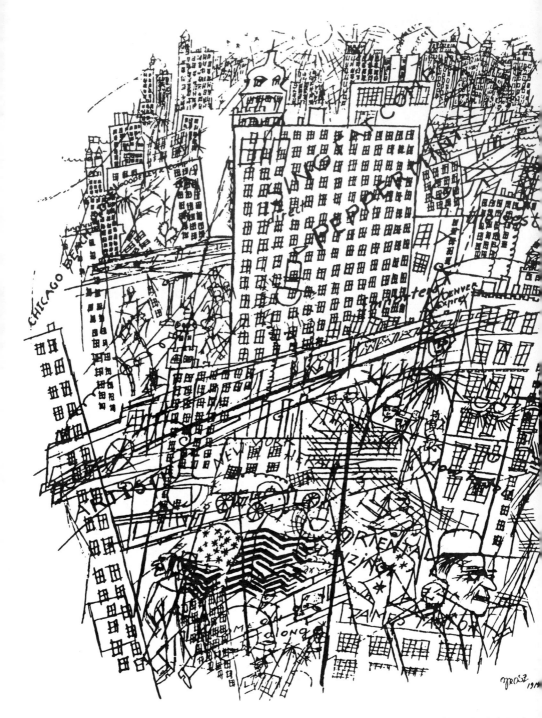

New York [1915]

coins on the counter, and (keeping his pipe in his mouth so his gold tooth was visible) would say in English, "Let's go! all hands to the bar."

Such a fairy-tale uncle was discussed for a long time after he had disappeared, and we secretly wished we could be like him.

My chance to see this beloved wish fulfilled did not come until much later, when the telegram arrived inviting me to teach a life study class in summer school at the Art Students League in New York. I thus embarked on the SS *New York* in June 1932.

◆

I stayed at the Great Northern Hotel on West 57th Street, right across from the Art Students League. The Great Northern had been recommended by my friend I.B.Neumann who knew lots of artists. He said its guests were the oldest people in the States, so the place provided the quiet atmosphere that artists need. In those early days Neumann was both my friend and my dealer. He could discuss art for hours on end with his soft, dark voice. His great enthusiasm unfortunately led him often to forget the financial side of art. After every visit I felt that I.B. should really not be a dealer but should have lots of money so that he could sponsor all those of us close to his generous heart.

I liked New York. It was exactly the way I had thought it would be. My wish had been fulfilled and I was not disappointed; that rarely happens. My classes began immediately. I had arrived in June, it was terribly hot, and I had only European suits. I perspired terribly. I literally had water running down my trouser legs and making puddles on the floor. It takes time for one's body to get used to the humid tropical heat. My late friend Max Morgenstern used to say it makes you feel like "jelly in a suit."

Prohibition was still on in 1932, so there were no public bars where one could get refreshed with a glass of cold beer. I tried the so-called "soft drinks"—you get thirsty from all that perspiration —but they did not agree with me. They made me feel as though I had swallowed bellows that pumped up my stomach from the inside like a balloon. Nor was I an ice cream eater, but I was nevertheless impressed by the variety as well as the flourish with which it was served. I enjoyed the cleanliness that I saw.

It was the depth of the American Depression. In winter you could see ladies in fur coats selling apples in the street, and many a well-dressed person stood in the soup lines. But for so many years I had seen far worse things, and recorded them, that these not very obtrusive things did not seem at all abnormal. I was much more

[OVERLEAF] GROSZ at the Art Student's League

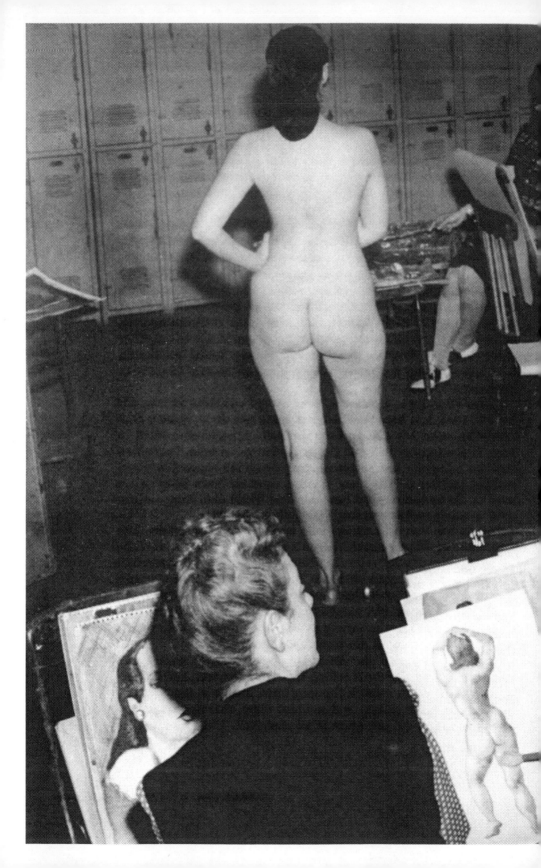

impressed by the general friendliness, even if it was commercially motivated. It was really quite a change from Germany at that time, when you saw so few happy faces and heard so much complaining and quarreling. You had the impression that Americans of all races, classes, and occupations were satisfied with the world, and actually, in spite of the Depression, their American world was still much more colorful and richer than the German. (In Germany one could only wonder what was wrong; why were German people so dissatisfied? why did they get annoyed so easily? why did they shout at each other? why did they take everything as an insult to their dignity?)

I liked New York. Perhaps New York liked me too: one has to love before one is loved in return. I did not have the common German habit of immediately comparing everything with home and criticizing it from that point of view. I lent myself to new impressions and took my time in making judgments. I tried to learn the language, and to absorb and understand what was unknown and strange.

I had a full class at the Art Students League. I had the good fortune of being the focal point of a disagreement even before I arrived. There had been a row about my appointment in which the student body was divided and the old scrapper, John Sloan, had resigned his presidency of the League in protest. The case got a lot of attention and was reported in the press. I had heard about it in Berlin but I could not really understand it from there. In any case the publicity which had fallen in my lap gave me a good start for that first New York summer, which I sweated out, not only outside my skin but inside too.

To tell the truth, I had no teaching experience whatever, had no "system," no "method," and was still pretty much at war with the English language. I did of course know the famous 300 words that are supposed to cover the basics, but sometimes there was more that I wanted to say, and then I was in trouble. I got around that by making little sketches to clarify my remarks or critiques, and thus managed to teach with great enthusiasm. The students seemed aware of that and were very nice to me. So successful was I as a budding American teacher that I thought of opening a private drawing and painting school myself.

I was less successful in my own work. (Here I must get a bit ahead of my story.) When I arrived on that memorable day in June, I had the dark feeling—a sort of premonition, I would say—that this was the turning point of my life. And it was. Quite unknown

to me, fate decided that I would become an American. Perhaps, I thought at the time, I can live in New York or elsewhere in America for a few years and go home once in a while, because, of course, one can make more money here. After all, I was not unknown. I was known as the man who had drawn *Ecce Homo* and *The Face of the Ruling Class*, as the merciless critic of German bourgeoisie and German institutions. Upon my arrival, *Time* magazine published an article with the caption "Mild Monster Arrives," and the *New Yorker* claimed that I always carried field glasses so as not to miss the smallest detail when I wanted to draw something. So why would not one magazine or the other commission something from me, or even hire me as a steady contributor?

PROVEN PROVERBS

"Mother was right, the first million is always the hardest"

Cartoon in Americana [1932]

Why not? The people who knew me here admired me as a satirist. They valued me as the artist who had drawn his fellow man for years in hateful, bitter grimaces. Almost everybody considered the period when I had been the sarcastic critic of postwar Germany as my best. For many I had almost become a legend, a leftover from the "roaring twenties." They, of course, thought I could do nothing but caricatures. Our prejudices, our limited comprehension and our ill will tend to stamp anyone with his one particular achievement, and thus I was stamped as a caricaturist.

I was soon to notice that my reputation in America was a so-called "small reputation." And hard to sell. I.B.Neumann arranged to have a one-man show for me at the Barbizon Plaza, where I shook hands with about a thousand people. It was wonderful; everyone was happy to meet me; they had heard "so much about me" ("Oh, sure!"), but unfortunately the success was in prestige rather than money, as was often true for I.B. I had no possibility at all of publishing my books. J.P.McEvoy, the well-known newspaper man I had met in Germany, was kind enough to help, but got nowhere. Occasionally, I was commissioned to do a drawing, but always told: "Not too German, Mr. Grosz. Not too bitter. You know what we mean, don't you?"

The commissions came primarily from the slick magazines for the upper ten thousand, where there was still some money. The leftist publications were out of the question for me; as everywhere in the world, that seems to be tradition among idealists, they wanted everything for nothing. God knows I had been doing that half my life; now I'd had enough of that. I had come back to the simple principles of production and money. The only person who took me as I was was my friend Alexander King, who put out America's first and only satirical magazine, *Americana*, and regularly published my things. He trimmed neither my wings nor my fingernails: "Scratch their eyes out, George," he would say to me, "the harder, the better!" Unfortunately his excellent publication perished later; but that's another story.

At that time, while I was trying so hard to give Americans what they wanted and to sell them the work of mine that they knew, I myself began to change. It is hard to describe how it happened. The way I feel about it is that the artist in me became predominant. In any case, I suddenly became disgusted with all those satirical distortions. Those years of clowning took their revenge. For smaller commissions I had to force myself, and managed to do

things of that sort, as my brain could command my hand. But I could not command my heart, and that simply was not with it. Art is not like shoveling coal. I was simply no longer interested in people as individuals with funny quirks. Were they not as alike as one egg to another? That was how far I had moved.

But as people receded, landscape and nature moved closer and closer. I saw trees and bushes more accurately, grass and leaves, and also flies, turtles and ants. There came a time when my landscapes became lonely and devoid of people. Was that a good or a bad sign for my development? I know today that it was good. It was not an escape, not a flight; it was an approach, a penetration. As for my dear fellow man—had I not expressed my feelings on thousands of pages?

So the second part of my life was in America, and began with an inner conflict with my own past, a past that I still reject today to some degree. More than ever I relegate caricature to a minor position in art; I believe that the times when it predominates are times of decay. Surely life and death are big subjects, not subjects for sarcasm and cheap jokes.

Such inner conflicts, however, are not exactly income producing. When I first came to America I was still willing to exploit my "illustrative" talents, but except for ridiculously small, poorly paid commissions, there was unfortunately nobody who had any use for my talents.

As things and people become increasingly remote, other, new worlds suddenly open up. Nature came closer to me in all its simplicity, unity and beauty, but also in the inexorable lawfulness of its elements. I could wander for hours over the dunes of Cape Cod, and humbly try to reproduce my feelings about nature as well as I could, neither adding nor omitting anything. Large, idealistic words and phrases fell away like deadwood. I wanted to be a free artist, and that is what I believe I have been ever since.

Terrors still live in me, but no longer are they visions, dreams or caricatures. They are neither invented nor contrived to help educate mankind. They are made of apocalyptic stuff and reveal the dualism of the world from its other side, not the blossoming side, but rather that of murder, arson, terror and death. I believe that I feel a good bit of old German tradition in myself. It is that tradition that makes me always see the dichotomy, life and death, so I can no longer literally and optimistically only exclaim: "Life! Life! Life!"

It was in October 1932 that I returned from that first visit to America. Though the summer months had been very hard, unspeakably hot and particularly unpleasant for me in that overcrowded oven-of-a-studio, despite these and other handicaps I liked America very much, especially that enchanted, magnificent New York. Some things I overlooked, or did not even see. My romantic inclinations helped my practical adaptability, and I decided to come back and live in America for a few years. The Art Students League renewed my contract; the salary was not great, but would perhaps cover the rent. And whatever I needed to live on —well, we would see. First let's be over there. There was always my ability to illustrate books or, if needed, the idea of a school.

I had taken Dennis McEvoy, the son of my newspaper friend, back to Germany with me; there were some famous, very progressive schools there at that time where he was to complete his knowledge of German. We landed in Bremen. It appeared to us, small and toylike, with houses as low as huts. But the wine and

small and toylike, with houses as low as huts. But the wine and food at the Ratskeller were very German and cozy. My wife had come to meet me at Bremerhaven, and I told her right away on the gangplank that I had only come to go back immediately. My decision was definite; right after Christmas I would take her and the children to America. There was no time to lose, and we had to prepare for the impending change immediately, both within and without.

I was like a boy of fourteen. My face glowed with wine and enthusiasm. I told story after story about the wonders of the new world, how we would make our fortune there and, of course, get rich too. I lied my head off; or, let's say, half the time, because I probably believed half of what I was saying myself. Don't you always have to exaggerate a bit if you want to make an impression?

In Berlin we started immediately to prepare for emigration. We had a big apartment in the Trautenauerstrasse, and I had my studio round the corner in the Nassaustrasse. We had a lot of beautiful antique furniture and the studio was full of all sorts of junk in addition to my pictures, my folders full of drawings and collected material; whole furniture vans full. After all these years of living in the same place it was a question of packing for overseas, giving away, or throwing away. Liquidating an apartment in which you have lived for so long is very peculiar; it is something like destroying a snail shell. Today somebody comes to get one piece of furniture, tomorrow another. Slowly it crumbles to pieces. Here I was with screwdriver in hand, ready to take down the chandelier. Our friend Pauli was watching, he was to get it as a memento. What could one do with a chandelier in New York?

Well, it was not really only the sentimental attachment to an apartment; fundamentally, it was my fear about my own daring. Suddenly, while I was standing on that ladder and working on the chandelier, the whole ceiling fell in—figuratively speaking. I suddenly realized that I, the braggart, had painted all my accounts from abroad in much too silvery, rosy colors. I was overcome by cold fright. The screwdriver fell out of my hand. Through the open door I heard my wife tell our friends about the wonders of New York and my alleged success.

Suddenly I was quite sobered. The rosy picture had gone. I saw New York in the rain, grey, with slippery streets. I saw ragged men lining up by a truck for hot coffee and rolls. One of them pointed at me, spat, and laughed sarcastically: "Haha, sure, wanted to conquer New York, you're a bit late, my friend, hahaha"—and in horror I saw that this was me myself, only much older, unshaven, with whitish-grey hair hanging over the greasy collar of my overcoat....

The old Venetian mirrors were still hanging. I got off the ladder and looked at myself; no, I was still looking all right, even had red cheeks, and was shaved. So let's not be discouraged! I climbed up to the chandelier again, and repeated to myself, in English and like a formula, "Never say die, never say die, never say die...."

I almost screamed that this was nonsense—nonsense, this whole idea of America—let it be, call it off. Leave the furniture where it is, leave the chandelier! We were dreaming, Eva, this was wishful thinking; what would we be doing in America? Do they have what we call culture? Who is even interested in art? Don't you see, you silly romanticist? Success and money, that's what matters. And those $150 that you're getting are the only reality; they are real, but a rather slim reality. How far will they go? Rent, erasers and tobacco for your pipe, that's all, George. Stay in the land of your fathers. There is a Hebraic saying: Seven years away, and the dog barks no longer. And you will have to serve for seven long years, for the seven lean years come first, and only then, only then the seven fat ones.

All this went through my weary head. I had bragged, I had exaggerated, and now in the grey reality of those Berlin November days I got the shakes. Eva was always asking me: "What is it going to be like? How are we going to live? Of course it would be nice to come over for a while, it would be new and certainly very interesting, but can we live there the way we do here? Just figure: there are four of us, we two, and Martin and Peter. How far will $150 go?"

Eva was very skeptical. She came from a practical family and was a realist herself, as was her grandmother before her. In her family there were miners and topographers, but no basket makers; nor had she read Cooper's *Leatherstocking Tales*. I had answered all her unpleasant questions with rose-colored lies. I would do illustrations, I said, and the school would be a great success— everybody over there said so—"everybody" being unfortunately only my rather unreliable friend I. B. But I told her neither that nor about my lack of success with illustration, nor about the little interest shown by publishers in my work, regardless of all "recommendations" and "connections." Even though dear J. P. McEvoy had gone from one publisher to another with me, the results amounted to nothing but pure courtesy and mutual compliments.

I knew that we would not readily be able to continue living as we'd been accustomed. In Berlin I had become known, I had made a name for myself. And not only in Berlin; I had some degree of fame in Europe, if I may say so. And in the past few years I had made some money, too. Publishers gave me work and I could do it in my own style. I had arrived. And I was now throwing all that away, for a mere chimera. I was aware that in America I would merely be one of the many. The competition was tough, and there would be no sitting back in comfort.

Nevertheless, something was driving me hence. I was being washed away like a piece of wood by a yet unknown subterranean stream. Of course, I was not innocent, and knew how things were going in Germany. I saw the cracks in the floor, and noticed that this or that wall was starting to wobble. I observed my cigar man was overnight wearing a swastika in the same buttonhole where there always used to be a red enamel hammer-and-sickle. (Perhaps he had simply twisted the sickle and the hammer into a swastika...)

It was like the first night of a famous play, or the start of a battle. People sort of cleared their throats and nervously watched the time because the papers were announcing daily that it was just before high noon. Just what would happen after noon was only hinted, but it was nothing elevating, nothing pleasant for me and my close friends. At that time I was still interested in politics, but my faith in the masses had become shaky—that is, to be honest, my faith in the "mission" of my art. I had gradually realized that this sort of propaganda was greatly overrated, that the agitators simply mistook the effect of the agitation on themselves for the effect on their beloved proletarian masses, and that the leaders with all their lovely slogans considered those masses as nothing but a herd of sheep with themselves as bellwethers, up front. My sobering happened slowly but surely, and had a lot to do with my wanting to leave Germany. And I did, after all, remain to a large extent a clear, individual artist who wanted to go his own way.

I was not very happy during those last months in Germany. I wanted out. I wanted to start a new life in a new place. Fear and insecurity blew away. It will work somehow, I thought, it will work somehow.

Then there were another few weeks of packing, of saying good-bye to my old, familiar studio where I had worked since 1918. Eva and I had decided to go alone first and leave the children—Martin was three, Peter five—with an aunt in Berlin. We would get things set first and see how they went, and then Eva could come and fetch both of them in summer. I still see that last day: the lamp over the large table at Aunt Lisbeth's alight, and I painted some funny pictures for the boys. Soon they will be sitting at an American table, I thought. Those boys are all right. I looked back once, across the Tempelhofer Field and down the Belle-Alliance Street; thought of those huge parades, with the fine uniforms, and the lonely tree where the Emperor had always halted. Eva was crying quietly. "See you soon," we said. But deep down inside I had the feeling as though I was seeing it all for the last time.

We embarked on January 12 on the SS *Stuttgart* of the North German Lloyd in Bremerhaven, and arrived in New York on the 23rd. The passage was rather stormy, but we were both good sailors and watched the raging ocean from the deck cabin.

On January 30 Hitler became Chancellor of Germany. Not only did the "proletarian masses" not protest, but ran in droves to the winner. I could never quite understand the collapse of the earthen

"red colossus," even though I did already have the feeling (not shared by many) of Hitler's total and long-lasting victory.

Then came the news of the Reichstag fire, which threw an awful light on everything. At that point I saw that Providence had wanted to save me. And in the little Hotel Cambridge in a New York side street, I thanked my God quietly for having so carefully guarded and guided me. Soon there were letters reporting searches for me both at my empty Berlin apartment and my studio. I have reason to believe that I would not be alive, had they found me there.

I immediately put in for my first immigration papers to the United States, and resumed my time-consuming job at the Art Students League. At night I would still sit and draw or do watercolors; I did not work in oils until much later. I loved New York and my new environment as much as ever. Every so often Eva got terribly homesick and I would try to comfort her as well as I could. We had moved out of the Cambridge to the somewhat larger Hotel Raleigh, where the express trains of the old elevated would roar by our room in the early morning: "Like the ocean," I would say, "wonderful!" We saw the neon lights of an undertaker's parlor from our window, but it did not remind me of death. I preferred the window of Isaac Gellis's Jewish restaurant where one could eat as much as one could manage. His sour pickles were particularly memorable.

Eventually even the worst horror stories paled, as had the exciting painted canvases in the booths of my childhood country fairs in Stolp. Furthermore, it was not only in Germany that there were concentration camps in the thirties, and deaths accelerated by governments. Seen from America, half of Europe seemed to have regressed to those same hellish conditions painted by Bosch, or by Breughel in his *Victory of Death*, at the very end of the nightmares of the medieval world. Had the world always been that way? Were the almost fifty years of European peace into which I happened to be born a mere illusion?

Germany—that was now a mere memory. Yet sometimes the horror came back again, and all the terrible things emerged from the bloody closet room to which I had relegated them. Then those memories streamed through my pictures: men wading through swamps and bloody fog, bones rattling, flesh wasting away, chasms that were flat and long and eternal and never ended; and the men trotting like ghosts in the crackling, blazing, smoldering glare of the burned cottages and poisoned earth, without hope or goal.

CITIZEN PAPER
PHOTOS

CROSS THE STREET

APPLICATIONS
FILLED OUT

CITIZEN BOOKS
FOR SALE

NOTARY ✹ PUBLIC

ON BECOMING AMERICAN

Once I had settled in the States for good and decided never to go back to my former home, I wanted to discard my "German" personality along with my citizenship, the way one would discard a worn-out suit. I was so bitter that I decided to forget who and what I had been and leave everything behind me. In other words, start a new American life.

I was just forty when I turned my back on Germany, not too old to acclimate, to fit correctly into American life. I did not want to be like some of my compatriots who were almost proud of their inability to adjust. After those mad, wild years in Germany, America seemed very normal to me, and that was exactly how normal I wanted to be.

I was severe with myself. I wanted to totally assimilate; I repressed everything in me that seemed too Grosz-like, too original, too Teutonic. Not only did I discard my European imagination, but in due course even my pride as an artist. I often had the feeling that I was really not an artist at all but merely an artisan, by which I meant no class distinction but simply normalcy: conscious absence of the anarchy, nihilism, "being different," so treasured by experts and snobs.

I found the attitude of the "voluntary exiles" repulsive, the ones that came here of their own free will, in contrast to the later "refugees." Their constant vague and pseudo-sophisticated talk of European culture and American nonculture seemed exaggerated, merely proof that these people neither wanted to, nor could, fit in. If they had been more successful in America, they would undoubtedly have talked differently. They made the mistake of setting themselves up as the standard; from the fact that their poems were not published in America, their plays not produced or their pictures rarely sold, they drew the conclusion that the country lacked culture.

My attitude was quite different. First, "Be humble," I told myself. "Make yourself small—no, smaller, smaller yet—wipe yourself out. Be like blotting paper, absorb everything useful, and admire. Let yourself be shocked at the hardness of the showy competition, be blinded by the surplus of talent. You are at a gigantic fair; make your booth as attractive as you can...."

Hurt nobody, please everybody—that became my motto. It is not so difficult to assimilate, once you have overcome the highly over-rated superstition of "character." We usually say a person has "character" when he is quite inflexible; a person who wants to get ahead and make money should preferably have no character at all.

The second rule, if you want to adapt, is to like everything. Everything, including things that are really not nice. The better you take this old Chinese wisdom to heart, the better you will adapt. One fine day you will notice that you actually do like every-thing—and look! after a few years of steady lying, the lies have become truth...(For life—I can testify from my own experience—is really much better if you say yes, than if you say no!)

I soon had the pleasant feeling that I was progressing in my adaptation. I developed the philosophy of a gambler at a roulette table; I lost my European arrogance, or rather I traded it for what I thought was American superiority. I got spells of hostility toward art. I tried to bend my talent into a sort of wishing rod with which to detect money. I came to the conclusion that power and success are the only purpose of life and everything else is more or less idle decoration. From that necessarily followed my admiration of great, pragmatic normalcy, my esteem for high paychecks and my respect of the big earners among American illustrators.

I fell in love with their meticulousness, their photographic like-ness, and became suspicious of any artistic explanation. I came to believe that imitation had always been the only purpose of art from the very beginning; it was as though artists had only been waiting for the invention of photography, as though the very first Stone Age painter would have preferred to use a Kodak instead of his stone pestle, had that been possible. All contemporary art, including my attempts with pen, brush and colors, seemed of dubious value. Elaborate phrases of explanation could hardly touch me, let alone pacify me. I was split down the middle, pulled back and forth between imagination and reality, between my marvelous secret fantasies and the simple, wonderful richness of a branch full of leaves.

When I behold the inventiveness of the reality that surrounds us—the agony of a dying leaf about to fall, the peculiar folds of a napkin thrown on the table, the cool and warm tones of a shell, the effect of wind on dune grass, all those rhythms and counter-rhythms—oh! how small and limited are the forms we humans can invent. How many artificial flowers has anyone been able to invent? None from pure nothing, and no more than three or four from unconscious memory. In nature, however, new discoveries and surprises abound. Endless and never dull, nature's forms are repeated by the million, alike and yet subtly different in every little shape, as best illustrated in Altdorfer's pictures.

At that time something remarkable happened. The more "American" I thought, the better I painted. I cannot explain that phenomenon even today, but my oils became richer, my colors and textures better, my modeling more plastic. On the surface I became increasingly cynical and occasionally had real fits of fury against art and artists. Both, including myself, seemed completely super-fluous, and I would have liked best to change my vocation. Those fits would, of course, always come when I was not selling; and that would often be for months at a time.

I lived by my wits, as Americans say; that is, I put my wits into my teaching. My drawing talent was occasionally politely admired, but this ability which had made my reputation was no way to make money. I seriously considered myself a failure. Since I no longer was interested in "inner wealth," my realistic interest was, "How much do you make per week?" So I was a failure.

I was waiting for a break like a gambler or a lottery player. I had nothing of the wandering minstrel and artist left, but a vague, romantic hope: "Just wait, my boy, be patient and humble, risk one more bet—just wait, one day you will have a comeback and be on top again!" Between times, however, I saw myself as an old, decrepit man sitting on the steps of a flophouse in downtown New York, sucking on a cigar butt, while a passer-by said: "See that character? He once drew *Ecce Homo....*"

I would have given anything to become an American illustrator, one of the chosen ones who do the pictures for short stories in popular magazines. When I was a beginner, and later in my crazy Dada or cubist days, I would sneak a look at those illustrations that stayed close to nature. They were truly something for the masses. Everybody could understand them; no explanations from grandilo-quent art historians were needed. It was folk art in modern clothing, with wide distribution. And the best thing about these full-color or half-tone illustrations was their absolute normalcy.

Certainly it was hackneyed, certainly it was glossy; it was this very sugary prettiness that appealed to me. I preferred it to the sour, pretentious experiments in unnatural form and color. The ideals of the American middle class were secretly closer to me than the partly mad, partly pseudo-mad special world in which the arrogant greats of the avant-garde lived and wanted to live. Unfortunately I myself was merely one of those puffed up frogs instead of a normal illustrator, and my drawings were caricatures of a slanted, crooked world, seen and interpreted from the pseudo-scientific viewpoint of Marxism and Freudianism. That stuff, I felt, belonged to the past; and had the Germans not burnt it, I myself might have heaped it up and put a match to it.

This neat American normality really attracted me. I took the embellishment and sentimentalization of our earthly life (since I had to have an explanation) as a sort of masked Hellenism. It was the world of the "little man" that was being idealized. The Gods had descended from Olympus and were walking around in tweeds during the day and in tuxedos at night. The high points were in expensive nightclubs, to the accompaniment of swing bands. Even the ads were powdered with this Greek sugar. Actually, these large, profusely illustrated magazines were simply picture books and fairy tales; they were the wish dreams of small, ugly mortal beings with bad digestion, heart trouble, cancer of the liver, incurable alcoholism, broken marriages and secret abortions. Not bad at all, those dreams, all freshly laundered, dry cleaned in fact, and beautifully wrapped.

We tried to imitate all that in Germany, but we never managed the real glamor and elegance. *Die Dame* and *die neue linie* (the latter, an imitation of *Esquire*) seemed somehow clumsier. Nor were our illustrators as good as the Americans. We had no Charles Dana Gibson, Dean Cornwall, Norman Rockwell, Harold von Schmitt or the first-rate Floyd Davis; not to mention fashion artists like Goodman, Fellows or the excellent Eric. Those American magazines were, of course, just large catalogues, with a few stories inserted between the ads; there was much to be said against them. But when you looked at them abroad, did they not seem like a breath of fresh air? A very attractive advertisement for a clean, appetizing, super-modern country where everything was fresh and friendly and smiling in contrast to sour-faced Europe. Of course I knew that this neat middle-class world existed only in the imagination of the ladies and gentlemen who were peddling the machine-made merchandise, but I preferred fiction to truth. I secretly longed for the fairyland of those pictures as I did for a fresh, clean-shaven, smiling dream.

I would really have loved to become a typically superficial American illustrator, a simple, obedient soul, who faithfully depicted his given subject and worried lest there be one button too many or one hair missing, in anticipation of his readers' mail. There were other types of illustrators too: nervous wrecks, influenced by ruins like Lautrec and that desperate Pascin, who were used by the more elegant fashion magazines. Next to Dürer, Menzel and Doré, their drawings looked like tired fly tracks dragged across the paper—fascinating, but completely morbid. Those are not the people I speak of, they were outside the mainstream and affected only the feeble and incompetent. What I wanted to become was an illustrator for the public at large. Even when I was a boy, had I not admired the deceptive likeness of Grützner's monks or the dashing hussars riding across the walls of the casino at Stolp? Had I not always loved our great Menzel who never misdrew a line, a popular illustrator to whom modern arbitrariness (often the result of ineptitude) was quite strange? He was completely normal and yet a great artist.

As an illustrator you had to master many shapes and be able to draw with great accuracy; the camera was a sharp-sighted competitor. I bought books about American illustration and got myself a triple mirror at Macy's in case I needed a model and did not happen to have one handy, so I could model for myself. Then I began to collect clippings. I clipped everything that I thought could ever come in handy and put it in a "morgue," as the press people call it (and according to my books, the illustrators too). As I am a collector by nature, folders and cardboard boxes filled quickly with clippings: costumes, operations, ships, animals, soldiers, floods, kitchen tables, faces, exotic trees, foreign landscapes, magnified materials, folds in wind, fluttering flags, flowers, beetles. A whole morphology and a chaotic world of shapes got heaped in my morgue.

I clipped and clipped, and every time I clipped I thought this was the exact picture I would need. At first I devised a method of arranging things. In one folder there would be "animals, tame," in the next "animals, wild." Here were "trees in landscape," there however "landscape with trees." I clipped and clipped. The folders swelled, the cartons flowed over, but the daily stream that poured out of newspapers and magazines could not be dammed. Whenever

I missed clipping a picture I was sure I had missed something of great importance—that very day I would get a commission for which this cowboy outfit....

Of course that commission came neither that day nor the next. It really was devilish: when I actually did have something of that sort to illustrate, I could not lay my hands on that particular clipping. My morgue was only vaguely organized and had gradually outgrown me. Somewhat pedantic as I was—not very pedantic, only a little—I had my troubles with titles. Where to put that wonderful tame lion? With the wild animals of course, or in Africa —no, wait a minute, he came neither from Africa nor a zoo, he was from some circus. So let's put him under circus. Anyway, he can be cross-referenced under four headings. Excellent, I tell myself, and let's leave that nice lion picture on top, for the moment, until I straighten it out. On the next rainy Sunday evening I'll look the whole thing over....

In the meantime I had a few drawings to do for *Esquire*, among others the interior of a laundry. I knew that I had recently cut something like that out of a catalogue, and spent the whole afternoon looking for the clipping. As usual, it had simply disappeared. So I had to do the drawing without any model, relying on dim memory. It looked right anyhow; I faked what I didn't know with lines and dots. Of course I would have preferred to be exact, but the damn clipping was simply gone.

Long after I had delivered the drawing and was thumbing through my beloved morgue, the laundry clipping was right on top. It did not surprise me in the least. That was the way it always went. But I gradually got tired of the constant search and the constant mislaying and the constant never-finding. Some of the clippings I had neatly pasted into scrap books but those, of course, were the ones I never needed. There was obviously a humorous but irritating hobgoblin at work here who arranged things so that you could never find the picture you were looking for. Crazy.

At that point I thought of my old friend Wieland. Hadn't he run a large publishing house? And been a master of organization. And of double-entry bookkeeping. And known everything about the newest filing systems. So I presented him with my troubles, and told him how neatly I had collected and clipped everything, but had not had the strength to arrange the collection that was going into the tens of thousands. Could he please at least teach me the first rudiments of filing?

Wieland opined that it was very simple to put such disorder into order. He had often done it for his publishing house and besides, he enjoyed it. We would of course need some material. I must order colored filing cards—he knew an inexpensive place—and then he explained how the whole collection must first be divided into different sections. "Something like this: inanimate things, let's say, pale blue or green; living things, red—" "O.K.," I said, "great." "So you immediately find your way. Red and green—if you should need an umbrella, you start out with the green box."

"Excellent," I said dutifully, "just what I've always wanted."

"Clarity and simplicity are my first principles. You see," he added, "when we get everything arranged under the large divisions, red, green and blue, then we make subdivisions, say, yellow, lilac, and white. So when you are looking for your umbrella and have the general green section 'dead things' before you, you proceed immediately to one of the subsections—perhaps pale green for old dead things, pale brown for modern dead things, and so on. And then I'll cross-index and double-index everything for you, so that you can look under weather—yellow file—or under rain—pale blue: nature and natural phenomena—or you just get to rain by way of water, and thereby to your umbrella. Even if you had forgotten your original cue—that umbrella—by this time, you are bound to hit upon an umbrella."

I had always been in favor of clarity and simplicity, and now I saw how simple a filing system really could be if it was properly organized. My head was swimming. Living things pale blue, dead things red. Look for umbrella under dead things, green file; subdivision: water, see natural phenomena, or see brown file for waterfall and cloud burst. Wonderful.

I got some large paper shears, two bottles of glue, black ink, and a heavy pen. Wieland sat for days at a long, improvised table in the living room of the small house that we had rented. The room was soon knee-deep in clippings. He cut and arranged every one of my clippings according to a system that he seemed to understand. It was a pleasure to watch how order came out of my mess.

In the meanwhile I was doing a few drawings for Ben Hecht. They were only margin drawings, but I still wanted to be accurate, and unfortunately I needed the picture of an old telephone that I knew for certain I had clipped from an article about Bell. So Wieland and I began to search. The clipping was not among the four thousand that he had already worked over. Once that fact was established, we sat down and rewarded ourselves with a few glasses of California wine. And gave up the search for that evening.

We did not go on looking the next day because we had to wait for the colored cards by which we would recognize the various sections. At last I would be able to find things, I thought. Wonderful, the way Wieland has it organized! It had already taken a few weeks by now for sure, but then it was a hellish job. Besides, this was July, and it was hot.

At last one morning the delivery wagon stopped in front of the house. There they were, the colored boxes, in five large, weighty packages. Paper is very heavy. Wieland and I both had to help to get them into the house. I was still finishing the solid shelves in my shop while Wieland carefully filled the containers with the four thousand organized clippings.

Whatever happened to the six thousand that had not been processed? I don't remember any more.

So here it all was in fine order, pasted up and labeled. The morgue was done, was perfect, and to this very day those pretty colored files are there, in the corner of my studio. Since the great reorganization I have never once touched it. Maybe my son will one day be an American illustrator; he can then use my clippings; unless they turn out to be a bit antiquated by then.

Amazingly I was never able to achieve the simplicity and normalcy of American illustration that I so admired. Paint seemed to melt somehow, especially when I used watercolors. The color flowed over the edges; faces got to look older and uglier than I intended. How I would have loved to bring neat, nice, and normal into my repertoire! I would often contemplate Raphael; true, he too had invented and exaggerated, but everything looked natural and could be understood by everybody, as in all "healthy" art. My disobedient spirit did not elevate me at all. I loved the mediocre, the widely understood language, but to my distress, I was unable quite to master it.

As early as 1933 Clifton Fadiman would say to me, "George, why for God's sake don't you work for *The New Yorker!*" "I'd love to," I would reply, "of course. Sure."

Fadiman was at that time not yet the pope of literature and the radio star that he later became, but he reviewed books for *The New Yorker.* He promised to speak to people; he was sure that my things were for that magazine; but of course—and he'd let me know. As is the rule in such cases, I never heard a word again. So that was not my place.

Esquire, a handsome magazine for college boys and bachelors, hired me later to do postage stamps. I mean this only in the pictorial sense, because my large drawings were reduced to the size of stamps to be reproduced as "spots" in the text. So I did become an American illustrator, but was not permitted the large, pretty, sweet, attractive pictures of my desire. But it was a good job anyway. I would get three or four short stories at a time, and allowed enough time; it did not pay much, but I had the luck to win a two-year Guggenheim fellowship, so I was free of immediate worry.

I was even able to move to a larger house and devote myself to my beloved oil painting again. After so many years, the colors had dried out and the camelhair brushes had been devoured by moths. On and off I still did some drawings for Frank Crowninshield's *Vanity Fair.* Or Mr. Brodovitch would give me one of the more hair-raising stories to illustrate for *Harper's Bazaar,* as I was reputed to be an expert in morbid and gruesome things. It was allegedly my "Teutonic" heritage that made me so good at depicting everything connected with death and skeletons.

My best commission—from George Macy, the publisher of Limited Editions—was illustrations for O. Henry's selected short stories: I did many full-page watercolors. I still look at those pictures and that whole beautifully made book with pleasure. I drew *Interregnum* for Caresse Crosby and her famous Black Sun Press, a sixty-page album of political and partly prophetic carica-tures at a time when Hitler was still considered a fairly local, harmless, transient problem. These two assignments, though they paid well, got practically no attention; today they may be collectors' items.

Soon my activity as an American illustrator ceased completely. *Esquire* dismissed me after two years; I was no longer needed. Those magazines operate almost like a fashion house, always needing and consuming new things or reconstructing old ones. Besides, there were a lot of young people ready to step into my shoes and do similar work for even less.

I have never been able to understand why I was not able to bend my talent toward illustration, this branch of art that I so admired (though scorned by other painters). I, who had started as an Amer-ican-type illustrator; who admired our Fritz Koch-Gotha and Hermann Vogel-Plauen; who once believed I could compete for the coveted Menzel Prize for young German illustrators. You can never tell what cards you will be dealt at the gaming table! I admit that my European development, my vocation as a German satirist could not—despite all my attempts at acclimatization—be wiped out and

The Spirit of the Century [1931/32]

bent back to the artistic leaning of my youth. I tried hard to emulate the great Walt Whitman who once wrote:

Do I contradict myself?
Very well then I contradict myself.
(I am large, I contain multitudes)"

That was my example. I had daily practice in self-abnegation, said "Yes" to everything, and gradually acquired the reputation of a positive, happy, laughing, contented optimist. And nevertheless there remained something immutable, something of myself—I do want to assimilate!—something schizoid and damned that lies inside me like a heavy, immovable weight of stone.

MAKING GOOD IN AMERICA

As I have said, in America I started all over again. I started with illustration, then I tried all sorts of things. That is the subject of this tale. I have changed it a bit because some of the people who figure in it are still alive; but if not exactly the plain truth, the story can be taken symbolically. I call it *The Story of the De Vilbiss Spray*, or, *How to Make Good in America*.

A long time ago, there were two families in southern Germany. One had been there a long time, and was very rich. The other had also been there a long time, and was poorer—not very poor, but not rich either, the way things are in this world. Both families had children, and one summer day the son of the rich family went to swim in the nearby river. By chance the son of the poorer family had also come to swim, so they met and both went into the cool water.

The water, however, was swift and treacherous in spots. There were nymphs and whirlpools that could pull a swimmer down into the depths. The very day when the rich boy and the poorer one went swimming, a cry suddenly came from the middle of the river: "Help! help! help, I'm drowning!"

The gurgling sound reached the ears of the rich boy who was basking in the sun after his swim. Experienced, intrepid swimmer that he was, he dove in headfirst, grabbed the drowning boy and pulled him out of the whirlpool. Only then did he notice that it had been the poor boy who had so agonizedly called for help. Cradling him in his arms, he swam on his back and pulled him to shore. There he bedded him on the soft moss, stood him on his head till the nasty water poured out of him, bent his arms back—in short, he revived him.

After a while the poor boy opened his eyes. Though the boys went to the same school, they hardly knew each other. The poor one seized the rich one's hand and squeezing it softly (he was still quite weak) whispered: "Victor, dear Victor...from the bottom of my heart I thank you for saving my life...dear Victor, I have nothing but words to give you now; but if I can possibly ever do you a favor, I'll do it."

"Alright," said Victor, "it's alright, Karl." Victor did not like to be thanked. What he had done was simply human duty, it did not call for gratitude. And that is where our story begins.

Years and decades passed. The war brought horror and misery to people, and then there was peace again. Victor had become a famous doctor in the large capital city and important people, even princes and princesses, came to him for advice.

And Carl? Well, Carl had emigrated over the seas to distant America and had never been heard of again. Only when the war was over and people dared look at the sky and stars again without fear of explosives falling on their heads, did Carl come back. Carl, poor little Carl, had become rich—allegedly even richer than Victor! He arrived with many brightly labeled trunks, some of them as big as houses. He came with an elegant entourage including princes and beautiful princesses, only that they were not born to titles like Victor's patients, but rather movie princesses and dollar princes. Carl brought many servants too, and a pack of trained dogs and colorfully feathered parrots who could repeat anything that Uncle Carl said to them. All of them rode in huge, brand-new, gilded cars.

The mayor received them at the city gate, of which only half was left; the other half had been blasted away in an air attack. To welcome Uncle Carl, the mayor presented him the key to the city (gold-plated in a hurry) because he was a shrewd man and needed money for the impoverished place. Uncle Carl had lots of money. A banquet was quickly set up and he gave the mayor a big bag full of beautiful gold pieces to build a new city hall and a brand new swimming pool.

Uncle Carl had brought along a poet to tell the story—in many verses, accompanied by a harp—of how this poor boy had become so immensely rich. He had started out by selling shoelaces; a few pairs at first, then many pairs, until he finally owned all the shoelaces in the whole country; at which point of course he no longer sold them personally, but merely stood by a huge cash register that automatically recorded the daily intake. Gradually, so the poet sang, all the metal rings through which the laces were threaded came to belong to him; then the shoes; finally all the leather for all the shoes. By that time Uncle Carl was richer than rich, but even that was not enough for his ambitions, as he wanted to go up in the world....

One day, in the big city of Chicago, called the windy city, where all the canned meat comes from, he stepped into a passageway and noticed people having fun looking into a peep-hole machine and

turning a handle at the side. As Uncle Carl had the mysterious ability to acquire anything that he wanted, all those machines soon were his, along with their many rolls of pictures that the handles turned. That machine with moving pictures was then further developed; it amused Uncle Carl, and as everything that amused Uncle Carl would turn into money, it was not long before he turned into a powerful movie magnate.

(I will have to change my style in the second part of this story, as I personally come into it....)

Years passed again, and it so happened that Victor and I and Uncle Carl also were in New York. Victor in the meanwhile had become my brother-in-law. He too had left Germany because a former corporal was in power there who not only set his hordes at people who did not obey, but also divided the population according to the shape of their skulls. Some skulls got a bad deal and therefore tried to emigrate before the law was applied to them.

There was nothing of that sort yet in America. It was still a free country. But though it was free, it was often difficult to make the money that enables one to fully enjoy that freedom. There were at that time many more people who wanted to work than there was work, particularly in my field; as an artist, I was producing something that was pure luxury. But I had to live too! Teaching was fine, but unfortunately badly paid. My wife and children were still in Germany. I needed money for their passage and their first few weeks here. But I was making only just enough to live on, and things were going just as they did for Tantalus in Greek mythology: golden fruits were within reach, I would put out my hand—and away they went....

America is not a country where you give up, so I didn't. I kept on looking for my golden opportunity. While worrying and figuring where I could possibly fit in, I finally had an idea. I used to do quite a lot of stage design. Maybe that talent could be put to use? As I wanted to make money, I immediately thought of Hollywood.

Sure, that was it. There was my hidden treasure; all I needed to do was to go and get it. Wonderful idea! But—there was a BUT: how do I get the right introductions? Obviously I could not just set forth with my portfolio under my arm, knock at the studio door and say: "Good morning, Sir, don't you need a first-rate stage designer?" That would not get me very far, I would in fact not even get as far as the door. You have to know somebody to get in, I mean the right somebody. Mere letters of recommendation would not be

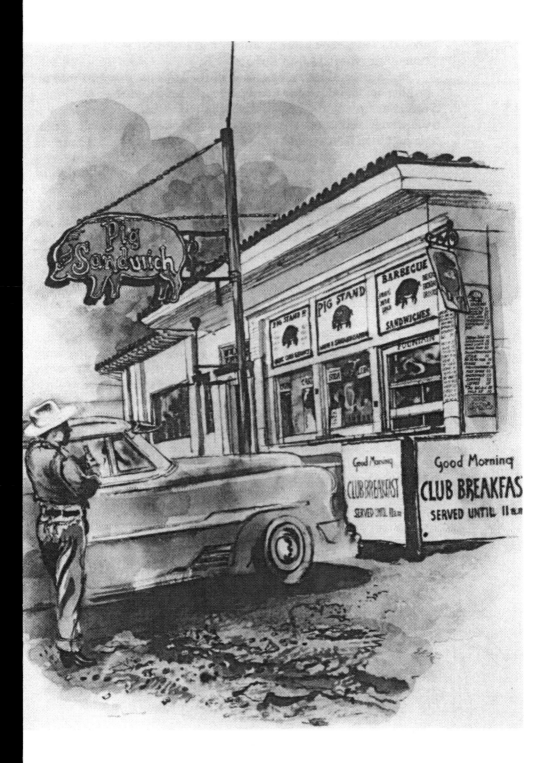

enough; for a good weekly salary, I would need the best connections. But where to find them?

Over dinner on the roof garden of the Hotel Madison, I told my brother-in-law of my worries and my plans, and that everything would be fine if only I had the right introduction to someone big in the movie industry. Victor thought a while, refilled our glasses with chilled Rhine wine and said, "Yes," actually he did have the right contact. "Uncle Carl is very big, even though not quite as big as he used to be; but anyway, if he'll take you on, you would be out of the woods."

He explained to me why Uncle Carl and he could not be close friends, but nevertheless maintained a certain degree of a boyhood friendship. And told me the lifesaving story. Well, said Victor, he hated to use people, and God knows this was the first time he had ever asked Uncle Carl for anything, but under the circumstances he was willing to make an exception. It so happened he would be seeing him at a reception, and I could be sure he would do what he could.

It went according to plan. I was asked to submit my stage designs, costume sketches and whatever else I had of theater work at such and such a place. I would later be notified of the date of my private audience with the near-legendary Uncle Carl, the little poor boy who had become one of the rulers of the movie world.

I was "walking on air," as Americans say, so beautifully light had life suddenly become. I saw everything in a rosy glow, made huge plans and built castles in the air. On wings, I cabled my wife to delay the shipment of our stuff—"highly paid job in California Hollywood possible." The word Hollywood I had specially inserted as an afterthought. I would really have liked to tell the clerk at the Western Union desk all about it, but she was not the least bit interested; for her it was merely a cable like all the others. I, however, saw myself as stage designer for one of the leading movie corporations—terrific. Sure, I thought, this is America. Boy, suddenly overnight you have this tremendous job. Of course I will save, and when I go back over there! I'll take the car along, sure—imagine! to look at Europe from an automobile, and with an American passport to boot—Wow, what prospects!

One day the awaited letter arrived: I was to be at the New York office of the great Uncle Carl on such and such a day. He wanted to meet me. Hurrah, I had won! He wanted to meet me, to look me over personally, that must mean of course that he wanted to hire me—of course that was clearly what it meant. If not, surely he

would not have had me come, he would have simply written a polite refusal. Victor was of course right; had not Carl once said, "Dear Victor, if ever I can do you a favor...?" Well, here was his chance. There certainly must be some place where he could use me. Oh, dear God in Heaven—terrific! No more tedious teaching, no more torture of poorly paid illustrations—off to the golden paradise of Hollywood! I am not exaggerating, this is how exuberant I felt.

So I prepared within and without, had my suit pressed, put on a particularly tasteful French tie, stuck a red carnation in my button-hole, so that the movie magnate would have a good initial impression of me. Respectful and at the same time free, cheerful and open was what I wanted to be. Nevertheless, there was a bad moment— can one ever get rid of those things?—when I felt as though I were being called to the high school principal's office in Stolp. That passed quickly, thank God. And riding the bus, well groomed inside and out, toward my destination, I was full of beautiful dreams for the future, full of grateful feelings for Victor (in which I generously included Uncle Carl) and full of satisfaction with America and the world.

This was my stop, and over there was the building with the administration and private offices of the great movie man. I went in, passed the usual newsstand and again studied the directory with its thousands of names. There it was—I knew it anyway—on the sixth floor. I got into the elevator, said "Six, please." The door closed, opened again, and there I was in the corridor.

The whole floor belonged to Uncle Carl's movie concern. Before me was a door and next to it a little window framing a lady with a headset. She took my card and the letter that I had been told to show and then said, turning toward me, "Mr. Smithold will be glad to receive you and give you all necessary information." She then gave me a white slip, and a uniformed boy took me down the corridor.

Everywhere I saw offices and heard the busy clatter of type-writers behind half-open doors. The walls were covered with posters and portraits of stars, larger than life. Then I was in a larger room. A big, very friendly man came toward me with a big smile, seized my hand, shook it for a long time, and exclaimed, "Oh, I am so happy to meet you. Yes, of course I know all your work. How very nice that you have come here!"

He spoke fluent German and was laughing all the time, but you had the feeling, despite all this cordiality, that he had been wound

Broadway [193

up by somebody and was running, purring his tune like a machine.

"Oh," he said and wacked my shoulder, "oh, how happy Uncle Carl will be to see you! Hahaha..."

With that, he took the receiver off one of the four or five phones on his desk, and suddenly a squeaky little voice spoke from the box next to it. The Friendly One answered, "O.K., Boss," while dialing a number on one phone, and listening to a second one. "All right," he said, "you can go in now." He motioned to me with the receiver. "There, down the corridor where those two men are, and show them your white pass. Good luck, haha, and I'll see you on your way back, won't I? Hahaha..."

I heard his roaring laughter all the way down the corridor.

The two men to whom he had sent me frisked me and asked whether I had any weapons. They looked closely at the pass, then one of them took it and disappeared through a door, came back, gave me the pass again, and said, gesturing over his shoulder, "O.K., buddy."

The door that I now approached seemed more intricately carved than the others. Suddenly I saw that this was not carving but iron grating, apparently put on afterwards to further strengthen the door! I remembered now having read (and that explained the detectives, too) of a kidnapping threat against a son or grandson of good Uncle Carl. Well, thank goodness I was not a kidnapper...

I knocked at the door. A weak "Come in," and there I was in front of the great movie magnate. He was quite short and walked with a stoop, but looked as though he had always walked that way, not just from the burden of age. His small, kind eyes looked at me from behind spectacles in a friendly way, a bit sideways, from bottom to top. "Yes, you can speak German to me," he said with a Berlin accent. My drawings were in full view, displayed neatly on a chair by the window.

Things looked good. Uncle Carl was standing, his hands behind his back, and asked me to sit down. I preferred to remain standing as I had the feeling that I could talk better that way, underline my words with my arms, do some acting. I told him my story and saw that he was moved. I became more dramatic, raising and lowering my voice. I noticed—one does notice such things—how Uncle Carl was softening...Slowly he moved backwards towards his large desk. I followed, continuing to talk. I was certain I had won. In a minute he would press a button—I was sure the contract was ready —and look! there he went and pressed a button without even looking that I had not even noticed....

Just as I wanted to finish with a dramatic summary, a side door opened and a liveried lackey appeared, balancing a De Vilbiss syringe on a silver tray. He put the tray down, took the syringe and went over to Uncle Carl. Uncle Carl bent his head back as though it had been rehearsed, and said nothing but "Squirt!" He kept his mouth open, made a sign with his hand, waited a moment, raised his hand again and once more said "Squirt!"

I was suddenly totally sobered. I had been interrupted in the middle of a fiery speech, and now I felt as though not only Uncle Carl's nose and throat had been sprayed, but I too, and with icy cold water. Some ending, just when I had him where I wanted him! Another two minutes, and I would have had that contract. No, it had all gone sour. Too bad that he had to ring for the syringe at that very minute!

After the man left everything had changed; it had become grey and ugly. Uncle Carl's new Hollywood suit with the wide stripes had suddenly become too juvenile for an old man. The rosy haze was gone. My drawings seemed to be wrongly placed. If a wind had blown them all out of the window, I would not have minded. And as in a Greek saga, it started to rain outside....

Uncle Carl consulted his gold watch, said, "Thank you, it was a great pleasure," and that my drawings would be mailed back to me. If there were an opening, he would let me know, and so on. He pressed the button again, and in going out, I still saw his head leaning back and the liveried lackey using the syringe.

I was terribly sad. I had really fallen flat. With one foot, I comforted myself, with one foot I really had stepped into that big lucky break; perhaps, I thought, while a huge actor's head grinned at me, perhaps I can get both my feet in next time? We humans never stop hoping...So what, forget it....

The friendly fellow through whose room I returned was still operating his four or five telephones like a juggler and talking to an artistic-looking visitor, this time in Polish or Russian or some Balkan language. "Hahaha," he was laughing to him, grabbing his hand just as he had grabbed mine, beaming and whacking him on the shoulder. Then he turned to me, spoke into a phone, listened to the squeaking box, said "O.K., Boss," put the phone down, came toward me and said, while ripping my arm out of its socket: "Haha, wonderfull, so wonderful to have met you, Mr. Grosz! Quite wonderful," he concluded, laughing loud, "haha, hahaha..."

I heard his laughter all the way into the elevator. And occasionally I still hear it, the way it goes when one is alone and thinks of all the things that have fallen flat.

I got my drawings back, nicely packed, and a letter full of nice phrases. Much later, I heard that the friendly fellow who laughed all the time was hired for that sole purpose. He was the "laugher," he laughed all the unwanted people away, or he laughed them into something, some false self-confidence or whatever that laughter aroused. For Uncle Carl had a motto: "Nobody, not even the most unwelcome person, shall leave me unsatisfied, even if he only takes with him that silly or admiring laughter and a handshake, hahaha...."

As to the De Vilbiss syringe, I am sorry to report that it too was phony. It was simply Uncle Carl's way of coming back to reality, and he used it whenever he felt himself getting soft and yielding. A touch of the button and the syringe then gave him the strength for stern decisions.

And that is the end of the story of how I almost landed a bigtime job in Hollywood.

ART LOOKS FOR BREAD

I was also once received at court in America. Not a real court in the European sense, of course, but yet it was the American aristocracy who asked me to teach painting for a month. The singer Lucrezia Bori asked me over one day, and told me that Mrs. Garrett in Baltimore wished me to give her painting lessons. All arrangements were made, and I went to Baltimore where the Garretts lived in a beautiful old manor house on large grounds. There was a guest house for visiting artists. That was where I lived.

Mrs. Garrett was very artistic. She loved painting, music and dance. While she had not exactly discovered him, she had "made" the Spanish painter Zuloaga in America; so successfully had she sponsored him that he was as famous before World War I as Picasso is today. True, he was a portrait painter, and many wealthy society ladies were happy to sit for him. Mrs. Garrett herself had done so several times. A large portrait of her was hanging above the main staircase. Zuloaga painted life size. She still raved about him, his private stud farm, his toreador friends, and the good old prewar days in Spain. "Poor Zuloaga!" she would interrupt herself, "who knows whether he is still alive. I read in the paper the other day that the Loyalists had shot his bulls and burnt his pictures." (That turned out to be merely a newspaper story, and Zuloaga was of course still alive.)

Mr. Garrett had once been the American ambassador to Italy. That was obvious by the many autographed photos of Mussolini on a table at the entrance to the library. Mr. Garrett collected valuable old books, so-called incunabula; when in a good mood, he would thump his cane on the floor, beckon me over and, with a superior air, show me his first editions. I would stand at a respectful distance, as I assumed he preferred that.

Mr. Garrett also had one of the finest coin collections in the world. When he wanted to show it, he had servants roll back the big drawing room carpet to reveal an iron trap door; an iron spiral staircase led to a small room below that looked like a bank vault of steel and iron; the priceless coins were neatly displayed on sliding shelves.

Mrs. Garrett was also a collector. She collected French paintings. Sixty water colors by Raoul Dufy hung in her little theater where she had annual chamber music concerts, and dance recitals. It was all done in grand style, in an era when style was ceasing to exist.

The drawing room adjoined a large terrace overlooking the well-kept and artfully landscaped garden, lighted at night by searchlights controlled from the house. Mint juleps were served in the late afternoon in silver beakers, frosted outside. It was very nice to sit out there sipping cool juleps ("May I replenish your drink, sir?") while the British accent disappeared and gradually gave way to more Southern tones.

Mr. Garrett used to spice our occasional conversations with remarks about my German origin. I had the feeling that he did not care much for Germans. Of course he did not say anything like "I don't like Germans" but rather, pounding his stick on the floor: "Your ancestors did not bring us much that was good. Look over there," pointing toward some sparrows on the terrace. "You see those sparrows? Your ancestors brought them over, and they have not been the best thing for our flowers!" I bowed and professed my innocence, mildly rebuking the earlier German settlers, and watching a bee humming round Mr. Garrett's head. I hope he doesn't blame us for the bee too, I thought.

"Those Germans," he growled, still a bit annoyed. I retired quietly on tiptoe. I had not contradicted him. I knew he needed to growl a bit—and yet, from that day on, every sparrow I saw seemed a nasty emissary from Adolf Hitler. Besides, I had adopted the manners and courtesy of a tutor at court....

Once I visited my friend George Biddle in nearby Washington. He was just working on his large fresco at the Department of Justice and as I had only seen his small pictures I was greatly interested in watching him work with a tiny palette (actually a saucer with a few colors round the edge) doing a real fresco, piece by piece. He later came with some of the boys from the W.P.A. fresco division to a party at the Garretts, given in my honor; Mrs. Garrett had heard in the meantime that I was not *merely* one of the obscure artists whom you helped by taking painting lessons.

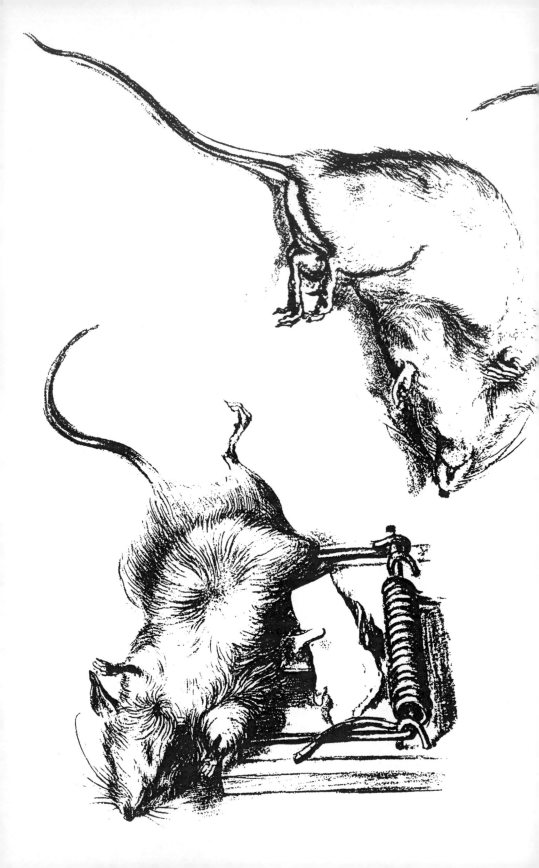

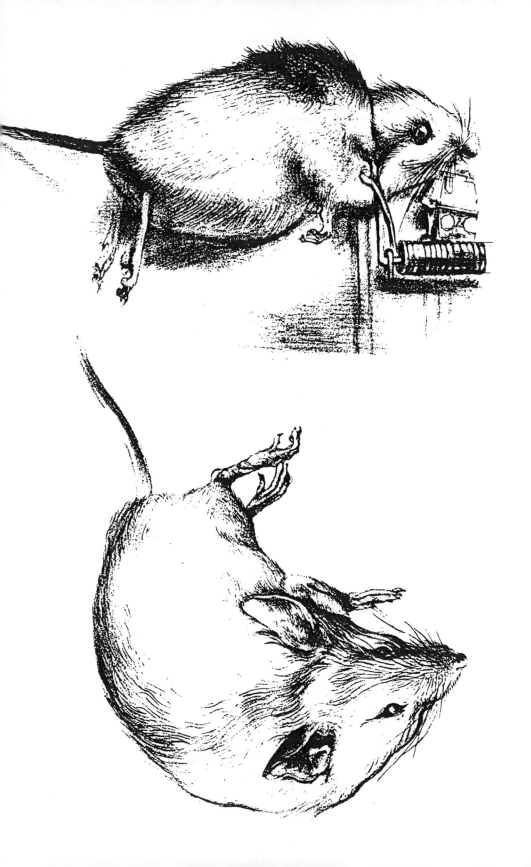

What Mrs. Garrett got from me in those lessons was mostly a running commentary. I also picked up her brush if it fell down. I figured that my contribution to this court was in the realm of entertainment, and that was quite all right by me. I was impressed with the Garretts because they were so rich; as a true artist, I preferred associating with rich people than with poor ones. Fundamentally, a rich man was just as boring as a poor one, but at least he had money. His money made the difference; with a little skill, some of it could end up in my own pocket.

A sensitive reader may take this as the confession of a parasite—but what else can a pure artist be in a society such as ours? That does not mean that I have any hope for a better one; the art of tomorrow will probably be nothing but continuous entertainment, and the society of a later date, the society of bureaucrats and commissars, will certainly need no art at all.

The best solution to my financial difficulties had always seemed to be running a school of my own. An opportunity presented itself when I.B.Neumann introduced me to the successful American painter Maurice Sterne, who was kind enough to let me participate in his well established school in the Raymond & Raymond Building, where Mr. Ben Raymond put a room at my disposal. So I began.

I had brought a monitor with me from the Art Students League, one of my most gifted pupils, the painter Marshall Glazier. He helped me bear my loneliness. And were we ever lonely! My "School for Painting, Drawing, Composition and Art Appreciation" consisted solely of Marshall and me. Students there were none. It was a bit depressing.

I did not tell my wife and her sister Cläre about it. I started out from our rather dark hotel quite cheerfully every morning, lying a little in my behalf by pretending that one or two students showed up every day. Eva wondered where the checks were? "Oh, the checks—well," I said, "you know how it is here. An art teacher is something like a dentist or a physician, and they aren't paid right away either."

I was like an ostrich, with my head in the sand. It must work somehow, I thought. My friend Alexander King advertised my school in his magazine. I had thought up smart captions, such as: "Cézanne knew how to make an apple out of nothing. YOU can learn that too!" I would illustrate that with a drawing of half an apple. Or we would cover a page with all sorts of squiggles, ink spots, dots, hooks, lines and random mess and print alongside: "DO YOU KNOW WHAT THIS MEANS?—These are the basic elements of graphics. Use them! Learn to DRAW!!!" Some of my other slogans were simpler, such as "Drawing makes you happy" or "By heart from nature."

I was very proud of my ideas, I thought they were quite American and was disappointed when they did not attract more students. The few that did come were all ladies—and I believe they came less because of my slogans than by recommendation of well-meaning friends who hoped to help me a little in this gentle way. That was fine, as long as I had students! Of course I had to furnish a model for my class and though Mr. Raymond was a kind, liberal and ever helpful man who never hurried me for the rent, I had hardly anything left. I was often quite miserable, and would there-

fore repair to a little bar for comfort; a few Planter's Punches would then turn the grey day into a rosy future....

There is an old English saying that claims, "Those who can, do; those who cannot, teach." As with most proverbs, it is only partly true. I did have ability; and I was also able to teach, in the sense of communicating with students and helping them along. I could even do that particularly well, as I came from an era where learning was made as nasty for us as possible. That was done by telling us the truth. "Well, finally, you've done it," the professor would say scornfully after the poor, twisted student had almost killed himself trying to *do* it....

I much preferred the American way of telling people the truth in indirect, almost covert form. Influenced by Dale Carnegie *(How to Win Friends and Influence People)* I soon learned to treat my students the way they wanted to be treated. I buried my former arrogance; a tendency toward nihilistic self-complacency was relegated to the deepest cellar of my being. Eventually I managed pleasant phrases and gave compliments that I only half believed. I learnt how by praise one could teach the difficult skill of drawing. As I did not have any ingrained judgment, it was easy to satisfy my students.

Despite widespread belief to the contrary, art can be learned. Copying an object can be learned, and later a head, and later a whole person. You can also learn to copy a pattern of a model and draw it "by heart," by memory from nature, as I claimed in one of my ads. Easier yet to learn is so-called creativity in art, and the easiest of all is the abstract. Just think of Rorschach tests, fabric design, graphs. Nobody really needs art any more, since everybody is practicing it. I really love the American optimistic belief that everything can be learned; but I don't quite believe it.

That was sort of a rainy time in my life, but the rain somehow did not make me sad. My dream of America remained as firm as ever—though once in a while I would wake up at night and, for a horror-stricken moment, ask myself: What if none of this were true? What if reality were even more real than it already is?

But that never lasted long, and I was right back in my own make-believe. Soon life really did brighten, when one day Maurice Sterne, who tolerated me as partner in his painting school, came and said: "George, I just got a big job in California. I am giving up my art school and will advise my students to continue working with you." That was very nice, and I was very grateful to Maurice.

Because of technical or whatever reasons, however, we had to move out of the Raymond & Raymond Building. We had to find another place for the school and that was not easy: where would we ever find another Ben Raymond? But my French-American secretary, Mrs. Brevannes, came up with an excellent idea. One of my students was the daughter of a very rich man named Palmer; and he owned the Squibb Building, at the corner of Fifth Avenue and 57th Street. "Mr. Grosz," said she, "why don't you simply write Mr. Palmer a letter? He knows who you are. Maybe he will let us have a garret in the Squibb Building."

I wrote the letter, and shortly thereafter was asked to see Mr. Palmer in his office. He was a busy man, as are all men of his age and income bracket. I knew how to behave: brief and to the point. And sure enough, as soon as I came in, he said: "I am a busy man; I can give you ten minutes. If you really have something to tell me, you can do it in ten minutes. So, what can I do for you?" And he looked at his wristwatch.

I was lucky. It took me only seven minutes, so he had another three left to think things over. I seemed to have made a good impression. He pressed a hidden button on his totally empty desk. A tall, Irish looking man came in. "I am handing you over to Mr. O'Leary," said Mr. Palmer. "Mr. Grosz—Mr. O'Leary." "Glad to meet you, sir," said Mr. O'Leary.

Mr. Palmer continued: "He will take care of you and settle everything to your and my satisfaction, I hope. By the way, something else. I hear you like Bougereau. Well, you must come over for cocktails some time and look at my Bougereaus. I have three. Thank you. Goodbye."

So I was now the owner of a fairly large art school on the thirty-second floor of the Squibb Building. I had inherited most of my students from Maurice Sterne, but my modest advertising gradually yielded some too. I was really proud. Before I entered the sky-scraper, I would often gaze at the thirty-second floor from the other side of the street and say to myself: "Boy, oh boy, your drawing teacher Papst should have seen this! God almighty, a huge studio on the thirty-second floor with a sun deck in front..." I patted my own back, and was whisked happily upward in the express elevator that did not stop until the 31st floor. Not bad at all. What a country, America. I was still comparatively young, only forty-four, and my dream more alive than ever.

The students (most of them were ladies I had taken over from Maurice) were almost all from upper income New York. That gave my school a rather feudal atmosphere. I liked that. But I also brought over some of my better students from the Art Students League to give it a more democratic look. And irony was far from my mind. I was proud of my students, and sometimes felt like the director of an exclusive club, what with all those mink coats on the hangers.

There were some memorable people among them. There was an elegant, wealthy man who was well along in years when he got interested in painting. He would bring his chauffeur to class with him and have me tell him which tubes to take from his brand-new, expensive English paint box; the chauffeur would squeeze the paint onto the palette which my student was holding in his white-gloved hand—an always much admired little ceremony.

Unfortunately I did not keep this student very long. He turned from art to Yoga. I happened to run into him again at a very animated, noisy literary cocktail party; he had retired to another room, where he was contemplating his navel and seemed rapt in deep meditation. He had unbuttoned his shirt over his no longer slender waist, so as to be closer to himself, he explained.

Another student of mine had been an abstract painter for some years, had shown his pictures, had some success, and now wanted to explore something else, another method. He was not untalented, but drawing from nature seemed rather a bore to him. I could understand that very well, after he had once explained to me what art was all about: impression. "Very interesting," I said. That's O.K. But what do you mean by that?"

"Gravity," he said.

"I beg your pardon?"

He explained his working method, which was as follows: he would take a pot of paint, and pour some from a specific height onto a canvas on the floor. "That makes an impression, right? Then I lower the paint pot. The impression changes. I go higher. Different again. Finally I get onto a chair. You wouldn't believe, Mr. Grosz, how that changes the impression!"

"Ever so interesting," I said, "Nothing wrong with that."

One day the art dealer Julian Levi called up. It was the year that the great Salvador Dali had such a triumphant success in New York. Levi was his manager and dealer; could Dali use my studio to draw a model? I said yes with considerable enthusiasm, as I expected a great deal of publicity from such a visit.

Dali arrived, in a thick coat of fake fur, a scarf in the Spanish colors of red and green, threaded with gold, round his neck. His famous mustache graced his upper lip but had not yet grown into the half-foot waxed antennae of a later date. My whole class was electrified by the presence of the greatest living painter beside

The Stick Man [ca. 1947]

Picasso. My cosmopolitan students almost unconsciously started to speak French. But Dali was exceedingly modest and unassuming; he asked for a small stool, squatted close to the podium, took out an old-fashioned sketch book with the gold imprint "Sketches" on it, untied the neat bow with which it was fastened —and drew, in great, silent concentration, without ever looking up, one very small drawing of the model's foot...

Then he invited me to the Russian Tea Room where his wife Gala, his immortal, much celebrated muse (incidentally, a shrewd business woman!) was waiting for us. Her first request was to see today's drawing. Dali pulled the sketchbook from his coat pocket; I politely asked to see it too, and was shown the miniature drawing of the foot that is now at the Museum of Modern Art.

I politely enquired what pencils he had used, and was told they were numbers 5 to 7; not surprising, as it looked as though done in silver point. I had forgotten my French, so I had a hard time saying anything much and we did not stay together long. That was the only time I met Salvador Dali, and I am sure I remember it better than he does.

My school lasted about four years. I gave it up when I got the two-year Guggenheim grant. I did not regret it. Teaching takes a lot of energy, and it always took me a while to get back into my own work. I did not have the wonderful American ability to do many things at once. As an art teacher I felt, and feel, as though I was walking up a different staircase with each foot and having a hard time keeping my balance.

The job as illustrator for *Esquire* came at the same time, so I was free of worry for the time being. There is a surplus of everything in America, and that includes pain and suffering. Only very few artists can make a living painting. Many painters who are not at all bad make their living in other ways; a few are dentists, one a barber, one even a butcher, and another works at the post office....

Art is considered a hobby. The old German joke "What does art do?—it looks for bread!" is well applied in America. There is, of course, a Bohemian world of young and older, mostly alcoholic figures who care little for material goods and often, following Van Gogh's example, wipe their brushes on their unkempt beards; but by and large that New York *bohème* is rather unreal, a cheaper copy of the Paris *bohème* that was already obsolescent by 1900, and kept alive only for tourists, along with the Apache dance and the Can-Can.

GERMANS IN AMERICA

I was now making "a decent living," as they say in America, but that was about all. War was in the air, but still seemed unlikely; somehow, the Depression was over. Roosevelt was president, Willkie had not yet started dreaming of "One World," the cost of living was reasonable, and we moved to a little house in Bayside, Long Island. It had a romantic garden not far from the Sound, and belonged to an old family named Lawrence. We bought a second-hand Willys Knight and had a girl working for us, who also taught my wife how to drive. My two boys, Mart and Peter, went to the pleasant Bayside public school, and everything was still full of sun and comparatively free of fear.

It was actually a carefree time. There was no atom bomb yet, Hitler was generally admired, and aside from some desperate refugees who were incapable of adjustment, things went well. We were again able to have a hospitable house. Friends from all over Europe came to see us when they arrived in the States. Due to the terror of that man Hitler, most of our friends were scattered. Some were living in Czechoslovakia, many had found refuge in France; always considered a free country, it unfortunately no longer was one. But my friends continued dreaming their dreams, just as I continued dreaming mine about the USA.

Paul Graetz, the wonderful Berlin comedian, stopped by on his way from England to Hollywood. We had German food and Paul talked and talked, and tears flowed down our cheeks and his. Bert Brecht came to see us, complete with bodyguard, a hoodlum who not only looked like one but talked that way too. Brecht left us a prospectus for a book whose printed motto was "Fighting Books Help the Fighters," from which we immediately understood: Berlin-Wedding. But at that time we could still have a laugh about such things. It was still half-past eleven on the big clock, not five minutes to twelve.

I had not seen Thomas Mann for a long time. I had met him at the house of his German publisher, S. Fischer, who used to entertain all sorts of interesting people at his villa in the Grunewald.

Had there been a wise gypsy at that party to tell our fortune from tea leaves or coffee grounds, not one of us would have believed her, least of all Thomas Mann and I who were seated across from each other at the same table. For she would have said: "You two will cross the big ocean. You will meet again in a large city, a splendid city with towering houses and many windows. I also see a shadow, a bad man with wild hair and a black upper lip. Beware of him, the tea leaves say, and close your shutters at night!"

That is how the gypsy would have spoken—provided she had been allowed into the progressive Fischer's house. We would have laughed of course, and would hardly have believed her prediction. We were sitting at laden tables; on the white damask of the table-cloths, festive candlelight blended with the shadow of the declining western world. Our conversation was a bit shrill and too witty; we knew it all and could discuss things objectively, paying no attention to the blood-red gleam on the far horizon. We were like hares in a hunt, trying to overcome our terror of what was approaching by means of wit and frivolity. And so we were looking to wise, restrained Thomas Mann, in whose honor this luncheon was given.

We admired him, because he had the gift of simultaneously saying yes and no with cool grace—a gift not given to every author. Cheap parodists had made fun of him as an equivocal, indecisive character, and it almost seemed as though he wanted to live up to that opinion. (Which was not entirely true: Thomas Mann's sense of humor was not so nihilistic as to mock or even parody himself.) He listened to our conversation a trifle too politely perhaps, but from the proper distance that was his due; it was always directed toward him as the center. He was the most famous among us, the secretly envied recipient of the Nobel Prize—the highest honor that a German writer could receive short of a hereditary title, which was out of the question in a republic.

This was the first time I had seen the famous man close up. Coffee and cognac had been served, a tray with Havana cigars, cigarettes and a lighted candle was being passed, and after a good meal, we were in a relaxed mood. Having discussed modern and old literature, the theater, and also various contemporaries, the conversation quite naturally moved to current events. Chief subjects were "good old" Hindenburg, who was actually not the good Santa Claus presented to the German people, and the very unfortunate part played by the Social Democrats in the government of an unbalanced state.

Thomas Mann was of course the center of the conversation, but did not determine its direction. Some of us self-important younger men with leftist tendencies would have loved to find out on which side and with which party this famous man stood politically. But Thomas Mann was not to be pinned down to any "direction."

He seemed to be standing coolly aside and somewhat above everything: many a fanatic held just this against him. Only rarely, when he could not dodge a question, did he approach politics, but even then it was with wise hesitation, consideration and restraint. He seemed even then to have harbored some doubt about all the party lines, as would befit a man of his heritage and birth.

Thomas Mann was not born into the working class. He was a gentleman. It showed in his long, narrow head, in his slender, narrow hands and feet. It showed in his posture, in his clothing, his ties and the cut of his collars. His collar, his suit, his hat are practically the same today as the ones he wore forty years ago, as though ordered and made to measure by the same tailors—probably the same who made the clothes for his father, grandfather and great grandfather—and changed only discreetly in cut and color to conform to current fashion. And just as conservative, changing and yielding as little to the shift in times and modes and phrases was the political writing of Thomas Mann.

I never saw Thomas Mann again in Germany.

One evening I learned from the *Daily News* that a former student of mine, Dr. Nathaniel Stein Wolf, was dragged out of bed in a pension on the Kurfürstendamm in Berlin, threatened, and taken away half-dressed, in a car. The caption read "American Jew beaten by Nazis in Berlin." The story was the usual one: taken out of bed, threatened with a weapon, and accused of possession of treasonable material. As he proved that he was an American citizen and they did not find any Red literature—how could they? he was only interested in art—they let him out of the car at the Charlottenburger Chaussee with threats of shooting him, and told him to run. "Run, and don't you dare turn round!" he was told. That was his worst moment, he told me later; "I really was terrified. I expected that bullet any minute...." Nothing further

A Writer, Is He? [1934/3

happened to him. He reported everything to the American consul, and left Berlin within 24 hours—the Berlin that he had loved as much as had his namesake and countryman Thomas Wolfe.

I then realized that the "Night of the Long Knives" had not been empty delusion. I had repeatedly been threatened with it; I had also been assured that when "der Tag" came, it would be no laughing matter for me. When it did come, however, I was lying safely in my New York hotel bed, looking at the Statue of Liberty out of my window; there on West 60th Street it was merely an inexpensive little copy, but still, it was a statue of liberty. How extraordinary, I thought, what whim of fate preserved you? The blow intended for me mistakenly hit the only American student I had in Berlin. I shuddered.

In days like those one thinks with bitterness of one's former home. It may have been partly because of this bitterness that my second meeting with Thomas Mann was no great success. It was shortly after Hitler came to power, in the summer of 1933. Eva and I were to meet Mann and his wife for lunch at a restaurant in Manhattan, with our friend Charles Lautrupp, a conductor who was an old friend of Mrs. Mann's brother.

The meeting was ill-fated from the start. It began with a bad breach of manners, as we arrived a full half-hour late. We apologized as best we could, telling of a Long Island train that happened not to be running today plus a punctured tire, which made the story hard to believe.

That was not a propitious beginning, and Mrs. Mann's expression was not friendly. We were soon seated at a small table, faced by glasses of fresh water. As I remember, there was no beer yet—or if so, it was still very thin, more like "nearbeer"—but Thomas Mann, thank goodness, was not one of those Germans who judge everything in foreign countries by the quality of their beer. Lunch in any case was plentiful, served on huge platters. We were soon in a debate about Hitler, his Nazis and their prospects. Thomas Mann was of the opinion that Hitler could not possibly last more than six months, an opinion shared at the time by many well-informed people.

Had not shrewd Dorothy Thompson taken one close look at Hitler, and declared that a man with a face like that could not last? Not only she but other experts on Germany, many influential industrialists, bankers, economists, journalists, many usually skeptical diplomats and professional politicians the world over predicted only a short rule for him. A ridiculous episode, for sure, but this amateur would soon be wrecked by his inexperience as a statesman. What had he shown to date other than his talent as a demagogue in the seduction of the people? Could one imagine the officer corps tolerating him as commander? And where would he get oil? And money? Oh, no—half a year at most.

I heard all that from Thomas Mann at our second meeting, in the summer of 1933. I must now interrupt my narrative to state that I have always had a slight talent for prophecy, probably from my mother's side. In addition, I am a skeptic with a tendency to say no rather than yes, and my observation has shown me that the masses are nothing but a herd of sheep who can contentedly be led to choose their own butcher. I have never seen much that was good in human beings, and when in a bad mood, I would become a real misanthrope.

That must have been my frame of mind when I met Thomas Mann and his wife again in Manhattan. Or was it that the author's wife had annoyed me by insinuating that it was not proper to speak so informally in the presence of her husband? However it may be, I was quite unnecessarily aggressive, sarcastic and misanthropic, and made quite clear that my contempt did not exclude present company. In other words, my behavior was really impossible.

I declared clearly and openly that Hitler was worthy of the Germans who had elected him. And though there was one sitting next to me, I no longer had any use for "better Germans." I opened the floodgates of my contempt over friend and foe alike; I was in a murderous mood; the diplomat I really like to be and sometimes am, was that day clearly Thomas Mann, not I. I might even have made a better impression on Mrs. Mann, had I controlled myself a little. But I thought—to hell with conventions, who cares about making an impression, and so all my accumulated bitterness and sarcasm poured out of me at the wrong time and place like an overturned barrel of poison. Eva kept kicking me under the table, but to no avail, so enamored was I with my own malice.

With an annoyed look at me, Mrs. Mann suddenly intervened: "Well, Mr. Grosz, and how long do you think that Hitler can stay in power?"

I replied promptly, and equally annoyed: "If you too are counting on the six months that your husband believes, you are badly mistaken. In my opinion, it will be more like six years, Madam." I added with a sting, "in any case, much longer than you and your husband imagine!"

At the time, that sort of prophecy sounded provocative and quite unreasonable. Only a completely irresponsible and malicious person could proclaim—and only for the sake of contradiction—that he could well imagine Hitler at the head of Germany for ten years.... Thomas Mann and I looked at each other angrily. We suddenly became aware that we couldn't stand each other.

Mrs. Mann came back into the conversation again: "You give this—this house painter six or even ten years? Shame on you, Mr. Grosz, you must be a horrid man even to be able to imagine such a thing!" For emphasis, she excitedly grabbed my arm. I suddenly noticed with horror that her nails had become sharp, like those of a cat.

Another kick on the shin from Eva suddenly sobered me. Why couldn't I have kept quiet and tacitly agreed with the illusions of the Mann's? Why all this fuss? Why not agree that we would all be back home in half a year, back in a better, liberated home? How silly to argue.

As always happens after such futile conversation, we were all feeling uncomfortable. Our real surroundings became suddenly very clear, with all the smells and noises of a restaurant. The dejected mood at our table was like thick air. I made an unsuccessful attempt to save the situation by saying: "Of course I might be mistaken—I probably am; it is utterly possible that six months is all that Hitler...." But these protestations sounded much less honest and convincing than my earlier pessimistic prophecies.

Thomas Mann was, however, very kind; he said in a conciliatory tone to his wife:

"Let Mr. Grosz talk! Everyone is entitled to his opinions—and as to my pessimism and my nihilism and my disbelief in the good—(he said nihilism!)—as to those matters, he continued with hidden sarcasm, he had had moments like that when he was a young man, and could well understand them. As in every question, there were two sides, on-the-one-hand and on-the-other-hand; you needed the ability to keep your thoughts under control and not to be overwhelmed by the present darkness and the inability to see a more optimistic view caused by it. Yes, certainly," he added, "I do know those feelings...."

Our discussion suddenly finished, as though someone had blown it out. All of us looked at our watches; simultaneously, all of us remembered urgent appointments. We all noticed that we had been sitting together too long. Before we had taken proper leave, we already were miles apart. Phrases of courtesy were uttered, and our conversation ended in the shallow chatter of distinguished contemporaries....

◆

We were sitting at supper in Douglaston where we were then living in a larger house a little further from the city. It had been a rainy, dark day; it was as dark in the morning as it usually is at six at night. It was still raining. There were a few friends with us

The Grosz Family in Douglaston [1940]

whom we had not seen for a long time. We had just opened some good wine to celebrate when the telephone rang and we heard that Ernst Toller had died.

It was May 22, 1939, and Toller had been found by his secretary, hanged, in the bathroom of a Manhattan hotel. He was reported to have had suicidal ideas for some time, had talked oddly to friends and enquired how to turn on the gas in a cooking stove. He had been in a state of depression, where everything seemed to turn against him. Ever since the collapse of the Spanish Loyalists he had not been the same....

My memory of him goes further back, to Germany, where we saw each other often. One evening at his house we had a lively discussion with the writer Emil Ludwig about the chances of Hitler, who was about to become Chancellor. Ludwig relied upon Hindenburg and the conservative influence of the army, Toller relied upon the working class—I however saw nothing that I could have relied upon. We separated in ill humor.

Toller had a part in the Red Republic in Munich in 1919, at the same time as his plays were being produced with considerable success all over Germany. That put him into the position of having forever to justify his great popularity. Instead of disappearing and writing more plays, he tried to become a sort of leader. But he did not have a leader's personality; he confused poetry with politics, and his considerable, much acclaimed gift of speech with true superiority. He never became more that a passionate agitator.

He may have dreamed of being another Ferdinand Lasalle, an inspiring figure waving a red flag, loved by the masses, a superior idealist, yet firmly among them. But he had none of the necessary attributes of leadership, not the hardness of will, not the contempt for the masses. He was romantic and sentimental and had a poetic view of swallows and human beings.

He was good looking. His large eyes blazed under heavy, dark brows; his dark hair fell in waves over his forhead. Women liked him—and he them. He liked to live well, was not ascetic and did not disdain the pleasures of life. After a fiery speech you could often find him in a little French or Russian restaurant, and this was stupidly held against him by the typical leftist petit bourgeois. Unfortunately he was not cynical enough to ignore that sort of talk, but felt hurt every time it happened. Everything about him had a certain nobility, and he never learned that you had to carry a horsewhip to rule, even if you never used it.

He had all sorts of conflicts. Toller plays gradually became obsolete and were only produced occasionally in small theaters. His hope for the victory of a large social movement with him as leader collapsed. As happens to many a noble but mixed-up idealist, he fell between two chairs: the Communists attacked him because he was not following the Moscow party line, and the Social Democrats were not revolutionary enough for his taste. Other worries and physical pain accumulated. Writing became difficult. He should have retired, gone away from the telephones, the busy life, taken to the woods for a while to rest, to collect his thoughts. But that Ernst Toller could not do.

He had to keep his act going till the end. People said he was a prima donna—I never thought so. He was vain, as are many artists. He was ambitious, but aren't we all, more or less? You would have to have enormous success, or be a pathological hater of people, or possess the wisdom of a Brahmin in order not to be. When you were alone with Toller, he was quite different and often quite natural. But as soon as he had an audience, he had to put on an act. In the zenith of his fame he had been the center of attention for too long to step aside of his own free will.

He once came out to see us in Douglaston. I met him at the train. It was spring and the landscape was in full bloom, but in Toller's soul it was autumn and the trees were bare. I saw how depressed he was. We walked arm in arm through the flowering countryside, all was peaceful and calm. Ernst said I was lucky; he too would like to live out here, work in peace and start writing plays again; he wanted to give up the whole rat race and be himself again. Could I not find a place for him, somewhere in this neighborhood?

It sounded real, but it wasn't. He was trying to convince himself. But he still craved being the center of attention. He had to have cables coming in and reporters appearing; he had to feel needed and wanted. I remember his hotel room when he arrived in New York: half a dozen newspaper men were there as I came in, two secretaries sat writing, Toller was giving a dramatic description of the execution of an anti-Nazi worker named André, a bellhop brought some telegrams, there was action. And Toller was happy.

Unfortunately he never saw through it all. Then, when he sat in a lonely room and there were no more reporters and cables...

Early glory is often dangerous. You cannot build a new life out of old newspaper clippings.

Never will I forget the day I went out to Ellis Island in the scorching heat to assist a friend who had just arrived from a

German concentration camp: Hans Borchardt—he had a name
again now, not just a number.

E. C., ever helpful, had managed to get us papers so that we
could board the vessel before it docked. I should really have met
this E. C. earlier. Flechtheim told me in Berlin about E. C., the
noodle king from the USA who had arrived and bought a few of my
things. It did not work out at that time; the important man had to
leave, and so we did not meet until 1932 in the famous Café Royal
on Second Avenue, where you could sit almost the way they do in
the cafés of Vienna, over a newspaper and a glass of water.

Doctor Plaut brought me and E. C. together there. Everything at
our lunch was with white. I did not yet know that white was the
favorite color of this art lover. E. C. had bought quite a lot of
pictures by the painter Kleinschmidt, who used much white. This
Kleinschmidt painted with thick color that he spread like butter, in
various shades of white, from the lightest yellowish-white to cool
blue-white. Now, both gentlemen were wearing white linen suits,
reasonable in this awful heat. But they also ordered food that
looked just like their white suits, and drank milk with it. I would
really have liked to eat something blue or red but suppressed my
wishes, always ready to conform.

In due course, E. C. showed me his collection; he had almost all
the graphics of Lovis Corinth, who was hardly known in America,
and everything by Käthe Kollwitz. He was one of those rare
collectors who bought things for the pure pleasure the object gave
him, regardless of fashion or theoretical concepts. In addition he
was a marvelous model who seemed actually to enjoy sitting. His
circumference was kingly; he looked something like a French chef,
peace and solidity personified, but animated with the specific grace
and lightness of fat people. I did his portrait several times.

We were allowed to board Han's steamer from the press boat.
But the technicalities of immigration were severe—Borchardt
could not land because he was missing a finger from his left hand.
He had been asked to wait because they wanted to know what had
happened to that hand; but he knew no word of English. So he sat
there, bewildered and frightened, without a jacket, in a raincoat
over a shirt, a conspicuous figure under the scorching sun.

Hans had been a master teacher in a so-called progressive school.
He had loved his job, unlike many of his colleagues who were
working at the wrong place and were caustic and angry. They too
were idealists of a sort, as was Borchardt, they too were hypnotized
by the promise of a glorious future, but theirs was a different

hypnotizer.

Hans was not alone in the concentration camp: his number was a high one. Already many thousands of idealists had been brought in and shackled. Alone he was certainly not, but he was terribly lonely. He had always had a cleanliness compulsion and was unhappy if he could not have three showers a day. A bad person smells bad too, he used to say. Where he was then, everyone smelled bad. Many years later, long after the nightmare was over, he could not get rid of the smell, no matter how much he bathed.

He saw the concentration camp as a gruesome insult, as a hell where those who were damned together did not gain in solidarity. Fellow prisoners became completely transparent, like gelatine, their screams padded with straw. It was very quiet there anyhow, much more quiet than in the real world. Even the machine-guns had silencers. And the loud camp music covered all suspicious sounds with Wagner and sentimental songs.

Those who knew how to garden were allowed to beautify the execution grounds. "You have a nice place here," a high leader once said when he came to see them. "Flower beds around the barracks." "What is your vocation?" "Assistant principal, Sir." "Well, look at him. Assistant principal, hm? I'll tell you what you are. An old Jew swine is what you are...So what are you now?" "I am an old Jew swine, Sir." "Well, there we are!"

A mutilated ear got infected. The mud was endless. Was there still such a thing as a shower, followed by a clean nightshirt? "Assistant principal, hm, just look at him! Are you brave?" "Yes Sir, I am brave." "Well then, if you are brave, what do you want to do?" "Die, Sir." "Well, great! The assistant principal wants to die!"

"Let's have a little fun again, so what. So let's have a few men to dig a grave, it seems Mr. Assistant Principal wants to die. Are you afraid?" "No, Sir, I am not afraid. "You just look at this one, you swine, you can learn something from him!"

"And how some of them hurried forward to bury me," Hans told me later, "you should have seen with what vigor they were digging, just to curry favor with the troop sergeant. And with what joy they dropped heavy, hard clumps of earth on me! Anyway, everybody except for me had their fun, not only the sergeant who eventually got bored and had them stop as the earth was already up to my mouth. Too bad, they would really have liked to see me buried alive," said my friend Hans Borchardt as we were sitting over a whiskey in Douglaston.

So Cain Killed Abel [1936]

"Prisoner #189654 punished by 24 blows on the buttocks and back for propagandizing his idiotic god Jehova in the potato kitchen. That was what happened to an indomitable Bible scholar who was beaten half dead for refusing to raise his hand in the Hitler salute or rendering any sign of respect to the ruling powers. Those were the most upright," Hans told us, "no torture could intimidate them, so convinced were they of their belief in the Day of Judgment."

And then there was the "Rosenkavalier." Hans thought of him when we were watering the garden in Douglaston on Long Island Sound one morning. He had called prisoner Borchardt in once more before his departure, for more instructions and intimidation. He got his name from his passion for roses; prisoners who knew how to grow them fared slightly better. As Borchardt entered, he was waving a rose before his nose in his gloved hand: "You are now to be dismissed and are going to America. You are forbidden to talk about Camp Dachau either as a hell hole or as a health resort for body culture; both are equally prohibited!" He sniffed his rose. "Remember one thing. We have excellent ears, and a long reach. All the way to America!"

Now this hell was over for him. Once in a while the "Rosen-kavalier" did still appear behind him, holding a Maréchal Niel to his nose. Surely he could not have spent *all* his time torturing people? Surely he must have been a family man afterwards, a father, a lover of Brahms, a grower of roses?

And the finger? "Oh, that was lost in loading stones. We loaded trucks from both sides, hurried on by supervisors. I suppose it was sort of fun to throw pieces of rock at each other's hands, and the bored watchman liked games like that. Well, so I lost a finger, and in the field painkillers were used very sparingly. It is due to sanitary assistant Klangwardt's comparatively careful handling that I did not lose my whole hand, black and swollen as it was."

Hans always kept that hand hidden; it was ugly, looked like a claw. No, he was not proud of this reminder of his hideous humiliation.

In New York, Hans Borchardt wrote a thick book, *The Conspiration of the Carpenters*, a confusing book, hard to read, with more than a hundred characters. Franz Werfel wrote the introduction. Some reviewers considered it brilliant, but it was quickly forgotten. There are a few plays by him too; for one, written in Germany, *Die Bluttat von Germersheim*, I did a few drawings. But he could never get that, nor *Pastor Hall*, written in America, produced. He died in 1951 in New York. The doctor said afterwards that he had practically no heart left. So one morning he fell back onto his bed, and was dead.

AMERICA, THE BIG

America is big and wide, and it often actually frightened me how this size pressed upon you in the cities. Fortunately I had brought things with me from my past that made me feel at home here. I would stand on the little bridge over the railroad in Douglaston and think of the same sort of bridge in Stolp where I used to stand, many, many years ago. From there the rails led into the wide, wide world, all the way to the ocean where a mighty vessel with three funnels was waiting to take me across to distant America.

So I felt doubly at home when I stood on the bridge in Douglaston and spread my arms. Yes, really at home! For now my romantic youthful dream had become reality.

Until then I had stayed in small hotels or small apartments; the noise of trucks would come straight through the walls, as they were swallowed up or spewed out by the Holland Tunnel, right across the bed in my little room. Yet I had been happy there. There is an excitement in Manhattan that stimulates work. And did I work! When I came home from my class at night, the watercolors simply poured onto paper so as to hold my impressions of the day. The city was bursting with sights, and I was bursting with the desire to take them all in. The dark little hotel room with its simple wooden table did not depress me—I was filled with light and color and joy. Many little notebooks were filled with sketches that were to be used later in my pictures.

I loved the big buses that rumbled through the streets, and more than ever I loved the fabulous shop windows, the likes of which did not yet exist anywhere else. Fairy palaces.

Germany had frozen something within me that was now melting, and in America I rediscovered the joy of painting. I deliberately and carefully burned part of my past. And learned English. My occasional deep depressions had nothing to do with America. Lightning seemed threatening, distant conflagrations and the smell of blood. I painted those visions of ruins with raging fire. That was long before the war....

◆

Thomas Craven and I have liked each other from the first day we met. He immediately became my good friend and advisor. I was living in a small apartment on Christopher Street, and Craven came there to interview me for an article for his book *Men of Art*. I admit that at that time I still knew very little about American art; besides Whistler, practically nothing was known in Germany other than the names of Maurice Stern, Hunt Diederich and Marsden Hartley. Even they were only known by the small circle round Flechtheim and his magazine *Der Querschnitt*. I have Thomas Craven to thank most for my knowledge of American art; it was through him that I got acquainted with stage designer Thomas Benton, John Stewart Curry, Reginald Marsh and Grant Wood.

Once Craven, Thomas Benton and Charles Henry (who later became my student) took me to the German quarter in Hoboken. We went to a Bavarian restaurant there, and the owner played Bavarian dances and songs for us on the harmonica. On the walls were primitively painted pictures of Bavarian mountains. We could almost have been in Bavaria, except for the beer, which was rather thin. Tom Benton sat there with his cane and his little black mustache, full of energy and loaded with sharp wit. Unfortunately I missed a lot, as my English comprehension was still quite limited. Later we landed in one of the eating places round the harbor and warmed our innards with delicious, fragrant clam broth.

I spent many a weekend in Woodstock with the newspaper feature writer J. P. McEvoy, an old friend whom I had known in Germany. There I met a different group of people. We went to see the painter Yasuo Kuniyoshi and watched him establishing a small rock garden. I saw Archipenko again, whom I had not seen for many years. McEvoy had enormous vitality, worked all day long in his bathing trunks, writing and dictating; every so often he would rush out of his room to read us a gag that he thought would amuse us. He would have half of Woodstock in his garden in the afternoon; not only was he very hospitable, he also had the largest swimming pool in the whole neighborhood.

He was a really well-adjusted person, never moody or

unfriendly, and combined work and play into a harmonious way of life. On one of our night trips to Woodstock he explained to me the secret of his vitality and success. He tried to live in harmony, to never overdo anything, and always to have time for wine, women and song as well as his work. He needed no drugs for stimulation: it was his work that did it. He used to admonish me: "Easy, George, easy! Don't run after things. Let them come to you." Or "You have to treat your luck badly." He opened my eyes to many things that a newcomer does not usually get to see.

He once took me to a club where Huey Long was to speak. He was said to have made himself dictator of the State of Louisiana, and to be aiming to become dictator of the United States. When I heard him speak, I got quite a different impression of the man. He was obviously a very shrewd politician, and spoke with wit. He had absolutely none of the cold, ugly traits of those misanthropic rulers in Europe. In no way did he act like a man with a mighty mission, as did Hitler or Mussolini.

It was really touching how much time McEvoy spent dragging me from publisher to publisher. Certainly it was not his fault that nothing came of it. He remains in my eyes the generous, big-hearted and hospitable patriarch from Woodstock.

In the course of events I saw less and less of Mac. He moved from Woodstock and our paths separated. I shall always remain thankful to him for his encouragement about staying in the States. His advice may have saved my life.

At the house of other friends I once met the Italo-Greek painter Giorgio de Chirico. As I came in, he was leaning dejectedly against the piano, a man with a head of a horse and a long nose, very much like his horse pictures. It was he who introduced the white horse to modern painting, and the broken pillar. He gave me the impression of proud loneliness, of wanting to be part of his yearning, rigid pictures. He must have felt rather lonely in New York, like the little girl guiding her hoop between the stone walls of the city in one of his most beautiful melancholy paintings.

Marsden Hartley once came out to see us. We had known him in Germany, and in one of those funny coincidences I had once had a studio in which, unknown to me, he had formerly lived and painted. The landlady showed me some oil paintings that he had simply left on the floor. He was a virtuoso whistler. But he would always turn his head away because he thought his mouth looked obscene.

Thus, a lot of friends came and went, appeared and disappeared,

Summer [1950]

such as that nice Dane, Charles Lautrupp, who conducted the Imperial Orchestra in Japan, and claimed to have the distinction of being one of the very few people permitted to turn his back on the Emperor. That is the way it is in America—like ships in the night. Everything goes fast here, and is quickly forgotten. A bit alarming.

◆

In 1935 I spent the first of seven summers in Cape Cod. That landscape with its beautiful high dunes was the exact inner landscape that I had been carrying with me for so long. There it was in real life! By now Cape Cod is flooded with tourists; there are art schools at every corner, and somebody with an easel and paint box wherever you look; the very bushes along the way are smeared with paint and the paths are littered with empty beer cans, squeezed paint tubes and dirty paint rags. A painting craze had seized the whole nation like a St. Vitus' dance and was polluting the countryside.

The house that we had taken was "cursed," as was an older building on the same grounds, and the greenhouse of the nursery-man who hated the flowers he grew. He should have been an ornithologist as he loved birds and had made a name for himself in that field. For financial reasons, however, he could not get out of the flower business, and he loathed it. He would even vent his fury on one of his valuable orchids by tearing it apart or squashing it before the eyes of a horrified customer, grinning, and breaking into satanic laughter. His wife was of German extraction, weighed almost three hundred pounds, and had a whole library of cookbooks.

There was no lack of "voices" and "whispers": what old country house does not have peculiar sounds? This one had a pump in the yard too that would sound like a distant heartbeat when activated on a sleepless night. It was hard to get used to it—we may have been a bit on edge—and the house next door was haunted too. The two "bad" Bowers boys lived there long ago; they drank a lot, and were forever fighting over their inheritance. Supposedly they were often seen chasing each other round the house like grey squirrels. There came a time when they not only ran out of money, but gin too. Our rather superstitious neighbors claimed to have seen a small two-wheeled carriage suddenly pull up and a lame man get out, wearing a very long black coat on a very hot summer day. He did not stay long; but shortly thereafter the two boys disappeared without a trace. Pious fishermen had no doubt about who that black visitor was. It was obvious to them that the two boys had sold their souls to him for an enormous amount of liquor. When some fearless local people got together with some enlightened summer folk and a Protestant minister, and went in to the house, they were said to have found lots of strange, enormous barrels. Nobody could figure how they got there, and the narrow door had to be taken off its hinges when they took one away. Once outside, the barrels were decomposed to ashes by the sun, leaving a penetrating sulphur smell behind. As late as 1946 even we could still occasionally feel a slightly sulphuric tickle in our noses.

After a lively party we drove past that grey house one night—the painter George Biddle, the Spaniard Gonzales, a young Irish poet, Eva and I. The moon was full and it was rather misty. Biddle was telling us about the two boys whom people still claimed to see occasionally chasing each other round the house. Said the Irish poet, "Superstition or not, I just saw something moving over there." "Nonsense," said Biddle, a very enlightened man of the world. We slowed down, and finally stopped. "Yes," said Gonzales, "there's something moving." I was of the opinion that there was nothing mysterious: it might be summer people, or possibly art students who did not care where they lived. Why not go in and look, and who knows, maybe we'd find something to drink. So we got out and approached. And what did we find? A clothesline with all sorts of garments fluttering in the moonlight. We laughed, got back in the car and ended the adventure with a few nightcaps at our house.

The next morning we talked about it to our Portuguese boatman and handyman who happened to come by for a friendly chat, and said we were surprised that any summer people had moved into that dilapidated spooky house. "What?" he said, "in the Bower house? No, no, certainly not, that's quite impossible, no thank you, Mr. Grosz, I would not care for another drink, no, I have to get along now...."

Further along the road there was another house, called the suicide house. We once wanted to pick some of the marvelous berries that were growing there and went up by the garage door. It was closed and there was no one to be seen, though it was obvious that people had been there frequently. The odd thing was that the door was riddled with bullet holes. Had somebody indulged in target practice until he felt sure enough of his aim to shoot himself? An oppressive thought. We quickly picked a few berries and went home.

But nothing on this haunted road was more frightening than the newly established art school. As you entered, you were greeted by a

man who seemed to have a mild form of St. Vitus' dance. His arms flayed in the air like the bent wings of a windmill. He was the "philosopher" of this art school. We would look down to avoid his eyes lest his stutter become unbearably confusing. He came from Texas and wore elaborately embroidered cowboy boots. To my mind, that man was the perfect symbol of an art school where students learned nothing except to "express themselves." Their self-expression looked exactly like the tall St. Vitus' dancer.

In all my life I have never heard more nonsense; but in a way it was fascinating. That wise guy seemed to be trying to confuse the students completely. The school produced a peculiar transmutation in your brain, like an old fashioned coffee grinder grinding up all your concepts. You would begin to talk in a way that was contrary to your own intelligence and convictions. In that hellishly modern studio light, objects of life and nature would take on hideous outlines. Well-considered ideas became distorted, producing something like mental seasickness. You could in fact not help rather liking what was going on, as long as you stayed there, chiefly because the owner of the school was a pleasant, goodlooking fellow who always trotted out drinks and was fundamentally all right. He had some money, and had been an actor, which is always an advantage. It enabled him to make fun of his own teaching, and after a drink or two he would give marvelous imitations of the guides in the Museum of Modern Art explaining the works of Picasso.

We knew nothing of all the madness, hatred and devilish goings-on behind the surface when we rented our summer quarters. Fortunately they did not manage to talk us into buying the haunted cottage with the greenhouse and other buildings. Only later were we to hear that the whole neighborhood had an absolutely poisonous reputation....

Cape Cod was interesting in other ways too. Half hidden, submerged in the dunes were so-called Cape Cod houses that looked like stranded ships. The beach was covered for miles with large fish that had taken refuge here at certain times of the year from the ocean, and perished in the sand. They reminded me of Breughel's picture of the big fish that ate the little fish. Some of the people who lived here year-round were like that too, washed in by the tide to disintegrate sooner or later. Many of them were old retired sea captains with their papers and mementoes; or people escaping

from the destructive rat race of the cities to a dream retirement. In another category were the Portuguese fishermen who had settled here around 1830. For some oversexed or perverse tourists these dark-haired, young, Latin fishermen provided a great attraction, and gave Provincetown a rather shady reputation.

John Dos Passos had a lovely house in Provincetown; from the terrace at the back you could step right into the water. That happened with almost religious regularity, for the purpose of rinsing off your hangover. Dos had a green thumb and tended his little flower garden with great loving care. After his wife was killed at his side in a car accident, a bookdealer friend from Chicago took over his house. He became a fixture. Before that, however, we spent many a lovely hour there and met lots of people, including the eminent critic Edmund Wilson, who not only summered on Cape Cod but actually lived there year 'round.

I remember Edmund Wilson best coming down the steps in his beach coat; like all fat people, he looked most impressive viewed from below, like the anonymous fat gentleman in the Prado, attributed to Velasquez. My other image of him is on a bicycle, looking like a character straight out of Dickens. Our conversations usually ended in the dunes where his house was—conversations about American painting, Félicien Rops, and lots of other things. Edmund Wilson is more a lobster person than a fish person: you have to use a nut cracker to get to the meat.

At night we would often go calling on people, on Eben for instance: as the son of a big theater agent, he could afford to paint without worrying about shows or selling and could destroy most of his works. He had kept the house he inherited exactly the way his parents left it, a true relic of the nineties, full of curlicues and mahogany. We would usually sit in the kitchen with our highballs, the Cape Cod wind howling round the house.

"Come with me," said Dos, "I want to show you something." I thought I was dreaming. Suddenly we were standing on a first-class promenade deck, complete with lifesavers and lifeboats. Eben's father had it built to look exactly like an ocean vessel; he could not stand sailing, but loved looking at the waves, so he had his own private piece of ocean voyage built.... "Those people really knew how to live" said Dos, "and the ones who had money, used it. These days they are more apt to conceal it—oh, where are the sixteen-course dinners?—Gone...Just look at that moon!" Suddenly you could have thought you were in Italy, with that Provincetown tower, and us high above the waves on a dream ship at anchor. "Well, I suppose we had better go back in," said Dos. "Yes, I suppose...."

We were somewhat befogged as we drove home from that excursion back into the eighteen-eighties. Now and then a deer would cross the highway, here and there the headlights would show blood: a turtle had been run over, or a skunk whose stench clung to the wheels, staying with us for a long while. I was pleasantly aroused, thought of Buffalo Bill, and imagined immense herds of buffalo crossing our way. "See?" I said to Eva, "we're on the Oregon trail." "Drunk is where you are," said she, "and to bed is where we're going." Virgin forests whizzed past us—but they were mere poles denuded by hungry moths. They really were impenetrable, however, full of poison ivy and poison oak. This was America, not Europe....

Grosz with His Wife, Eva [1959]

THE PAINTER ENTERS HIS STUDIO

The first things you see when you come in are the cartoon of a pig and the two horseshoes, both of which are known as bearers of good luck. This is my room, this is my world. Grünewald's Christ is fastened on the wall with thumbtacks, as are some bills and a color chart. To the left is a Rogier van der Weyden reproduction: men and women falling head first into the blazing flames of hell.

This is my world. The red dumbbells in the corner I painted myself; next to them, that big, heavy stone that I dragged up from the Sound. Both of them are symbols of the senselessness of life, but also signs of how to combat this senselessness or chase it away with dumbbells, rock-lifting, kneebends and stretching. Maybe tomorrow I'll paint the dumbbells and the heavy rock with butterflies, symbols of the brevity of life with their graceful fluttering over flowers.

Many canvasses are there, turned toward the wall. You cannot stare at your own pictures all the time.

This is my room, my life! It is also the shell of an oyster that quickly snaps shut. Or at times the house of a sensitive snail. The sound inside is sometimes hollow and empty, as is the infinite melody of the ocean. The pictures have their faces toward the wall, humbly and modestly. They are a piece of me. They are standing there like flats on a stage, waiting to be brought forward again to take part in the play. Who will take a look at them tomorrow? Who will buy us, where will we end? Those ridiculous and yet beloved frames! How much joy they contain, how much contrition, how much disappointment—and how little triumph! A bit of canvas, a few sticks of wood—and possibly a piece of eternity?

Here is my drafting table. I painted it blue, and made the footrest

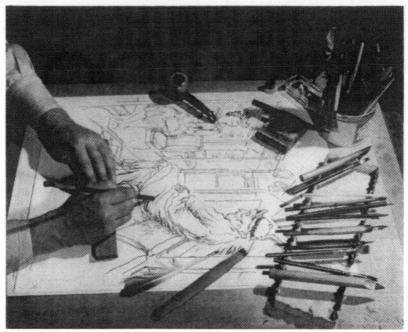

myself. What experiences that patient board has shared as the companion of my dreams and hopes! Here I have sat through many a night, drawing until morning. Here paper was covered with dark lines of angry accusation, but also with forms of pure pleasure. A pen traveled over the paper like a big black fly, its legs dipped in ink. From scribbles that nobody could decipher something like a map took shape. A drawing board is like a battlefield, or a place of execution, or it can become an amusing diary, or a bitter one. What will succeed, what will go wrong? Will I fill the order to the patron's satisfaction? The dumbbells, painted red, have at times taught me to manage seemingly senseless things.

I have lots of brushes. I love the ones shaped like fans, you can spread and stroke with them as with your fingers. Closest to my heart are my smallest brushes. Amazing, the drops of light that they yield when dipped in thick, old linseed oil that has been seasoned by sunlight.

So this is my world, my room. It has not become a business office, calculations here are different. And nothing is sold—or only rarely. A rectangular white canvas, as prescribed by Euclid, puts a little bright order into the confused darkness around us. I am here with all my imagination. By painting upon it, I can record something about myself and my inner world: lines, shadow, light and the eternal, infinite spiral. There is a market somewhere for all that.

No, mine is not the world of commerce; inspiration and mood are what matter in mine. No margarine is made here, no tires, no bicycles, nothing edible. At best products of imagination are fabricated here, and though this world is useless, it secretly continues to exist. The world consists essentially of useful things and pretty things, and the ivory tower was built much more solidly than many a supposedly practical construction.

The more practical the world becomes, the more permanent will be the concealed, romantic-irrational world of the useless. This does not mean madness, but rather the result of eternal law. Man is becoming more peculiar or, to state it more clearly, some people get deeper satisfaction from the image than from the thing itself. An old legend has it that the painter Apelles could paint such lifelike fruits that birds and insects would come down from the skies to feast upon them. The rationalist, intimidated by natural science, has a rational explanation: certainly they came, but not because of their lifelike appearance; insects have different organs of perception than humans. No, Apelles, they were attracted by the fresh oil in the paint, possibly linseed oil or beeswax...

That is typical of the times in which we live. We are all so beautifully enlightened, and have left imagination to the geopoliticians and the technocrats.

Once more I sing my little song for closeness to life, against intellectual theories and construction—once more, before all is wiped off the grey slate of approaching time, obliterated with a sponge soaked in blood.

EPILOGUE

I n 1959 George Grosz moved back to Berlin. He died there July 6. The following account is translated from Lothar Fischer's monograph, published by Rowohlt in 1976.

After his arrival in Berlin, he seemed full of force and energy. He arranged for a night on the town with the journalist Martin G. Buttig who, in turn, brought along the sculptor Joachim Dunkel, whom Grosz had not yet met. They were joined in Grosz's apartment by Robert Bell. From afternoon until evening Grosz and his companions chatted and drank in the garden of the restaurant, Habel am Roseneck. He acted out his New York meeting with Thomas Mann for them.

In The Death of the Old Dadaist, *Martin G. Buttig wrote, "Grosz lit his n'th cigar, a yellowish-brown, very strong, Havana, and enthusiastically offered them around. None of us had any idea how many bottles we had emptied. Eva Grosz gently suggested going home. Grosz agreed, saying they had spent enough time in one place. Out on the street, when she asked whether he would not call it a day and come home with her, he spoke of the lovely evening that had just begun and could not possibly come to such an abrupt finish. 'There is something interesting that I really have to show you,' he said. He was referring to a photo in the former prizefighter Franz Diener's tavern that showed Grosz with his gloves on, from the days when he was painting Schmeling's portrait. Sure enough, that posed photo was still on the tavern wall, among the framed pictures of all prominent fighters of the past. Grosz posed again and said he would henceforth patronize Diener's restaurant. The owner asked him to inscribe the autograph wall. Grosz promised to do that, and to add a drawing. He would come back very soon, some morning when there would*

be no interruptions. Then of course he ordered champagne, and beer from Czechoslovakia....

"It was shortly after midnight when we left the restaurant and strolled the short way to his house. Grosz embraced us under the starlit sky. He walked up the steps, clicked his heels, tipped his hat and started a speech with 'Ladies and Gentlemen'...(in English), praising the day and friendship, night and stars, Berlin and mankind in general. Afterwards the door opened again a crack, and out came his straw hat with the wide black band, and waved to us. Then the key turned in the lock inside. We saw his shadow as he mounted the stairs." The account ended with the statement that Grosz was dead a few hours later.

At dawn, a newspaper woman discovered him in a heap on the landing inside a side door. He must have gone out again, unable to end the night, overrating his capacity. An ice man came along and alerted some bricklayers on their way to work. Grosz was still alive when he was carried to his apartment; he died shortly thereafter, suffocated by his vomit...The physician wrote heart failure on the death certificate.

Breinigsville, PA USA
16 February 2011
255661BV00001B/46/A